Politics of Conscience

A BIOGRAPHY OF
MARGARET CHASE SMITH

Patricia Ward Wallace

PRAEGER

Westport, Connecticut
London

Library of Congress Cataloging-in-Publication Data

Wallace, Patricia Ward.
    Politics of conscience : a biography of Margaret Chase Smith /
Patricia Ward Wallace.
        p.   cm.
    Includes bibliographical references and index.
    ISBN 0–275–95130–8 (alk. paper)
    1. Smith, Margaret Chase, 1897–1995.   2. Legislators—United
States—Biography.   3. United States. Congress. Senate—Biography.
I. Title.
E748.S667W35   1995
328.73'092—dc20
[B]   95–4288

British Library Cataloguing in Publication Data is available.

Library of Congress Catalog Card Number: 95–4288
ISBN: 0–275–95130–8

First published in 1995

Praeger Publishers, 88 Post Road West, Westport, CT 06881
An imprint of Greenwood Publishing Group, Inc.

Printed in the United States of America

(∞)™

The paper used in this book complies with the
Permanent Paper Standard issued by the National
Information Standards Organization (Z39.48–1984).

10 9 8 7 6 5 4 3 2 1

Copyright Acknowledgments

The author and publisher gratefully acknowledge permission to quote from the
following material:

Selections are reprinted from *Declaration of Conscience* by Margaret Chase Smith,
Garden City, New York: Doubleday, 1972. Used by permission of Jensen, Baird,
Gardner & Henry, Attorneys at Law.

Selections are reprinted from the Margaret Chase Smith Library archives. Used by
permission of the Margaret Chase Smith Library, Skowhegan, Maine.

For the best friend I ever had

CONTENTS

PREFACE

Margaret Chase Smith was the most influential woman in the history of American politics. Her only significant rival was Eleanor Roosevelt, who influenced more as symbol than as policy maker. For thirty-two years Smith served in Congress and worked with committees on military affairs, appropriations, government operations, space, and intelligence. Twice Republicans considered her a vice presidential possibility, and in 1964 she launched the first campaign by a woman for the presidential nomination of a major party. Indicative of her longevity and her bid for national office, Smith served both a state constituency in Maine and a larger group of supporters in the nation. She went from being Maine's daughter to America's heroine, and she did it with her conscience and reputation intact. Along the way Smith developed a unique political partnership with William C. Lewis with whom she lived and worked, in both office and retirement.

History does not allow for heroines any more than heroes when recounting human activity, and Margaret Chase Smith, revealed, was as replete with petty rancors, vengeances, ambitions, and self-doubts as anyone else. Her public persona, however, was the New England lady: gracious, reticent, frugal, hard working, and honest. From this mixture came a skillful politician who found her way through the congressional labyrinth of conflicting interests as an independent. No one ever took her vote for granted, and she never acknowledged the sexist discrimination and patronizing of her colleagues unless it denied her rights due a senator. Then she responded with a fury that taught others to be wary. In this manner she challenged Joseph McCarthy, Dwight Eisenhower, John Kennedy, and Richard Nixon. As prototype for female and minority politicians, Smith succeeded in her goal to be a U.S. senator, not a woman senator, and she did this by overcoming gender instead of championing it. Never a feminist, Smith did not practice sisterhood or work for the significant women's legislation of the 1960s and 1970s. Instead, she worked for Maine and the nation as a cold warrior and became an unrepentant proponent of the military-industrial complex and of nuclear power.

I illustrate the anomalies of Margaret Chase Smith by beginning each chapter with a revealing vignette. Each opening scene is based on fact, and quotations are documented, but in some of them, I supply dialogue illustrative of the situation.

I first met Senator Smith in 1977 when she, accompanied by Bill Lewis, came to Baylor University as a distinguished lecturer. For me and my students in women's history and in foreign relations, she was history come to life. I arranged for Senator Smith to return in 1979 for a week of seminars with students and faculty. Again in tandem with Lewis, Smith enthralled as she recounted her political experiences, which illumined twentieth-century American history. We corresponded during the following years, and eventually an invitation came to research her newly opened library. Bill Lewis was dead by then, and Senator Smith generously shared her memories with me in hour after hour of interviews. But then our relationship changed when I began interviewing her family, friends, and political colleagues and asking Smith about conflicting interpretations. My use of the historical method Senator Smith saw as disloyalty, and to my keen disappointment she told me in a final interview on 28 September 1988, "When you ask me something and I give you an answer, there can't be any other interpretation of that."

Her attitude was not shared by the professional staff at the Margaret Chase Smith Library, and I thank the three respective directors, James Mac-Campbell, Russell Fridley, and Gregory Gallant, for administering as well organized a research facility as I have visited. Graciously assisted by Angela Stockwell and Reginald Collins, Gallant, in particular, ensured my access to every one of the eighty file drawers of correspondence; more than four hundred scrapbooks; over a hundred volumes of statements, speeches, and hearings; and thousands of photographs and objects in the museum and storage room. For all their historical value, the scrapbooks proved a problem in documenting because Senator Smith's Washington office seldom indicated the source and date of newspaper clippings, magazine articles, and other memorabilia.

Apart from my research, the best memory I have of my stay in Maine is of my friendship with Evelyn Worth. To this day when in search of solace, my mind returns to her cottage on North Pond, which she made available for my use, with its island, ospreys, and loons.

I also thank those in Maine and Washington who allowed me to plunder their memories of Margaret Chase Smith. I will always treasure Barry Goldwater's telling me, in response to my asking if his health permitted an interview, that he felt good enough to wrestle a bear. Sadly memorable, J. William

Fulbright, after being unable to recall an incident, said that he did not intend to have any more interviews because his memory was failing. Strom Thurmond's office with its four high walls covered floor to ceiling with awards, commendations, and photographs was as striking as the man is. A modest George Mitchell, in the splendor of the majority leader's office, praised Senator Smith, but when I asked if he had criticisms, he replied that he would leave it to others to criticize. Robert Dole, pressed as to why Maine became one of the nation's poorest states despite Smith's influence, responded with sharp humor that the state had two senators. Other memories include John Stennis's frail voice over the telephone, Edmund Muskie's dour unpleasantness, Liz Carpenter's raucous good humor, William Cohen's office library (the only one I saw in visiting dozens of congressional offices), and Edward Brooke's special empathy for Senator Smith's separateness as female.

My daughter, Devon Ward, shepherded me through this project, as she has through life, by accompanying me to Maine, sharing research responsibilities, and exploring with me the joys and Beans of Maine.

I especially appreciate my colleagues Paul F. Boller, Jr., Robert A. Divine, and Robert G. Collmer who showed me the extraordinary courtesy of reading my early chapters and pointing me in good directions. In addition, I thank my research assistants—Jay Shobe, Douglas Doe, Patricia Santa-Cruz, Mary Margaret Adams, Ron Capshaw, and Charles Muskiet—for searching out the forgotten dates, lost books, necessary facts, and names for the index.

Lynnette Geary, administrative assistant and bedrock of the Department of History at Baylor University, typed the manuscript with the admirable efficiency that she employed on my preceding six manuscripts.

Baylor University's generous sabbatical and research grant programs, instituted by President Herbert H. Reynolds, made this project possible. In fact, President Reynolds hosted the luncheon for Senator Smith and General Lewis at which we first discussed a biography. As long as universities like Baylor encourage scholarship, careers as significant as Margaret Chase Smith's will not be forgotten but will be recorded to educate us all.

Introduction:
Showcasing a Legend

The mammoth bus, filled with Quebec-bound tourists during the summer of 1988, turned off highway 201 in the small town of Skowhegan, Maine, and lumbered up Neil Hill, then pulled off the narrow road in front of a small, white frame house, an unlikely tourist stop. Without disembarking, the passengers stared through the bus's large windows into the house's glass-enclosed atrium while the tour guide explained why they had stopped and whom they were viewing.

On exhibit inside, as in a department store window, was a small, white-haired woman with a fresh rose on her lapel. She was conducting an interview with yet another aspiring historian. Startled when the bus blocked out the sun and darkened the room, the interviewer looked out in puzzlement at the gaping tourists with their cameras poised. With vision in decline like body, the object of the unmitigated curiosity perceived the sudden shadow and asked, "What is it?"

Appalled at the blatant intrusion, the interviewer managed, "A busload of tourists." The unexpected response was a quiet smile, as erect a posture as the stooped shoulders allowed, and a practiced lifting of the prominent, squared-off chin. With the interviewer now watching this performance in miniature as awestruck as those on the bus, the woman, still seated, raised her right forearm from her lap and opened her hand in monarchical wave.

In the five minutes that the whole incident took before the bus continued on to Canada, the interviewer realized that the wave was a pleased welcome to a not-unexpected occurrence. Indeed the room—brightly lit overhead by a sky light, spartanly furnished with wicker chairs, and colorfully contrasted with white walls, black slate floor, and red door—resembled a stage set facing an audience on wheels. Until her death in 1995, passers-by on their way to Shop 'n Save, the post office, or the Old Mill Pub as well as to Quebec City could view Skowhegan's, and possibly Maine's, most famous resident from early morning when she read and answered her steady stream of mail until late afternoon when the last of her visitors departed. Admittedly on a reduced stage with a declining audience, Margaret Chase Smith in her ninetieth year nonetheless continued, as she had most of her life, to live in public view.

Already in history textbooks as the first woman to be elected to both the U.S. House of Representatives and Senate, Smith spent the years since her defeat in 1972 lecturing on college campuses, serving on boards of directors, and planning the Margaret Chase Smith Library Center. Dedicated in 1982, the center, more museum than library, is an addition to what used to be Smith's home. Only a red velvet rope separated the exhibit hall from the atrium where Smith spent her days. Almost daily, retired couples, groups of schoolchildren, or women traveling in twos or threes stopped by the secluded location overlooking the Kennebec River and viewed the memorabilia of Smith's thirty-two years in Congress. On entering, the visitor saw hanging overhead in the high-ceilinged room some of the ninety-five colorful academic hoods presented to Smith with honorary degrees from colleges and universities throughout the nation. On a dress form was the uniform Smith wore as a lieutenant colonel in the Air Force Reserves, and in a display case was the makeup kit she used on her around-the-world tour with Edward R. Murrow's "See It Now" television crew. There was the hat she threw into the 1964 presidential campaign, "Margaret Chase Smith for President" posters and buttons, and a red and white "Smith for President" pot holder. Everywhere there were elephants and roses of innumerable sizes, descriptions, and materials: sculptures, paintings, jewelry; realistic, comic, imaginative; gold, sterling, ceramic, wood, bronze, plastic, china, pewter, ivory, and crystal. Lining the wall were photographs of Smith with Presidents Dwight David Eisenhower, John Fitzgerald Kennedy, Lyndon Baines Johnson, and Richard Milhous Nixon, all of whom, along with Franklin Delano Roosevelt and Harry S Truman, passed through the White House while she was in Congress. On the walls were wonderful photographs of a lovely, young, smiling Margaret Chase Smith inspecting a World War II battleship, conducting a hearing on the Korean War ammunition shortage, and meeting with Winston Churchill, Chiang Kai-shek, Jawaharlal Nehru, Gamal Abdel Nasser, Pierre Mendès-France, and Francisco Franco. Most prominently displayed was the cornerstone of Smith's political career, her 1 June 1950 Declaration of Conscience speech against Senator Joseph McCarthy.

Always there were uninformed visitors motivated by curiosity, lacking anything else to do, or fleeing the hot or cold weather outside who wandered in, looked awhile, and then asked the receptionist if Senator Smith was dead. Well-mannered visitors, after thanking the receptionist for their free souvenir postcards and pencils, frequently remarked that Smith was a remarkable woman. During her last years there were also those who meandered down the display hall past the childhood mementos and political cartoons to the red velvet rope and the silent, near-blind woman working just beyond. These hastened back to the receptionist to ask if "that woman" was Senator Smith and then joked about a "living museum exhibit" and "a senator on display." Emboldened, some of these visitors asked for an introduction or permission to take a photograph for some aunt, grandparent, or friend who once met Senator Smith. More often than not, Senator Smith agreed to pose and chat for a minute in a manner reminiscent of her receiving visitors in her congressional office long ago when her days were so full. To this day the most striking, and probably the most common visitor to this unique memorial to a political career, is the one, usually young, who walks in, looks around for a minute, and then asks, "Who was she?"

Chapter One

MAINE'S DAUGHTER

The top shelf was six feet off the floor and, adding to Margaret's incentive, contained boxes of assorted candies, but despite standing on tiptoes and stretching, she had to admit defeat. The manager of Green Brothers five-and-ten-cent store smiled indulgently and told the twelve-year-old job applicant to come back when she was taller. He knew Margaret as a regular customer and also because her mother often worked for him. Amused when Margaret had seriously approached him "in a business-like way" to say that she "would like very much to be considered as a part time employee," he had used her height as an excuse to turn her away. His mistake had been to say that when she could reach the shelved merchandise "to come back and he would talk to her seriously."[1]

Green Brothers on Water Street was Margaret's childhood heaven. She and her friends had spent more time than money there for years as they roamed the aisles to look at the staggering assortment of items, most of which cost five to ten cents. There were tortoise shell combs and velvet ribbons, pearl necklaces and gold rings, rubber balls and jump ropes with handles, sweet-smelling perfumes and real (not homemade) soap, and hundreds of ceramic figurines, what-nots, and glass vases, bowls, and boxes. Junk to many, unobtainable luxury goods to Margaret, but if she worked there among them, they would be hers to smell and touch and sell, and, better, with her own money to buy.

Determinedly, Margaret returned time and again through the sixth grade and the following summer, and always she eyed her nemesis, the six-foot-high top shelf behind the counters. Finally, when she was thirteen and in the seventh grade, more desirous than ever of Green's exotic goods, she came back to remind the manager of his promise. She still had to stand on tiptoe,

but this time she could reach the top boxes of candy, and with a trium-
phantly expectant smile she faced the manager.

Participants in the pioneer settlement of Maine, members of Margaret
Chase Smith's family were as rock-ribbed New Englanders as it was possible
to be. Her father's lineage proudly went back to early colonial America and
the founding of New Hampshire, but specifically to the colony's criminal
court records. The first American Chase, Aquila, was probably born in England about 1618 and emigrated to New Hampshire as a young man. By 1639
he, his wife Ann, and his brother-in-law David Wheeler were "presented"
before Hampton's court, "admonished," and fined for "gathering pease [*sic*]
on the first day of the week." Breaking the Sabbath was a serious offense in
Puritan New England, but Chase practicality held that the peas had to be
picked when they were ripe.[2]

The Chases continued to live in New Hampshire for two more generations,
but a third-generation son, Isaac, born in Concord on 30 December 1766,
departed for Maine. For Isaac Chase, Maine was the unsettled frontier, an
unknown area for most Americans, and one with promise. Dawnland was
the Indian name for Maine, and other tribes referred to Maine's Indians as
Dawnlanders, from *Wabonaki,* or "living at the sunrise."[3] Norumbega was
the earliest English reference to Maine, somewhere on the "back side" of
Nova Scotia and vaguely located on the Penobscot River. Originally a place
name from a 1529 map drawn by the explorer Giovanni da Verrazano, the
first European to see Dawnland, Norumbega became an English Cibola, a
golden city with "pyllors of Cristoll."[4] More practically, Captain John
Smith—mercenary, mariner, and former commander of the English colony
of Jamestown—in 1614 designated the area New England and advocated
settlement. Another English soldier, Sir Ferdinando Gorges, formed the
Council for New England and by 1629 named and was proprietor of the
Province of Maine. Although he never reached Maine himself, Gorges motivated early settlements there and earned the title Father of Maine.

Margaret Chase Smith's ancestors had to contend not only with fierce
Indian determination to hold on to their lands but with a successful alliance
between the Abnaki Indians and French colonizers to the north. From first
sighting, the Abnakis had been damned as "bad people." In that incident
the Indians had agreed to trade with the explorers on their ships but only
through a basket raised and lowered from "some rocks where the breakers
were most violent," and "when we had nothing more to exchange and left
them, the men made all the signs of scorn and shame that any brute creature
would make, such as exhibiting their bare behinds, and laughing immoder-
ately."[5] In lightning attacks the Abnakis burned hundreds of farm houses
and killed or captured over seven hundred colonists in settlements from
Pemaquid, Berwick, York, and Kittery. The devastation brought Maine to
the attention of the Puritan divine Cotton Mather, who decided for the sake

of both God and Massachusetts that Maine should come under the direction of Boston. Religious refugees had established Puritanism at Plymouth in 1620 and had considerably strengthened it at Massachusetts Bay in 1630. Military expansion followed by religious dominance penetrated Connecticut almost immediately, and beginning in 1637 Massachusetts assumed control of New Hampshire. Now Boston extended its defense perimeter into Maine, and by the end of the 1600s Mather's missionary army of young parsons had followed Boston's political commissioners north. So complete was Puritan hegemony that Massachusetts controlled Maine until the 1820 Missouri Compromise.[6]

Reflecting the hard work required to clear the howling wilderness in which they found themselves, the Puritans sanctified work and taught that worship of God included dutiful attention to a secular calling. The Puritans made sins of idleness and luxury and virtues of industry and thrift. Like centurions taking Roman law throughout the empire, Massachusetts's ministers spread their practical doctrine throughout New England.

Isaac Chase, like most other Mainers, accepted the philosophy but rejected the politics and agitated for independence from Boston. In perceiving themselves as different from Massachusetts citizens, Mainers developed a unique—some would say peculiar—self-image. Their peculiarities became a cherished aspect of their collective character and as integral as their verities of hard work, economy, and prudence. Mainers valued their own practical wisdom and natural wit over that of outsiders, particularly learned ones, and developed a distinct, salty, downeast dialect so that even language separated them from Massachusetts. Mainers also acquired a self-confident identity as independent, self-sufficient, assertive, and conservative, even among other New England Yankees. This early, Maine was as much a state of mind, an attitude, as a place, and Isaac Chase was shaped as much by geography as by genetics.

With a 3,000-acre land grant from the government to encourage settlement in Maine, Isaac Chase married Bridget Delano in Winslow in 1786 and lived in Sidney before settling eight miles south of Skowhegan in Fairfield in 1805. Becoming Captain Isaac Chase in the War of 1812 and commanding an artillery company, he also fathered eleven children, one of whom he named Isaac, after himself. This second Isaac Chase, born 15 May 1800, married Rachel Emery in 1825. Their sixth child, John Wesley Chase, born in Fairfield on 6 May 1837, was the father of George Emery Chase and grandfather of Margaret Chase Smith.[7]

The 3,000 acres of land were gone by the time of the second Isaac Chase. With primogeniture and entail, which had required property to be passed intact to the first-born son, no longer the law, the land had either been divided among the many Chase children or sold off in parcels for income. Probably a combination of division and sale accounted for the dissipation of the land grant by the 1820s and for Isaac to be earning his living as a minister. Acknowledged as "famous for the preaching of the gospel in many parts of the state, and a man of great power and influence," Chase, according to an 1822 document, "visited the opening in the forest" and "reported there had been a revival, the fruits of a pious school teacher."[8]

His son, John Wesley Chase, fought with the Union army in the South during the Civil War but returned to Fairfield to become a Methodist minister. He married Margaret Nolan, had a daughter, Alice, and two sons besides George Emery. The three other Chase children attended school, but George refused to go. Both John Wesley and Margaret died young, John Wesley at thirty-nine and Margaret in her early forties. George Chase first worked as a hotel clerk, then learned the barbering trade through a long apprenticeship, and eventually moved to nearby Skowhegan to open a barber shop.

Less is known about the lineage of Smith's mother, Carrie Murray Chase. Her grandmother, Mary Boulette, born in 1850, probably came to Maine from that section of New Brunswick that the Scots had settled. Her grandfather, John L. Murray, was born in St. Georges, Canada, in 1846, and soon afterward his parents, Mr. and Mrs. Lambert Murray, without a land grant, moved to Skowhegan with him.

Whatever illusions the Chases and Murrays had about opportunity in Maine, they quickly learned that nature had the upper hand. The huge granite slabs that pushed up through the ground stood as barricades to use of the good soil. The towering forests of huge trees cowed those who sought to cut them, and on the rocky seacoast there were no white, sandy beaches but, rather, the angry North Atlantic that dared men to wrestle for its wealth. Then for nine or ten months of the year, there was the cold to battle as the world turned white and icy with body-numbing gale-force winds. Those who survived—and many did not—became as rugged as the land and sea and lived an unrelenting life of work. Mainers earned their clear, blue-eyed squint of suspicion, thin-lipped smile of hard-fought triumph, and craggy, weathered faces, and they passed what allowed them precarious survival on to their children.

The village of Skowhegan, which attracted the Chases and Murrays, was, like many of Maine's other towns, determined by a waterway. In this instance, it was the Kennebec River, which flows from the great northern Moosehead Lake southward for 150 miles to Bath and the Atlantic. As a prospering mill and factory town, Skowhegan required and achieved a predominant population of laborers. Immigration south of land-poor Canadians from Quebec supplemented the continued migration north and made for a colorful ethnic mix of French and English languages and Catholic and Protestant churches. By 1900, 33 percent of the residents were French-Canadian. For long hours and limited wages, residents, male and female, sawed shingles, fashioned brooms, felted cloth, carded wool, and stitched shoes. With little wealth in town, there were no sharp class divisions but rather a middle-class population of hard-working home owners with large families to support.

As a young man John Murray began working at the Dane Sash and Blind factory. He earned $1.25 for a twelve-hour day and continued there for forty years. About 1860, using his woodworking skills, John built a six-room, white clapboard, two-story house on a maple-shaded lot on North Avenue for his bride, Mary. The Murrays had a daughter Annie, a son William who soon died, and on 10 May 1876 Carrie Matilda. Mary died at age thirty-two when Carrie was six, but her father soon remarried, to a woman named Addie Lessor, with whom he had a third daughter, Laura.

A pretty child, Carrie Matilda learned to play the banjo and accompanied her sister Annie who played the piano. She easily made friends at school and was a good student, but as she grew older, her great desire was for a job and the independence that she thought would accompany work. Carrie's closest friends were older girls, and when they left school for jobs that seemed glamorous to her, she too decided to leave school. Believing she was making a mistake, her father tried to keep Carrie in school by pointing to the better jobs that she could acquire with a high school diploma. Unpersuaded, Carrie chafed under the restrictions of Skowhegan High School until her senior year in 1894 and then, not quite three months before she would have graduated, quit. Since 1875 education had been mandatory in Maine but only up to age fifteen. Carrie continued to live at home but found a job with her friends at a shoe factory and was happy with her escape from academia. When she proudly showed her first week's wages to her father, he said that since she was now an employed woman, she would have to pay him five dollars a week for room and board. Startled at having her grand salary depleted by the necessities of shelter and food, Carrie nonetheless understood the lesson her father was teaching and contributed to the family income. Two years later at age twenty, Carrie married George Chase, twenty-one, and John Murray asked the young couple to move in with him. Gratefully, they accepted and were surprised when John also gave them a wedding present: a bank book for an account with over five hundred dollars on deposit. John had deposited each of Carrie's five-dollar payments to him to demonstrate another New England verity, thrift. In 1896, five hundred dollars was a munificent gift and an unexpected bonanza for the young couple. In the few months of marriage before obvious pregnancy forced her confinement, Carrie continued working at the shoe factory and became a skilled "fancy stitcher," one of the better positions.[9] George's three-chair barber shop was prominently located on Madison and Water streets, and his personable, easy-going manner attracted a steady clientele.

On 14 December 1897 Dr. J.N. Merrill delivered a baby girl to twenty-one-year-old Carrie and twenty-two-year-old George Chase in their home on North Avenue. According to her certificate of baptism from Notre Dame de Lourdes in Skowhegan, Margaret Chase Smith was christened Marguerite

Mandeline Chase on 18 December 1897. While the certificate lists her father as George Chase, it lists her mother as Caroline Morin and sponsors as Lambert Morin and Adile Lessard. The rumor that Smith was French-Canadian, which carried stigma, haunted her entire political career, but the speculation was always that *Chase* had been anglicized from *Chasse,* not that *Murray* was originally *Morin* or that *Margaret Madeline* was *Marguerite Mandeline.*[10] Margaret Madeline became the eldest of six Chase children born during the next fifteen years. A son, Wilbur George, followed in 1899, then two more boys, Roland Murray and Laurence Franklin, a second daughter, Evelyn in 1909, and finally Laura in 1912.

Margaret's parents were poor, hard working, barely educated, honest, and proud—Mainers. Home and family were central in the lives of the Chase children. "I can't stress that enough," Smith said years later. Her parents "were very, very particular about the home and the family. The home was everything to them."[11] For the family, there was the stability and permanence of the home always being the house on North Avenue in Skowhegan. The kitchen, "good-sized," was the heart of the house and had a wood-burning range stove, a large sink, and a pump that grandfather John Murray had connected to the well in the yard. There was a pantry with cupboards off the kitchen on one side and on the other a porch with a hammock, chairs, and a clothesline for Carrie's wash when the weather, more often than not, did not allow her to hang it outside to dry. Toward the front of the house was a combined sitting room–dining room, where the family ate all their meals, and close by was George's and Carrie's small bedroom. The front room with a bay window was the parlor, "a real parlor, dark and gloomy," and "closed except for funerals and weddings. If I ever had to go in that room I walked in and backed out," Smith reminisced. "I was afraid of that room." The front door opened into a hall with the stairway. The "sizeable" front room upstairs was always Margaret's bedroom; the other children shared the larger middle room, and Grandfather Murray had the back bedroom.

Out back behind the kitchen was a connected shed leading to an attached water closet and a barn, because extended cold winters required the attachment of outbuildings to the house. The family kept wood and later coal in the long shed, and the barn housed a hay loft, a horse ("we always had a horse"), a pig ("we never had more than one"), a cow, and some chickens.[12] Village life was synonymous with farm life except that the family did not raise a cash crop, just a food crop. George kept a large vegetable garden behind the barn on his lot, milked the cow, gathered eggs, and butchered a hog each fall. He was particular about the lot, and Smith joked that he would not let people walk on his grounds unless they took their shoes off. In the spring Carrie planted a flower garden and kept flower boxes on the windows.

Carrie's work was constant. In addition to sixteen years of being pregnant, caring for an infant, or rearing six young children, she was responsible for preparing the family's food: cooking three meals a day for eight people; canning, preserving, smoking, salting, and drying food from the garden and livestock; separating cream from the cow's milk to churn into butter; baking bread; and keeping her kitchen stove burning. Then there was the cleaning up of the dishes, pots, and pans, the house, clothes, and children, which required pumping water to heat on the stove each time she washed dishes, mopped floors, did the wash, and bathed the children. Lamp chimneys had to be cleaned each day, wicks trimmed, and bases filled with kerosene in order to light the house each evening. That left ironing clothes after she had cut them out and sewed them, and mended them countless times. Carrie's generation made their own mattresses, quilts, and bed linens, as well as their own soap and cleansers and many of their medicines and cosmetics. The children remembered that Carrie was "a very good cook" and that the house was always "immaculate."[13]

With all this to do, there were still times when Carrie had to work outside the home to supplement the money her husband and father brought home. Sometimes she could take her old job back at the shoe factory or get on at the five-and-dime, but most often Carrie found part-time work at the Coburn Hotel waiting on tables. The most elegant building in town, the Coburn was built in 1882 on the northern corner of Elm Street and Madison Avenue where the Old Red Dragon Tavern had been constructed in 1811, only to be replaced by the Skowhegan Hotel and then the Brewster House. George Chase had also worked as a waiter at the Coburn, and the work allowed Carrie to come and go while caring for her young family.

During one of the many hard times, George moved his barber shop to a room he built on to the left of his father-in-law's house on North Avenue. Hair cuts were fifteen cents and would only get up to thirty-five cents, so even with a rent-free shop, he did not earn a large income. Chase's shop had one barber chair, one ornate gilt-framed mirror, and one shelf of shaving mugs, each personalized with the owner's name. A few blocks away, Ed Sayers had another barber shop, and then there was the problem with George's health. He had migraine headaches, which frequently kept him from work. Driven by pain, he would retreat through the door that connected the shop to his home and lie in darkness as Carrie applied steaming hot packs to his head. The children grew up remembering his face a "fiery red" and Carrie "hovering over him with packs." Bucknam's headache powders, which cost twenty-five cents, did not do much good. George's affliction proved hereditary and affected Margaret, Evelyn, Laura, and some of their children. Over the years George became "a rather retiring kind of man. He didn't say too much," as Evelyn remembered. He also lost his hair quite young and was completely bald. Barber sensitive, he wore an artificial hairpiece, which many never knew about.[14]

"My father was a good father," Smith maintained, "but my mother was a wonderful mother." She remembered George Chase as "strict," "particular," and frequently ill, but Carrie was loving, fun, "strong-minded," "active and capable." As the oldest child and daughter, Margaret became Carrie's partner in caring for the house and the other children. They forged a lifetime bond that not only provided Margaret with the certainty that she was treasured and needed but also that she could be as capable and independent as Carrie. In her immediate family Margaret also had another role model, Grandfather John Murray. For the first twenty-four years of her life, she lived with him and observed that he was "very energetic, hard-working," and frugal and that he had "principles by which he lived." "My mother was like he was," Smith concluded, and she would be like her mother.[15]

Margaret grew up, according to neighbor Wallace Bilodeau, in "a plain working-class neighborhood," composed of families with similar backgrounds, incomes, and values.[16] On North and nearby Heselton, East, Winter, and Lawton streets there were numerous children and two grammar schools, Lincoln and Garfield. Their mother and father "didn't care for us to go to other places," Smith said, but they welcomed other children into their home.[17] "Have as good a time as you want, but have it at home," Carrie and George taught. Possibly they kept their children close to home because they had two children who had died suddenly. Roland Murray, their second son, developed pneumonia when he was one and a half years old and died overnight. "My mother never did get over that child being taken," Smith believed, but it was the third son, Laurence Franklin, named after George's brother, whom Smith remembered best. As the older sister, she "loved to dress him up and take him out" for a walk because he was a "handsome child" with a "very, very bright mind." When Laurence Franklin was two years and ten months old, he became ill with dysentery and quickly died.

Margaret grew into a short, pudgy, round-faced child whose photographs depict a serene to solemn little girl with a quiet smile and startlingly blue eyes steadily fixed on the camera. She had long, dark curls parted in the middle with hair ribbons on each side or pulled straight back with a large floppy bow. She had a stubborn streak that could bend her parents' will to her own. Once when the other little girls were wearing their hair in a dutch cut, Margaret decided that she also wanted short hair. Her mother and father said no, but she insisted and went into the barber's shop and "did a little crying." Carrie gave in first; people said Carrie "would never deny her," but before her father capitulated, he held the scissors up threateningly. "It's about the only thing I remember about those early days vividly," Smith reminisced while running her fingers through her short, curly hair. "I can see him now holding those shears up." George said, "It's going to be too late in a second. You going to change your mind? And I said no, and he cut my hair." When he finished, Smith said, "It was not a pleasing sight," but all Carrie said when she returned home was, "Oooh, Margaret."[18]

In 1903 at age five Margaret entered kindergarten at the Lincoln School, a wooden two-story building built in 1869, just a few minutes from her house. She usually walked with her chum Pauline Bragg, whom Margaret complained always had larger hair ribbons than she. Her class began with about thirty-five students, and Margaret enjoyed school but said, "I wasn't much of a student, nobody paid much attention to me as I remember." In second grade Lizzie Higgins was her teacher, and Gertrude Townsend taught her in the third grade. Margaret moved next door to the adjacent four-room brick Garfield School for grades four through six. Rudimentary at best, Margaret's education involved one teacher each year attempting to instruct thirty to thirty-five students in a variety of subjects, especially the basics of writing, reading, spelling, and arithmetic. Little to no thought was given to science, music, art, literature, history, or geography. For working-class families literacy was more the goal than a broad education, and "learning was rote memorization and recitation to the teacher," said Margaret who remembered that she always had a good memory.[19]

Skowhegan was a good place to grow up: rural, slow paced, and small enough for everyone to know everyone else. Margaret's childhood was stable and secure. She accepted her parents' love and concern as her natural right, and like many other first-born children, knew that she was uniquely treasured, especially by Carrie. Never touched by tragedy or want, Margaret grew into a remarkably mature person who was ready for independence, and in the Chase family, as in the state of Maine, that meant work. Without her even knowing, Maine was working its magic on Margaret, molding her, as it had her parents and grandparents, into a born-and-bred New Englander.

Work for increasing remuneration became the quintessential focus of Margaret's youth and surpassed school, friends, boys, and even family. "I must have been very ambitious," was Smith's understatement.[20] Years later there were frequent references to Smith's going from working in a five-and-ten-cent store to the U.S. Senate and having to work because she was from a poor family. Not only was she a young girl when she worked at Green's, but also there is considerable question as to whether her family was poor. They owned the two-story house in which they lived, took regular vacations at East Pond, and soon gave up the rented cottage there for one her father built at Lakewood, where he also bought a boat. There were the piano lessons, a six-party telephone, and a car, costing five hundred dollars, for George early in the 1920s. "Somewhere along the way, I presume, it sounded good for a girl from a poor family to do what I did," Smith said. "I didn't go to work because we were poor. I went to work because I wanted to be independent. I wanted to spend my own money as I wanted to. And I did. That is exactly what I did."[21]

Margaret's next job was with the telephone company as a substitute operator. By this time she was in high school and had a reputation for wanting work. The night operator called and asked if she would like to come to the telephone office upstairs in the Masonic Hall on Water Street and let her teach Margaret how the switchboard worked. Then when the operator wanted time off, Margaret could work for her for ten cents an hour or all night for one dollar. From time to time the "day girls" who had to work until 8:30 P.M. wanted off an hour or so earlier and would also be willing to pay Margaret. Accepting immediately, Margaret knew how she would spend the money: on shoes. Because of her height she had started wearing high heels and became "a great shoe woman."[22]

Skowhegan had battery telephones in the 1870s, and during the 1880s Bell Telephone Company opened an exchange in the Western Union office. The switchboard Margaret learned was manual, with four sections of numbers and plugs. Although there was a published directory of numbers, callers commonly asked the central operator to connect them with a person by name, not number. This practice meant Margaret had to memorize the telephone directory as well as learn the mechanics of the plugs. Smith maintained that the work "helped her memory immensely" and seventy-five years later illustrated by remembering that the insurance man John C. Griffin who would "kind of bark at you when you would . . . say, 'number please' " was himself number thirty-one.[23] Margaret also learned patience. "Goodness, if there's anything you need it's patience with people on the telephone," Smith remarked. She developed an ingratiating telephone manner and retained it. Witnessed talking on the telephone at age ninety-one, Smith metamorphosed into a young woman who slid down in her chair, stretched her legs out in front of her, and crossed them at the ankles. Vivaciously and with notable charm, she teased, laughed, and even flirted with her male caller for an obviously enjoyable and long period of time.

Working alone all night in a large building was spooky and tiring, although there was not much activity after 11:00 P.M. and there was a couch on which to sleep. One thing it was not to a teenaged high school student was boring, because Margaret listened to as many of the conversations as she could. "Oh, indeed, I did," Smith chuckled, "that's how I knew what people were doing."[24] One school couple whom she knew talked every evening from nine until ten, or at least they kept a line open without saying much except to inquire every so often if the other person was still there. Margaret not only knew a great deal about what was going on in town, she also became well known; in a small town in the early 1900s the telephone operator was an important person—a vital link to the doctor, fire department, police, and everyone else in town.

Number fifty-nine became a regular caller to the switchboard every evening at about a quarter to eight. Margaret first noticed that "this pleasant voice would come in and say would you please tell me the time. And I would give him the time. The next night he'd do the same thing. It went on night after night."[25] Margaret learned that he was Clyde Smith, "the first selectman in town, very prominent," recently divorced, and twenty-one years older than she. Intrigued, she told Pauline, "He has the most fascinating voice. I always try to answer him just as impressively," and she carefully gave him the time, in hour, minutes, and seconds. "It was kind of pleasant," Smith concluded later, and although "I didn't offer to talk to him for awhile . . . I did later on. I kind of dragged my voice."

Impressionable sixteen year old or not, Margaret was among many in Skowhegan who were impressed with Clyde Smith. He was by many accounts a handsome, dynamic, articulate man at a time and place when dependability was valued over appearance, solemnity preferable to charm, and reticence appreciated more than rhetoric. From birth a peacock among Maine loons, Clyde Harold Smith was born north of Skowhegan on a farm overlooking the village of Harmony on 9 June 1876, the same year as Margaret's mother. His father, William Franklin Smith, and mother, Angie Bartlette, both farmed and operated a store. Clyde started school in the "little red schoolhouse" at Harmony and helped his father by driving a team to deliver groceries.[26] The family, including two other sons, Kleber and Myron, moved to nearby Hartland in 1891, and Clyde attended the Hartland Academy. No more of a student than Margaret, Clyde left Hartland Academy for Shaw Business College and business school for politics.

Blessed with an unusually pleasing personality and a persuasive style of speaking, Clyde began discussing political concerns with customers at his father's store. Lawyer Bill Brown said that at seventeen Clyde knew more about the tariff than most adults and would argue for a high tariff while filling a customer's order. During family meals, Skowhegan photographer Lyndon Huff observed Clyde arguing politics with his father. One night Clyde would speak as a Democrat, and the next night he would argue as a Republican. Rather than play baseball, skate, or go to dances, Clyde studied political issues as he had never studied in school and began his first campaign at age twenty-two for state representative. No one expected him to win against his experienced opponent, but Clyde had a bicycle, which he rode all over his district to talk to voters. With notable energy and enthusiasm he talked of putting his campaign posters "on the pig and the jersey cow" while his confident opponent did not bother to campaign.[27] Clyde won a surprise victory and in 1899 found himself the youngest member of the Maine House of Representatives. Clyde served two terms in the house with little impact and in 1903 chose not to run again, accepting instead a position as superintendent of schools.

In 1905 he reentered politics as a candidate for sheriff of Somerset County. Prohibition was the controversial context of the election, and Clyde, who never used alcohol or tobacco, promised to enforce Maine's law "without fear or favor."[28] With prohibition laws since 1846, Maine had pioneered regulation of liquor in the United States, and Clyde's first speech in the legislature had been in opposition to resubmitting temperance to the public for vote and was for enforcement instead. In Somerset County enforcement meant closing the flourishing open bars that flouted the law, and with twenty-five more votes than the presumably entrenched Democratic incumbent Clyde was elected. At twenty-nine the youngest sheriff ever elected in Somerset County, Clyde seized the largest quantity of liquor in county history: twenty-two barrels of hard cider, two quarts each of gin, whiskey, and alcohol, and seventy-five gallons of wine.

Since Skowhegan is the county seat of Somerset County, Clyde Smith moved there when he was elected sheriff. He lived on High Street across from Edward Page, the president of First National Bank, owner of significant northern lumber interests, and one of the most influential men in town. The two became close friends, and Page became Clyde's mentor. He saw Clyde as "a young man who was going places" and encouraged his daughter, Edna, and Clyde to marry.[29] On 17 April 1908 when Clyde was thirty-two years old, he married Edna and continued as sheriff until 1909. Then he became involved in several business ventures: lumber, autos, real estate, and banking among them. Clyde and Edna also bought a controlling interest in the *Somerset Independent* on 19 May 1909 and later renamed it the *Independent-Reporter.* In 1913 Roland Z. Patten bought the paper from Clyde but left him one share in the company and the title of president.

While Clyde prospered financially, his marriage deteriorated. By several accounts a beautiful and kind woman, Edna never had children with Clyde and separated from him in 1913. Their divorce, apparently a bitter one that estranged Clyde from the Page family, especially Edna's brother, Blin Page, was final on 27 January 1914. Persistent and widespread local gossip was that the marriage failed because Clyde was a "ladies' man," a phrase used by several Skowhegan residents, although others more bluntly referred to his "womanizing" and "skirt chasing." "Very suave and very smooth," "a very, very attractive figure," and "admired by women" were common observations made about Clyde Smith. He was known to have "kept company" with several women. "I guess nobody would dispute that if they knew anything about him at all," Lyndon Huff said.[30] Divorce was rare in early twentieth-century America and carried palpable stigma. More deleterious in its effects on women than men, certainly divorce would have required significant cause for Edna to have risked social ostracism.

Clyde's prurient predilections did not harm him politically, and there are those who maintain that the titillation of sexual innuendo had a positive political effect. Whatever the undocumentable truth, Clyde Smith was elected first selectman in Skowhegan the next year, 1915, and held this foremost town position until 1932. Since Canaan's first town meeting in 1788, Skowhegan had elected selectmen to administer the community's business. Along with fence viewers, tree wardens, and as overseers of the poor, selectmen reported to interested citizens at the most democratic of American institutions, the town meeting. As first selectman Clyde presided at the meetings, which were held at the Opera House after a 1904 fire destroyed the original town hall, Coburn Hall. Renowned as "the smoothest talker that you ever heard" and "a beautiful speaker," Clyde put on a good show for the town folks as well as efficiently doing his job. During the meetings he stayed on the left corner of the stage, and "anything that came up, he had to explain it," one Skowhegan resident recalled. "He had a powerful voice and it was a good voice. You could hear him very clearly. . . . He knew the ropes and he knew how to carry everything out and carry everything on."[31]

Reportedly Clyde also carried on more flagrantly than before with women. His office was in the Opera House, and he was said to use the dressing rooms upstairs from the theater for assignations. Women could come and go from the rear of the building by using the back stairs. Once when Clyde was up for reelection as selectman, a citizens' group, presumably led by Blin Page, circulated a list of women with whom Clyde was believed to have had affairs. Instead of denying the charge, Clyde walked into the loud, packed town meeting and said that it was all true, of him as well as of the men who opposed him. He was reelected.

Margaret Chase was an innocent sixteen year old when Clyde first talked his way into her life and heart. When she was seventeen, he offered her what most appealed: a better-paying job. The selectmen needed a part-time assistant to record tax assessments in the town books and would pay twelve dollars a week, more than double her salary at the telephone company. Because the work had to be done during the day, Clyde arranged with the high school principal for Margaret to take her typing and shorthand classes in the evening at night school. "Talk about your experiences," Smith said. "That was one. I learned a great deal about politics in those days."[32] Clyde and the other two selectmen, an elderly Methodist deacon, Judge E. D. Packard, and a short, stout Franco-American, William Demo, went all over Skowhegan, by the early 1900s a town of over five thousand, and personally assessed property. Then they discussed their findings and had Margaret record their consensus. For about six months during her senior year and the following summer, Margaret learned about real estate, taxes, and budgeting and observed the political process from a rare vantage point. "Mr. Smith was very popular," Smith concluded. "A great many people came in and talked with him."[33]

By her own account Margaret learned little in high school. "All I was told from the time I went to kindergarten was that I had to go to school so that I could get my diploma," Smith lamented. "Nobody said why I had to get my diploma," except that it would lead to a better job. Margaret thought of school as a "necessary evil; it was like serving so much time in prison," and she "resented going to school." During her freshman and sophomore years, Margaret took the regular curriculum of English with Dorothy Elliott, mathematics, botany, language, and her downfall, ancient history with Gladys Wilson. The latter, Smith vividly recalled, was "a young, attractive, very bright woman" who was herself a graduate of Skowhegan High School and Colby College. "I never thought she was much of a history teacher. There wasn't anything about history that she made alive, interesting. She would give you the subject and expect you to recite the whole page." Margaret flunked history, with a grade of "sixty-nine and a fraction" when seventy was required. "Very unhappy about it," Margaret refused to take another history course and "almost left school," but Carrie talked her into continuing. Margaret also had difficulty with Latin—"never could see why I had to take Latin"—and with French—"I never could get the pronunciation."[34]

Margaret switched over to the commercial course of study in her junior and senior years and took typing, shorthand, bookkeeping, and a course in office etiquette. Along with eight others in her class of thirty students, Margaret prepared for a job under the guidance of teacher Pearl Meader. With Pauline Bragg, by now nicknamed Polly and who continued to be Margaret's best friend and who also was one of the commercial students, Margaret did better in school. Her highest academic accomplishment in high school came when she received a certificate for proficiency in typing forty-five words per minute.

Along with work and school, Margaret developed a social life apart from her family. Pauline played the piano at dancing school and at Skowhegan dances, and Margaret went along with her. Churches alternated in sponsoring socials for high school students each month, and Pauline and Margaret in their best sailor suits with pleated ankle-length skirts regularly attended. Respectable boy-girl contact in early twentieth-century Skowhegan allowed dancing together, sharing a cup of punch, even walking home together afterward, but not much else. There was no dating as such and little privacy for young couples allowed. Almost no one had a steady boyfriend or girlfriend, classmate Lewis Brown recalled, although there was some pairing off for hay rides. "My mother didn't think much of those things," Smith said. "Actually I think I worked so much outside that I didn't do a lot of those things that most young people did. I was after that ten cents an hour that I was getting."[35] Pauline remembered, though, that she and Margaret once had a crush on the same boy, and he might have been Lewis Brown, better known as Bunny in high school. Margaret believed that he was the best-looking boy in their class, but "Bunny Brown had so many girls chasing him I didn't get much chance with him."[36] Brown had worked as an office boy for Clyde Smith when he was selling automobiles and borrowed from his "great collection of dime novels" about "the Wild West and the Liberty Boys of '76," but he was not interested in girls at the time.[37] Margaret "had two or three boys" that she "thought were nice," and Smith recalled that they would "walk us home from school, take your books home. That kind of thing."[38] One time a boy asked Margaret to go canoeing at Lakewood, but when she jauntily stepped into the boat, it tilted, and she went head-over-heels into the water. Pauline also remembered that Margaret carried a photograph of Clyde Smith while they were in high school.

Bunny Brown recalled that Margaret was an "average" student and "thought of her as a big girl."[39] She does look surprisingly large in her high school photographs, with a big, squared-off face, plump body, and dark hair. Both the pretty little girl of the past and the slim young woman of the future are difficult to see in these rather unattractive, sullen pictures. There is, however, one account to the contrary, and it also came from Bunny Brown. On 2 June 1915 Margaret's class staged their Junior Exhibition, a popular school tradition that required every member of the class to participate. A recent college graduate, Pauline Oak, had returned to Skowhegan with theatrical ambitions and directed the performance, which was presented on the city hall stage. Due to the remodeling of the high school building, classes were being held in the city hall that year. Because there were more girls than boys in the class, Brown had to dance with six members of the class in a musical number depicting the history of dance, titled "A Dance Dream." The scene began with a sedate minuet and progressed to the foxtrot, but the liveliest dance was Bunny's and Margaret's "The Girl of the Spanish Hop." Margaret wore a rather risqué knee-length flamenco dance costume with black hose and a long black wig. The next morning Bunny was working at Sampson's Drug Store where, as usual, Skowhegan's businessmen gathered to visit and buy a newspaper. The local publisher, who had to be either Roland Patten or Clyde Smith, said, "Well, I'll tell you one thing, boys, that Chase girl has got the nicest looking legs as you'll see on any ladies this side of Boston." "That was shocking at that time," Brown observed, and correct he was because in nineteenth-century America women did not have legs (they had limbs), and they were never on display.[40] "Dresses were never off the shoe tops," Bunny said, and under the dresses, he may or may not have known, there were high-top boots, dark knit stockings, several petticoats, and long bloomers. Smith's excellent memory failed when asked if she remembered this incident, but she smiled as she said, "No, I don't remember that dance, no."[41]

A vivid memory, and the best time Margaret had in high school, was playing basketball. She had the good fortune to be in school at the time the Gibson Girl was fashionable. The creation of artist-photographer Charles Dana Gibson, this popular look was of a healthy, active woman who exercised, played golf and tennis, and rode a bike, albeit in a long skirt. Competitive women's athletics in public schools began during this fad, and Skowhegan organized its first girls' basketball team in 1912, with Margaret one of six girls on it. The team played "the old style three-court game," and Margaret's position was side center, "but I played all over the lot."[42] Charles Smith and Marion Stewart coached and took the team on overnight trips by train to play Cony, Waterville, Rockland, and Augusta high schools. For the first time in her life Margaret was traveling farther than Smithfield Pond and in a vehicle not pulled by a horse. Trains had not reached Skowhegan until the second half of the nineteenth century and were still awe inspiring, although the accommodations were more suited for freight than passengers. Once when playing in Augusta, Margaret spent the night in Blaine House, the governor's mansion. The home team commonly provided overnight facilities, and the governor's daughter was one of the Augusta players. "The Augusta team was a very aristocratic kind of team," Smith said. "They came from homes of great wealth" and had "raccoon coats, and we, of course were just poor Skowheganites."[43]

The girls played in full, knee-length, blue serge bloomers and pleated white middy blouses worn outside with large black silk ties. They sported white tennis shoes, long black stockings, black headbands, and bouffant white caps, with elastic to hold them on, and Smith thought the players were attractive. "I do not mean pretty faces," she elaborated. "I mean healthy, well-proportioned and well-poised, with good personality and good sportsmanship attitude."[44]

Coach Stewart said Margaret was "fast," and she must have been competitive and successful also, because in the senior year she both managed the team and played. On 3 January 1916 the newspaper reported that "the Skowhegan School team composed of the girl students won from up-river girls [North Anson] by a score of 13 to 3. So far the girls have not lost a game this season."[45] The girls went on to win the Central Maine championship after defeating Waterville five to four, Cony six to two, and Oakland six to one. Helen White was team captain and did almost all the scoring. Margaret, Helen, Geneva Smith, and Marion Adams lettered in basketball and received considerable local publicity. "The 1915–1916 Girls Basketball team of Skowhegan," the *Independent-Reporter* crowed, "has without a doubt established a precedent in Athletic History of the school by winning every game out of the fourteen played."[46]

Margaret's other memorable experience in high school was her senior class trip to Washington, D.C. According to Bunny Brown, the class of 1915–1916 was probably the first in Skowhegan history to make such a trip, and the planning began a year in advance. The ten-day trip cost sixty dollars for transportation, hotels, and meals, and the students required the advance notice to earn or for their families to save the money. Brown worked at Sampson's Drug Store before and after school each day and all day on Saturdays and Sundays for $2.50 a week. The boys had to wear long overcoats and hats on the trip, and Brown saved for a new coat and shoes as well as spending money. He remembered most of the students working to save the money, but surprisingly not Margaret. Although she was working at the telephone company at the time, she considered, as did her parents, the sixty dollars beyond her reach and Washington beyond comprehension. Except for Grandfather Murray, Margaret would have missed what was her most edifying experience to date. Without any prior comment on the family's assumption that the trip was impossible for Margaret, one day Murray asked her to meet him at the bank. Still earning $1.25 a day as he had since he was a young man, Murray went to the bank every Saturday after he received his pay at noon and deposited fifty cents. Margaret's eager anticipation on meeting her grandfather was that "he was going to give me the sixty dollars. I was as excited as could be." Indeed, Murray did ask Mr. Merrill, the bank teller, to draw that amount out of his account, and "well, I thought it was all set."[47] But when the money arrived, Murray asked Merrill to draw up a note for Margaret to repay the sixty dollars with 6 percent interest.

Seniors with teachers and parents as chaperones departed Skowhegan by train to Boston and Fall River, where they embarked by ship for New York City. By train again they traveled briefly to Philadelphia to tour the city and then on to Washington. Congressman John Peters from Ellsworth, Maine, met the exhausted but exuberant group at Union Station and after settling them in a local hotel took them on a tour of the White House. To their astonishment they ended up in the Oval Office to shake hands with a former teacher, President Woodrow Wilson, "which, of course, was a great thing in the lives of us from Skowhegan," Smith said.[48]

On the eve of expansion during World War I, Washington in 1916 was still a genteel southern city in the midst of a leisurely beautification program. The Park Commission had drawn up and was slowly implementing a plan to build congressional and judicial office buildings facing the Capitol; a reflecting pool, gardens, and fountains on the Mall; and a memorial to Abraham Lincoln. As it was, railroad tracks crossed the Mall, "uncouth poles" from Western Union and the telephone company outnumbered trees in some areas, and new electric trolley tracks meant torn-up streets all over town.[49] A city of about 330,000, Washington awed the students with its bustle and beauty. They toured the Capitol, attended sessions in the House and Senate, visited the Supreme Court, went through the Library of Congress, and saw Mount Vernon. "For some crazy reason . . . perhaps to show off," Emery Dyer and one of the girls walked to the top of the Washington Monument.[50] "We went everywhere," Smith exalted.[51]

Less historic but as memorable, Margaret tasted multicolored harlequin ice cream for the first time. George Otis Smith, the father of one of the boys in the class, worked in Washington, and he and his wife invited the Skowhegan group out to their home on Bancroft Lane. Experiencing her first elegant, if casual, entertaining, Margaret Chase Smith remembered little cookies with the "colored ice cream" and, as striking, a napkin and said, "It was a lasting memory for me."[52] Margaret saw Alice Roosevelt Longworth driving an automobile down Constitution Avenue, and recalls, "That to me was the greatest sight."[53] She also had her picture taken with "three little black children," and said, "I probably had never seen a black child before. We didn't have black people in Maine." For Margaret blacks were another tourist sight, and she left Washington with no awareness of the "secret city" in which the children lived. Off the tourist route but close by the marble monuments and glistening white public buildings, there was a hidden city of alleys festering with poverty, disease, filth, and crime and inhabited by some 16,000 segregated blacks.

For all of the pleasure derived from her senior trip to Washington, Margaret did not return to Maine with a prescient desire for a career in politics. Life was once again circumscribed by the slow seasonal rhythms of Skowhegan. "Our idea of the world," the Washington interlude aside, "didn't go much beyond the state of Maine," Bunny Brown observed.[54] Fewer than a hundred newspapers arrived in Skowhegan each day, and even the "fact that there was war in Europe didn't disturb us very much," Brown continued. "We had no radios. . . . Not too many people had telephones. Only occasional automobiles."

Senior year was the impenetrable fact of 1915–1916 for Margaret, and the school term began on 20 September. Skowhegan High School, for the first semester still located in city hall, had a student body of 150, 31 of them seniors, and 9 faculty members. The class yearbook, the *Lever,* recorded the yell of the class of 1916 as "Rizzle dazzle, Fizzle frazzle, Sis boom bah, '16, '16, Rah, rah, rah!"[55] and commented humorously on each senior with a quotation. For Pauline there was John Dryden's "who thinks too little and talks too much," and for Margaret there was the unattributed, and inexplicable, "She walks as if she were stirring lemonade with herself." The class will gave "to Karl Genthner the little green fruit dish in which Pauline Bragg keeps her dates," and for Margaret, in presumed reference to Clyde Smith who drove a Maxwell, "We give to Ruby Dyer, Margaret Chase's permission to ride in a Maxwell car."[56] The quotation that Margaret dedicated to Ruby and other students was, "The wages of sin is death," and the song the *Lever* attached to Margaret was, "I Wonder What My Love Is Doing Tonight."

Graduation day was 22 June 1916, and the school held the exercises at the Opera House. "High over the stage," the newspaper reported, "was conspicuously hung the class motto, 'Labor Omnia Vincet,' Labor Conquers All."[57] All the seniors sat on the stage, decorated in the blue and white class colors, flowers, and evergreens. One student read an essay on the evolution of the typewriter, another presented a travelogue on the Washington trip, and a third orated on Shakespearean heroines. Polly received one of the Shepherd Prizes for having the best grades and showing the most improvement in her business courses, and Greg Warner was valedictorian. Then, as in graduation exercises of time immemorial, each student responded to name called and stepped forward to receive diploma as parents applauded or sighed with relief. The Reverend George Merriam gave the benediction, and the audience tittered as the principal said, "The audience will please remain seated until the class of 1916 has passed out."[58] Drunken staggers and laughter notwithstanding, the long-anticipated completion of high school was fact for Margaret Chase. Margaret's accomplishment was also her parents' because she was the first member of her family to be graduated from high school.

The "winsome maidens and stalwart youths" of Margaret Chase's class of 1916, as the *Independent-Reporter* referred to them, had limited ambitions upon graduation.[59] In writing the class prophecy, Bunny Brown did not have any of the girls leaving Maine but did have them becoming "house-wives and clerical workers and secretaries." Two of the boys entered Bow-doin College, and two attended the University of Maine, but "I don't think any of the girls went to a four-year college. As I recall, we were kind of an undistinguished group."[60]

A week after graduation, war's long reach touched the lives of young people in Skowhegan. In distant Mexico, Pancho Villa had perpetrated the massacre of eighteen American miners at Saint Isabel in January and had raided Columbia, New Mexico, in March, which resulted in seventeen American deaths. President Woodrow Wilson in response ordered General John J. Pershing and twelve thousand troops to undertake a punitive expedition into northern Mexico against Villa. Seventy-seven of one hundred twenty young men from Scowhegan who reported for National Guard duty passed the physical examination and were organized into Company E of the Second Maine Regiment.[61]

The next year the army activated Company E again, this time for service in World War I.[62] Pauline Bragg's new husband, Matthew Greene, was drafted, but Emery Dyer did not pass the physical. Also drafted was the first boy Margaret ever dated. They had gone to the movie theater his father owned, and now this young man was in uniform. For the first time Margaret began to watch the news for reports of injuries and deaths, and she and her friends "were troubled."[63] Tobey Mooers came home in December after six months in France and reported that Company E was fighting in the Champagne area. He had been assigned ambulance duty there and stated that he had been taking the soldiers "from the ambulance in pieces."[64] Matthew Greene returned unharmed, but one classmate was crippled with a leg injury, and two others were killed, one of them the boy Margaret had dated. After the war ended in November 1918, Clyde Smith, characterized by the newspaper as a "magnetic orator," welcomed Skowhegan's soldiers home in a "monster celebration."[65]

Enigmatically, the *Independent-Reporter* in its story on Margaret's high school graduation had mentioned that she would "become a teacher for a time at least."[66] Margaret did not want to teach any more than she had wanted to stay in high school, and working her way through college was simply not a consideration. Several of the girls who had been good students entered two-year colleges, but for Margaret and her family a high school diploma was the epitome of educational achievement. Margaret's goal was, as it had been and would be for years to come, a better-paying job. She had applied for a full-time position as a telephone operator but had learned with disappointment that there were no jobs available. When she heard that District 5 needed a teacher in the one-room rural Pitts School "on the back road about 5 miles from the village" and would pay $8.50 a week, with little enthusiasm and some trepidation she requested and received the position.

Since there was no accreditation procedure and a shortage of applicants, the school administrators required neither college training nor a degree.

Margaret's eighteen-year life reached its nadir at Pitts School. For five dollars a week she arranged room and board with a local family, whose home was in a beautiful apple orchard, and reported to work in September 1916. Serving an area of large farm families, the schoolhouse was a small, white clapboard building with windows all around and an outhouse in the rear. Inside there were blackboards on three walls, slant-top student desks, "a great big black stove," and up front Miss Chase's desk and chair.[67] Margaret had nine children, ages six through fourteen, in first through ninth grades, and she was expected to teach them all of the required courses. Reminiscent of generations of first-year teachers, Margaret the night before learned the lessons she would teach the next day. She calculated that in order to accomplish what was required, she had to teach "about two minutes to a child a subject each day," and maintained that she "worked very, very hard that year," probably again like most new teachers, harder than when a student herself. "No one will ever know how hard I worked," she said.[68]

She rang a hand bell to commence and dismiss school, seated the youngest children directly in front of her desk and the oldest in the rear, and assigned each class its work in reading, grammar, geography, or arithmetic. Learning was still a matter of memorization, and one by one she would call the students to the recitation bench by the stove to hear their lessons. Then she would make a new assignment in a different subject and continue recitations. At noon she and the children ate their lunches out of a lard pail, drank water from a common dipper and bucket, and brought in more wood for the stove from the pile outside. At recess Margaret organized games and calisthenics to run off pent-up energies, hers and the students', and then continued classes until 3:30 P.M.

Margaret's problem was loneliness. "How I got through that year I don't know," she said, "lonely, I was so lonely."[69] She had never lived away from home before, and although she returned to Skowhegan every Friday and stayed until late Sunday, she was miserable. She paid Carrie $1.50 of the $3.50 she had left after she paid for room and board and lived off the remaining $2.00. Margaret's internment at Pitts ended while she was home for Easter recess. She received a message that the telephone company finally had a position for her, and with no remorse about leaving her students she asked the superintendent of schools to find someone to finish out the school year for her. Although later she would frequently be characterized in teacher stereotypes, Margaret fled Pitts and academia forevermore after her scant twenty-eight weeks of teaching. She happily returned to her front bedroom in the Chase house on North Avenue and remained there for the next thirteen years.

Secure in familiar surroundings, Margaret began work as a daytime telephone operator. She convinced her friend Pauline Bragg Greene to apply for a position also, and once Pauline was hired, it was like high school again. The two could walk to and from work together, eat and shop on their lunch breaks, and enjoy their "fascinating" jobs. "We worked 63 hours a week," Pauline said, "and the starting pay was $4 but we liked it and we felt we had good jobs. Discipline was strict, but we were used to that. Our school discipline had been strict too." One of Pauline's duties was to shovel coal into the furnace of the telephone company building, "counting the shovelfuls to make it last" because of the wartime shortage.[70] The measure of Margaret's misery at Pitts was that she accepted the operator's position for less than half the salary she had made teaching.

The manager of the telephone company, Frank Matten, offered her a promotion to chief operator, "which was," she thought, "a big job in those days."[71] Margaret decided, however, that she "didn't want to be a telephone operator for the rest of her life" and declined the offer, recommending Pauline instead. Pauline happily accepted and worked as chief operator in Skowhegan until her retirement in 1962. Apparently impressed with Margaret, Matten offered her a second position with him in the Maine Telephone and Telegraph commercial office on Madison Avenue. There from 8:00 until 5:30 she sat behind a large iron grate on a bench at the counter and waited on customers who came to pay their bills or to use the public telephones. The usual salary was $13.00 a week, but because of her experience Matten paid her $16.00, her top salary to date.

Happy with her economic advancement and ready to have a good time, Margaret became part of the Jazz Age generation of financially independent, fun-loving young people. With Skowhegan's population going from 5,000 in 1910 to 5,981 in 1920, the town had changed more than grown over the years. The train brought in large numbers of traveling salesmen who frequently made telephone calls from Margaret's office. With this surplus, if somewhat disreputable, group of men in town, public entertainment facilities increased. To the delight of young people, there was a speakeasy connected to Pomlow's Restaurant, a beer parlor on Madison, and a couple of movie houses like the Bijou and the Empire. Clyde Smith converted the Opera House to show movies, and immediately his former brother-in-law, Blin Page, decided to open the Strand Theatre, as much out of bitterness as good business sense, several townspeople believed. The most fun was always to be had at the Lakewood Country Club, "The Playground of Central Maine," as the *Independent-Reporter* referred to it.[72] Located five miles north of Skowhegan on Lake Wesserunsett, the inn held dances on most Tuesday and Friday evenings on its cool, screened veranda. George Chase still had a cottage on the lake and kept a motor boat there for the family to use. Too tired from being out dancing the night before, Margaret seldom rose early to go fishing with her father anymore. Now she was more interested in picnics with her friends, steamboat rides around the lake on the *Margaret B,* Sunday band concerts, and the movies made of the dances at the inn. Most tempting to many was the nationally recognized Lakewood Theatre, in operation since 1901 and considered the oldest summer stock theater in the United States. Pauline's husband worked at the theater, and sometimes Pauline would usher. "That was fun," she said. "I saw all the plays, met the stars and collected autographs."[73] Among the stars in the summer productions were Milton Berle, Cesar Romero, and Ed Wynn who starred at Lakewood in the first production in the nation of *Life with Father*. Lyndon Huff as a boy played tennis at Lakewood with Humphrey Bogart and Vincent Price and later became the theater's official photographer. In addition to its "tumble-down hotel," Lakewood had a "modest restaurant, a cage of monkeys, a bear," and a bowling alley.[74] For twenty-five cents, a person could take the open trolley from Skowhegan to Lakewood, see a play, stay for the dance, and have something to eat and drink. Margaret loved to dance and learned to do a modest Charleston and shimmey but seldom had to ride the trolley to Lakewood. For just under five hundred dollars her father had bought a Model-T Ford, and daringly Margaret learned to drive.

When hemlines went up, Margaret gave up her ankle-length skirts and the hated black stockings for shorter skirts and flesh-colored stockings, shocking at the time. Her weakness for high heels continued, but she contented herself with lipstick and never used the obvious eye shadow, mascara, and rouge of the new cosmetic craze. When the young women of the 1920s began having their hair shingled, Margaret hesitated, but Carrie encouraged her with news of a friend who had her hair "semi-shingled" and added that she hoped "you have yours done."[75] Even Margaret's sister Evelyn, who was still in elementary school, reported that their friend Blanche Bernier "had hers done yesterday and I may have mine done this week."[76] Margaret did have her hair cut but never resorted to the obviously fake black, red, and platinum dyes so popular among the flappers of the twenties. Something of a "semi-flapper" with "semi-shingle," Margaret never drank or smoked, but she enjoyed a good party.

Margaret apparently continued to see Clyde Smith during the 1920s, to an extent that caused considerable gossip. On 23 December 1920 Clyde Smith wrote a Mrs. Richardson that "friends and foes alike give you credit for being able to spread more gossip than can the scandalous tongues of a whole community." He added that he did not know how "Mr. and Mrs. Chase will treat your charges of contamination relative to their daughter," but he intended to lose no time "in placing you in true light."[77] On the same day Clyde Smith wrote Lena M. Dyer that her "reference to Miss Chase's contamination exists only in your own evil eye. How thankful you could be if your own life had been as clean and as far above reproach as has hers."[78] He added that he had not given Dyer a "reputation" and that he had not "stated to you or any other human being that I did not care for Miss Chase or that I would or was not going to marry her." Once on a rare and unexplained trip alone out of town in 1924, Margaret received a letter from her mother with the provocative instruction to "do what is right and come home soon." Carrie added that "Mr. Smith called up here tonight to see if we had heard from you and said he had." Carrie closed with a final admonition to "be careful."[79] Several of Margaret's contemporaries, interviewed in 1988, speculated that the purpose of the trip was to have an abortion, but there is no evidence for their assumptions.

Semi-flapper or not, Margaret still considered work her life and preferred economic advancement to dances, plays, and movies. "Guess you think I was rather strange," she said, "but as a young woman I was always busy. I had other things to do so I did not do those things."[80] After working for two years with Matten, Roland Patten, the owner of the weekly *Independent-Reporter,* came by the office to ask if Margaret would be interested in working for him. He offered eighteen dollars a week, and since "that was two dollars more than I was getting," she accepted on the spot, although she had four weeks of unused vacation time from the telephone company. In addition to two dollars more, changing jobs meant crossing the street, because the newspaper offices were upstairs in a two-story wooden frame building across Madison from Maine Telephone and Telegraph. Patten, whom Margaret considered "very eccentric," put her in charge of circulation, gave her a rolltop desk at the entrance in front of the windows, and had her collect for subscriptions and take changes of address. Margaret came to consider herself "a girl about town" who knew everyone and was active and involved in the community. "I knew everybody and everybody knew me," she said.[81]

Increasingly, like many other young working women of the 1920s, Margaret became involved in club work, for purposes of both camaraderie and self-improvement. Sorosis was a social club for young women, Smith said, who believed that having a club "was the thing to do" and "we thought we'd like to try it."[82] A member asked Margaret to join, and she enjoyed the meetings with entertaining programs on the "Social Psychology of Laughter," book reviews, "Personal Efficiency," and travel opportunities. With little pretense of purpose beyond pleasing themselves, the young women held numerous social events: card parties, picnic suppers, moving picture benefits, dinners, and dances. One year Margaret served as president of Sorosis, and while she did not attach much importance to it, she learned that other people liked her and that they would follow her lead.

Organizations for working women had developed more slowly than women's social clubs and men's business clubs, because there were not significant numbers of interested middle-class women in the workplace until after the turn of the twentieth century. Poorer women in unskilled factory and mill positions seldom had the energy, inclination, or leisure to organize, but the large numbers of women in clerical, secretarial, and sales offices and stores did. The Business and Professional Women's Club (BPW) pioneered the organization of these women, and by 1921 their efforts reached into Maine with chapters established at Lewiston, Auburn, and Portland. In March 1922 word reached Skowhegan, and a group of older women, among them Elizabeth Dyer and Dr. Julia Kincaid, assembled women, including Margaret, to travel to Portland to hear the BPW's national president, Lena Madison Phillips, speak on the relevance of the club to their lives. Persuaded, the Skowhegan women returned and founded a local chapter, with Margaret as vice president. The club's stated purpose was "to promote good fellowship and the spirit of unity" and "to create a deeper sense of the dignity of the professions and of business and to advocate and maintain a higher standard of workmanship and of business and professional ethics among women." More succinctly, the group's motto was "A Better Businesswoman for a Better Business World." The emphasis was on making better workers of women, not on improving the workplace with salary increases, safer working conditions, or better hours.

Margaret became BPW president in 1923 and had as her objective "to get the girls to be able to stand up on their feet and say something."[83] She assigned them two-minute speeches on their work for presentation at meetings and set the example by participating herself. Public speaking was a lifelong disability for Smith. Articulate and ingratiating in informal speaking, Smith became wooden with a prepared address in front of her and read every word with little to no expression or contact with her audience. For Margaret the problem had begun in high school, and the one time she had been scheduled to give a speech to her class, she had suffered "a very serious headache, and so I never performed." That she understood the importance of women's being able to communicate orally in public was surprising and that she attempted to help others with a similar limitation commendable. As president of a mostly older and unmarried group of women, Margaret carefully prepared for her meetings. She studied *Robert's Rules of Order* and "learned those rules by heart," and she carefully typed an agenda with her statements written out in full.[84] Obviously successful in her leadership position, Margaret, like generations of women who use clubs as political incubators, learned to chair meetings, marshal votes, and organize programs. Margaret's effectiveness in Skowhegan brought her to the attention of the state federation, and she was appointed editor and manager of the organization's newsletter, the *Pine Cone.* Using the skills she had learned at the *Independent-Reporter,* Margaret solicited 1,900 subscriptions for $686.44 and spent $625.66 in printing and mailing.

Again, her success brought reward, and in 1925, at age twenty-seven, Margaret was elected president of the state federation, the youngest to date. The incumbent BPW president, Flora Weed, secured Margaret as a candidate for the presidency because the other contender, a Republican, intended "to politicize" the organization.[85] Since Margaret was still apolitical, Weed, a Democrat, believed she would see to it that the "Republicans won't take over." The position was significant, because the BPW in Maine now had twenty-four chapters with a membership of 1,563, and when Margaret organized the annual convention for the federation in Skowhegan, she secured Maine governor and Mrs. Owen Brewster as honored guests. Margaret also represented Maine at the club's national convention in Des Moines, and when she returned to report on the meeting to her local chapter, she received a briefcase as a gift and as an acknowledgment of her status. As state president, Margaret spoke at other chapters, continuing to read her addresses and to praise BPW as a "common meeting ground" for working women who wanted to improve the business world by becoming "finer, more understanding" women.[86] Margaret finished her year as state president with a $4.60 deficit but was reelected, and at the second convention she organized in Skowhegan, she had Clyde Smith give the welcoming address.

All this time Margaret had continued to work for the newspaper. Her duties had expanded to setting slug for subscription blanks, providing information on employment opportunities, preparing the mailing list, and estimating costs for engraving and printing. When Patten decided to move her from circulation to advertising, Margaret also began writing ads. To learn how, she bought a copy of the *New York Times* each morning, studied the ads in it, and tried to rewrite them for the *Independent-Reporter,* "which wasn't too bad an idea," she said.[87] After a couple of years in advertising, Patten moved her to the editorial department, where she had difficulty writing but stayed two years. Accounting was Margaret's final department at the paper, but "this I did not like," although she credited herself with becoming a "very good ordinary bookkeeper."

The newspaper had two signal successes while Margaret worked there for which she later received credit, deserved or not. The first was a significant increase in circulation, which led to an award for reaching the largest circulation among New England country weeklies. The second was a citation for being one of the ten most successful country weeklies in the nation. Margaret also received credit for writing the paper's slogan, "There are eleven Bostons, many Londons, but only one Skowhegan," although the idea originated with Patten.[88] One-time local resident George Otis Smith, the director of the National Geological Survey, provided the inspiration by mailing postcards from around the world that always were delivered with only the name of the addressee and Skowhegan.

In 1928 Margaret changed jobs again. She was at her front desk one day when the woolen mill owner Willard Cummings came in to place an ad with her for an office manager. He explained that he was moving his office from Boston to Skowhegan where the mill was located, but his male office manager, whom he paid $118 a week, could not make the move. Cummings wanted to employ a woman in Skowhegan to do the same work for $50, which surprised Margaret because "that was big pay in Skowhegan. No woman ever received anything like that." Boldly, Margaret inquired as to the qualifications for the job, and Cummings responded that what he wanted was a woman who was a combination of Maine's U.S. senator Wallace White and state senator Frank Holley. Admitting that "that's quite a big order," Margaret nonetheless asked, "What about me?" After ascertaining that she could type, take shorthand, and keep books, an apparently impressed Cummings said that he would have to talk to Patten. After a brief private discussion, Patten came out of his office and told Margaret that he could only increase her salary to $28 and did not want to keep her from the better-paying position. When Cummings hired her on the spot, Margaret "nearly had heart failure. I couldn't take shorthand for a man like that. I couldn't type sufficiently. I'd taken those things in high school, but I hadn't done them since, and I began to see that I was way in over my head." Margaret went to Clyde Smith for advice, and, having political differences with Cummings, Clyde adamantly said, "You know better than that. You know you can't do that. I said who says I can't do it. He said, well, we had quite a discussion anyway. And I did it. I took the job. Fifty dollars a week, and I went home and cried every night for six months."[89]

The Cummings mill was located on Water Street by the North Channel bridge; Margaret's office, in the front of the mill, extended out over the boulders lining the Kennebec below. When she timidly reported to work, she learned to her consternation that she had a staff: a bookkeeper, a secretary, a clerk, and a general assistant for errands, "each one of them far ahead of me in . . . experience." Overwhelmed but determined to succeed, Margaret worked diligently and concluded that after six months she was "in charge of myself and my job."[90] Cummings was "difficult," and Clyde had assured her that nobody could work with him. But once Margaret learned not to contradict him or make changes, they got along well.

One of Margaret's responsibilities was making up the payroll and handing out pay to, as she called them, the "little people," the mill workers in the dye house and carbonizer room. She came to have "greater feeling about the ordinary laborer" as she witnessed their hard work in "an unhealthy atmosphere" for twenty-six to twenty-eight cents an hour. Aware of the wealth of the Cummings's family that allowed them to educate their children in Paris, Margaret "cringed" as she doled out the workers' weekly pittance. Her heightened awareness of salary inequities was not personally applied, however; she never questioned Cummings's paying his former male office manager more than double her salary. "I just took it for granted that he could get [a woman] cheaper," she said.[91]

Cummings was in Paris during the 1929 stock market crash, and Margaret, in charge of his financial records, feared that he was destitute because of his heavy losses. He was not and believed that being away instead of frantically trying to remedy the crisis kept his losses to a minimum. Cummings kept his mill open and Margaret's job secure, but Skowhegan's banks ceased operations for a while. When they reopened, they limited withdrawals to ten dollars per person per week except in emergencies and for commercial transactions. "Times were very good in the Twenties up till the crash came,"

Lyndon Huff remembered, and then Skowhegan, like the rest of the nation, suffered.[92] The Emergency Relief Agency (ERA) brought surplus Florida grapefruit and canned beef to distribute from the ERA office in the municipal building. When the National Recovery Act (NRA) brought relief with a forty-hour week and a minimum wage of twenty-five cents an hour, workers staged Labor Day parades and passed out NRA buttons. In the parades each group of workers carried items symbolic of their work like Wallace Bilodeau's father who carried a cowhide on a stake for the shoemakers. For Margaret the Great Depression was "a pretty cruel time" when "everybody went without," but "we didn't lose a lot of money because we didn't have money to lose."[93] Her security in the crisis bred confidence, and she found herself ready for another challenge.

Chapter Two

IN TRAINING

Determined to be on time, Margaret gently edged the big black Maxwell above the speed limit. Warily she glanced at Clyde sitting next to her and smiled when he appeared too absorbed in his reading to notice. He did not like for her to speed and had warned her before that a fine was an unnecessary embarrassment for a highway commissioner.

They were on their way to Norridgewock for a meeting, but to Margaret it seemed like an outing, not work. But then campaigning was not work to Clyde either; it was life. The road followed the Kennebec River, and the water mirrored the many trees whose leaves were beginning to change color. Despite the bright sun, there was a chill in the air that Margaret knew signaled an early end to summer and made her all the more determined to enjoy the day.

"Slow down, Sis. We don't want to get there early," Clyde said. "I want the meeting to be underway and everyone there worrying that I'm not coming. Then we'll walk in with a lot of noise and apologies and take over."

Although only a dozen or so elderly people were seated around the dowdy parlor, Clyde boomed to the man who opened the door, "What a great turnout! Sorry I'm late, but some town business came up. I finally told them they would have to wait because I had an important meeting to attend."

Margaret watched as Clyde brought the meeting to a halt by going around the room and speaking to each person. He called most of them by name, asked about their children, and remembered the last time they had met. Then he told the chairman to please continue, and he would just sit over on the side and listen. The chairman insisted, of course, that Clyde go ahead and speak.

With an easy charm that worked on the room full of voters as well as on her, no matter how often she saw Clyde in action, he began by introducing her as not only his wife but also as a state Republican committeewoman and former state president of the Business and Professional Women's Club.

Then, standing more erect and using a more formal tone, Clyde continued, "From time immemorial kingdoms and nations have been confronted with the problem of how to provide for helpless old age, humanely and economically, for each succeeding year has revealed a larger number of aged persons who have lost in life's uneven struggle."[1]

Margaret recognized the words from a speech that Clyde had been giving since 1923, but she also silently acknowledged that it was even more appropriate now that depression stalked the land.

"Pensioning of worthy citizens is not a new principle or an unheard-of innovation," Clyde continued reasonably and persuasively.

Turning her attention from Clyde to his audience, Margaret observed the nods of agreement. None of those present appeared impoverished, but they were not affluent either. They were, however, staunchly independent, resistant to charity, and inured to the responsibility of providing for oneself. But they listened closely when Clyde argued that the 1930s were different, harder years, and with businesses and banks closing and unemployment rising, the government had to play a larger role than before.

A few minutes later Margaret signaled Clyde that it was time for them to leave for a labor meeting in Waterville.

This time Clyde drove, and Margaret, without being told, took out his black campaign book to add the names of the new people who had been at the meeting. Clyde had an excellent memory for names, but Margaret surprised him by correcting him on one person's name and adding the name of the man by whom she had sat who had arrived after Clyde had begun.

For the rest of the short drive, Clyde had Margaret turn to the Waterville list in the black book and read him the names of those who would likely be at the meeting.

That done, Margaret teased Clyde about leaving out sending mothers "through those gates ajar from whence no traveller returns, with a poor house insignia stamped upon her fair face." Clyde replied that those present were too old to have to worry about their mothers' old age pensions. He wanted them to worry about their own.

Stopping in front of the union hall, Clyde told Margaret that he wanted her to stay in the car and write him a new speech for the Somerset County Republican meeting that evening. When she asked, "What about?" he said, "Be positive. Write about what the party has accomplished over the years."

As Margaret wrestled the typewriter from the back seat onto her lap, she realized that she had been promoted from chauffeur and record keeper to speechwriter. Well, it was about time; she had listened to enough political speeches to know there was not much to them.

"I don't think he wanted to marry Margaret," Skowhegan photographer Lyndon Huff said, "but she kept pursuing him and finally he married her."[2] If this appraisal is accurate, convincing Clyde Smith to marry her had taken sixteen years, because Margaret was thirty-two years old and Clyde fifty-three when they married on 14 May 1930.

The depression aside, the timing of the wedding was not auspicious. Clyde had spent 1929 embroiled in a state highway scandal that had resulted in the governor's asking for his resignation. While continuing to serve as selectman in Skowhegan and as a member of the Governor's Council in Augusta, Clyde had been named chairman of the three-man State Highway Commission in 1927 by Governor Owen Brewster. A longtime champion of a rural highway building program when he was in the legislature, Clyde claimed credit for miles of improved roads in Skowhegan. As chairman of the State Highway Commission, he administered federal funds from a depression-era public works program of the Herbert Hoover administration. A bonanza for Maine, the program allowed the commission to employ some twelve thousand men on construction projects financed by an annual $700,000 federal grant.

Then rumors began of trouble on the commission, and rumbling from Augusta held that the commissioners would soon fire their chief engineer because he disagreed with their policies. The next election brought William Tudor Gardiner to the governor's house and fresh worries about a Department of Justice investigation of expenditures on Maine roads. The Department of Agriculture directed the rural roads program, and Secretary of Agriculture William M. Jardine asked for the investigation because of thousands of missing barrels of cement intended for road use. Although investigators failed to turn up the cement or guilty parties, Jardine held the highway commissioners responsible and demanded that they be fired or he would suspend federal funds. The governor complied and demanded resignations from all three commissioners. Two resigned, but Clyde refused, maintaining his innocence and demanding a legislative investigation. Not without influence after thirty years in politics, Clyde not only secured an investigation but was exonerated by it. After Clyde threatened to run for governor in 1932, Gardiner appointed him to another year's term on the highway commission, which the legislature had reorganized to satisfy federal authorities. As in most political scandals, the public remained uncertain as to who was responsible. The missing cement remained unlocated, and federal funds from a Republican administration in Washington continued to build highways in the Republican state of Maine.

Simultaneous with the highway corruption rumors, speculation began in 1929 that Clyde was responsible for the pregnancy of Cora Quinn, a Skowhegan shoe factory worker. In 1930 Cora gave birth to a daughter, Rita, who grew up in Skowhegan and was widely reported and never denied as being Clyde's daughter.

In addition to his personal and political problems, medical records show that Clyde had what he called "nervous breakdown tests" in 1930.[3]

Although the decision to marry at last appeared peculiar to many, Margaret maintained that she and Clyde had been engaged for two years and went to some lengths in her "Wedding Memories" book to record her marriage as a girl of eighteen might. She wrote that her first entertainment in celebration of their intention to marry was a "supper party" where they received "an electric flat iron," and then that her friends gave her a towel shower and later hosted a bridge party where her gift was a doily set. Margaret had her blue lace wedding dress "made to order in Paris" with a hat to match, and in Skowhegan purchased "crystal beads and beige stockings" to go with it. The rest of her trousseau, she recorded, was an "oxford grey traveling suit," "six of all underthings, silk," "a dark blue coat, and a tan lace chiffon dress."[4]

On 14 May in George and Carrie Chase's small parlor, the Reverend George Merriam married Margaret and Clyde. Margaret carried a rose bouquet and had her sisters, twenty-one-year-old Evelyn and nineteen-year-old Laura, as her witnesses. Only thirteen guests crowded into the house to observe the wedding, but some three hundred attended the reception afterward at Clyde's house, where the Smiths intended to live. Margaret wrote that they were "unusually well off in that we have one of the finest places in this part of the state, a large 30 room house with about twelve acres of land. The house is completely furnished in a most homelike manner."[5]

Clyde's was the largest house in Skowhegan and originally known as Fairview Farm when Manley T. Pooler built it in the 1880s and kept blooded stock in extensive stables. By the time Clyde purchased the Pooler estate in 1927, at the time of the highway commission scandal and with funds that were not investigated, the animals were gone, and the road on which the house sat was named Fairview Avenue. The three-story house had five baths, eight fireplaces, two kitchens, a sunporch, a second floor balcony, and a two-story barn. The front door was ornamented with stained glass windows, the hallways had tear-drop chandeliers, the fireplaces' carved mantles reached the ceilings, and the bathrooms had pink marble sinks. For the first time since Margaret's seven months as a teacher, she left her parents' home for another residence.

Margaret took two weeks off from managing the office at the Cummings mill, and the morning after they had married, she and Clyde left on a wedding trip to Augusta House. Because of rain, Margaret recorded, they soon returned to Skowhegan. Her last girlish entry in her memories book was, "We are still enjoying ourselves attempting to make our entire life together one long honeymoon."[6] Clyde completed his troubled term on the highway commission in 1930 but continued as selectman through 1932. All the time he had some business going on the side. As Margaret pointed out, "He was either in some automobile business or some real estate business. . . . He was in the road culvert business for awhile."[7]

Margaret credited her employer, Willard Cummings, not Clyde, with her personal involvement in politics. Politically active himself and impressed with Margaret's success as a club woman, Cummings suggested first that she be added to the Skowhegan Town Committee. Then in early 1930 when Cummings managed Wallace H. White's campaign for the U.S. Senate and before her marriage, Cummings told her, "Miss Chase, I want you to run for committeewoman from Somerset County."[8] Clyde did not want her to run, because, as she said, "he didn't like having two politicians in the family."[9] Margaret ran anyway and won a seat on the committee on 27 March 1930; she was reelected twice. "I didn't know anything about politics," Margaret said, "but I knew everybody and everybody knew me. It was just a natural thing. Call it destiny if you will, but I just fell into it."[10]

Although Margaret returned to the mill after her marriage, her work on the town and state committees took increasing time. Clyde took even more because his political ambitions had by no means abated, and he saw advantages to having his young, attractive wife at his side. Margaret quit her job early in the 1930s and devoted the rest of her life to politics.

In contemplating his political future, Clyde vacillated between running for governor or for Congress in 1932. He claimed that he had "an almost unanimous Labor vote" because of his persistent championing of a stronger workman's compensation law, a shorter workday, child labor restrictions, and old age pensions.[11] Considered one of the Republican old guard because of his successful involvement in politics since the beginning of the century and despite his liberalism, Clyde believed the highway scandal was behind him and the choice of races his to win.

Complicating his decision was the unexpected announcement of his foremost personal and political nemesis, Blin Page, that he was entering the Republican primary for the gubernatorial nomination. Blin was Clyde's former brother-in-law and longtime rival for the affection and respect of Edward Page, Blin's father and Clyde's mentor. Also a resident of Skowhegan, Blin was a wealthy timberland owner and banker, two-term state representative, and sitting state senator. The press referred to the two as "bitter enemies," and reporter Sam E. Conner elaborated: "For more than twenty years there has been a chasm wider than the grand canyon between the two of them."[12] Not wanting to be seen as responding to Page's initiative or, more pragmatically, risking a split in his Skowhegan base of support, Clyde decided to forgo the governor's race.

He announced instead for the Governor's Council, the predecessor of the current governor's cabinet but more powerful. The council, elected regionally, had veto power over the governor's appointments and other privileges, which must have amused Clyde in contemplating Page as governor. During the campaign "we were like a team," Margaret said. "We worked together very closely on practically everything."[13] Mostly they traveled the country. "I went with him and did part of the driving," Margaret continued. "He always made a good many calls on the rich and the poor alike. They had great admiration for him." Margaret scheduled Clyde's appointments and handled his correspondence, "some of it by dictation, more of it on my own," she said. Although always in Clyde's shadow, Margaret learned that she was as good as he in remembering people's names, a fact that she credited to her work as a telephone operator. There she had also learned the importance of courtesy, and naturally, without making an effort, she assumed the persona of a politician's wife: quiet, pleasant, attractive, and efficient. Longtime Maine politician Peter Mills, who observed the Smiths on the campaign trail, said, "She was the guy's wife. She wasn't there pulling his coat tails and telling him what to say or anything like that."[14]

Clyde succeeded in his campaign for the Governor's Council, although Page lost in his primary election. The election, phenomenally for Maine's traditionally Republican-dominated politics, brought Democrat Louis J. Brann to the governor's mansion in Franklin Delano Roosevelt's landslide. As a liberal Republican Clyde got along better with Brann than the other members of the Governor's Council, and he was frequently called to Augusta. Often Margaret traveled with him to the granite state house and, if she did not have a meeting of her own to attend, sat in the hallway knitting. Although the activity was appropriate for the wifely image she was cultivating, knitting for Margaret had more to do with industry than domesticity. She was as incapable of sitting idly for long periods of time as she was of finding pleasure, much less fulfillment, in "woman's work."

At first what Margaret wanted was to be with Clyde, and she accepted that "anyone who ever spent any time with him ended up going campaigning."[15] The only certain exception to their being almost constantly in each other's presence came late in 1932 when Clyde left on an extensive business trip to Massachusetts, New York, and Ohio. His letters home provide the only intimate view we have of their relationship. Addressing Margaret as his "Dearest Little Girl," Clyde wrote in his first letter, "Many times I have shed tears when thinking of being impotent yesterday morning. I am so sorry." "It seems so strange and unnecessary to be separated," he added the next day and vowed in another letter, "Never again little girl will we separate . . . that is as long as earthly ties are concerned. We live together so closely that we did not appreciate the comfort and happiness we were enjoying." From Middletown, Ohio, Clyde told Margaret not to "worry any more. If you could look into my head to-night you would plainly see you need not worry." Referring to Margaret as "the best girl in the world" and signing himself "Your lonesome boy," Clyde wrote Margaret every day and complained about the drunken behavior of the men with whom he traveled. He not only assured her of his own fidelity but added that it was "wonderful to go away and feel that the little girl you left behind is earnest and honorable." With excessive but revealing emotion, Clyde told Margaret that since she packed "his grip, tears come to my eyes every time I look into it." "Be brave little girl," he wrote in his last letter, "the sun will shine again."[16]

In 1934 to Republican consternation, Brann became the first Democratic governor since the Civil War to be elected to a second term. Clyde startled the press by announcing his candidacy for the governorship in 1936 on election day 1934, before the complete results had been announced. Once again, though, just a few hours before Clyde, Page released a statement to the press that he also planned to run for the state house in 1936. Press speculation was that Page had learned of Clyde's intentions and deliberately "had got the jump on him."[17]

In the newspaper coverage of the campaign, Margaret received early attention under the headline, "First Lady of Maine?" "There may be a couple of more attractive ways and pleasing personalities than Mr. and Mrs. Smith," the reporter wrote, "but we do not quite remember just when or where we have seen them."[18] Then Page launched what Clyde called a "dastardly attack" by resurrecting the highway scandal and charging in particular that Clyde had had an interest in a company that had sold tractors and trucks to the state. By March Clyde had backed off again and announced that he was withdrawing from the governor's race because he did not want to embarrass the party with a bitter contest. "He didn't like it," Margaret said, but at the same time he announced for Congress.[19]

In the ten-county Second Congressional District Clyde and Margaret distributed campaign cards asking, "Mr. Laborer: Do you believe in a fairer work day? Mr. Pensioner: Do you believe in a practical and permanent Old Age Reward?"[20] President Franklin Roosevelt's campaign czar, Jim Farley, had an aide assessing the Second Congressional District race, and he reported about Clyde, "There is plenty in his record to use against him. On the other hand, he is a clever politician, a man who makes a good appearance, and who has a charming wife who is of help to him. . . . His candidacy is a dangerous one. . . . There is great danger that Smith may be elected."[21] As the Democrats feared, the voters responded affirmatively, and the Smiths moved to Washington. They left Skowhegan by car on 27 December with their little black and tan chihuahua, Alice Betty, and arrived on New Year's Day 1937.

Friends had leased a "little red brick house" for them on Raymond Street near the Chevy Chase Country Club, and although Clyde and Margaret had difficulty in locating it, they were pleased with the choice. Margaret considered it "small" after living in that great big 32-room house in Skowhegan but "very, very comfortable." The two-story house had been freshly dusted by their friends, who had also left a welcoming bouquet of a dozen roses. After unpacking, Margaret held Clyde to his campaign promise to her that they would "take a trip South and get some sunshine and some rest" before Congress convened. They drove to Savannah, Georgia, but found four inches of snow, and, Margaret said, "Clyde felt we had had enough traveling so we turned around to go back North."[22]

Washington had been harder hit by the depression than Maine with salary cuts preceding layoffs and a somber sense of failure permeating the town's major industry, the government. The New Deal with its proliferating agencies had restored both purpose and confidence by, among other initiatives, increasing the number of federal jobs from sixty-three thousand in 1933 to ninety-three thousand by the time the Smiths arrived. Official Washington's new prosperity affected the community through a construction boom that made the city appear a disaster area to newcomers like Clyde and Margaret. Some eight hundred new office buildings, twenty-three hundred row houses, and eighteen hundred apartment buildings went up during the 1930s, as did the Longworth House Office Building, the Supreme Court Building, and the Library of Congress Annex. Awestruck by the grandeur of the city, which she remembered from her senior trip, Margaret walked the streets, gawking like a small-town tourist.

Clyde had assumed that Margaret would get them settled in their new home while he moved into his office and prepared for the 5 January 1937 opening of the Seventy-fifth Congress. In what must have been a major marital donnybrook, Margaret informed Clyde that she had no intention of staying home and missing the one great opportunity she had; she had assumed that she would manage his office. When Clyde argued that he would be accused of nepotism if he appointed her to his official staff as a paid employee, Margaret adamantly responded that she intended to work in the office—and for pay. Clyde was entitled to only two employees, and he had already hired Margaret's former boss at the newspaper, Roland Patten, for one of the positions and Lena Batchelder, an experienced secretary, for the other. "Perhaps I should have been willing to take the position without pay," Margaret said, "but I couldn't see how I could and be the kind of secretary that I should be and that he needed."[23] When Clyde did not give way, Margaret went over his head to the voters and informed them of the dispute. Sheriff Earl Ludwig in Knox County obligingly started a "strongly-worded" petition in support of Margaret in the congressional district and, after securing several thousand signatures, called Clyde to say that "they had voted for Margaret as much as for Clyde."[24] Margaret also showed Clyde a letter that said that he would not have been elected if not for her. "Sis," Clyde retorted, "you've been a big help to me but remember I did some important things before you were born."[25]

Clyde gave in but allocated only $3,000 out of his own pay as salary for Margaret, which she considered "small." "But I was satisfied," she added. "It made me official and gave me a chance to go to committee meetings and go to departments for the information needed in handling his mail."[26] All of this Margaret did with relish, unlike Clyde who was more overwhelmed than excited by his new role. Congressman Smith and his "manager," as he not inaccurately referred to his wife, moved into the office of Clyde's two-term predecessor, Edward C. Moran of Rockland, on the main floor of the House Office Building.[27] Then Margaret stood in a drenching rain in a sea of black umbrellas, as though on the front row of the greatest theater in the nation, to watch Clyde march in with the other members of Congress and sit on the east steps of the Capitol for the inauguration of bare-headed Franklin Roosevelt. For the first time she appreciated the enormity of Roosevelt's 60 percent victory at the 1936 polls, because the House had only 89 Republicans among 331 Democrats, and in the Senate there were only 16 Republicans. Margaret considered herself "quite dressed up" in a new beaver coat, "Maine beaver," but which, once soaked, did not "smell good."[28] Clyde's snow-white hair stood out among the hundreds of congressmen, and Margaret saw the gleam of his perfect teeth, now false, when he threw back his head to laugh at someone's remark. Old-fashioned with his diamond stickpen, possibly, but Clyde was more distinguished in appearance than most of his colleagues.

"On arriving at the Capital city," Clyde said, "a green and unsophisticated congressman begins by seeking committee appointments, for it is within this group that results are obtained instead of upon the floor."[29] Because he had served on the Committee on Labor for many years in Augusta, Clyde secured the endorsement of the Maine Federation of Labor for appointment to the important House Labor Committee. William B. Bankhead of Alabama, the formidable Speaker of the House, had no intention of giving a first-term Republican congressman that plum, but Clyde surprised the leadership by also securing the endorsement of the Associate Industries of Maine. For over twenty years in Maine, he had fought industry, but the association accepted that Clyde now represented them also and wanted him obligated. Judge Benjamin F. Cleaves, secretary of the association, wrote, "We differed on many things but I always found him a fair, worthy, honorable opponent."[30] None of Clyde's competitors could claim the support of labor and industry, and "in a few days," he said, "the appointment was made."

A reform wage and hour law was the work before the Labor Committee, chaired by veteran congresswoman Mary T. Norton of New Jersey. Although Clyde had called for the repeal of New Deal legislation in his campaign, his liberal Republican record was in his favor, and Norton welcomed him as an ally. Southern Democrats opposed the legislation because it meant more government involvement in private enterprise and threatened low wages in the South. Their opposition made Clyde's support all the more important to Norton. She named him along with herself, Hugo Black of Alabama, and Claire Hoffman of Michigan to the subcommittee that actually wrote the bill. Clyde became a hard-working congressman who studied the issues, responsibly sat through the interminable hearings of the committee, and, Patten said, "set himself the self-imposed task of being present at every roll call" at the same time.[31] "For months and months," Clyde said, "hearings were held, evidence sought, and facts determined" before the Norton bill emerged.[32] In his first statement on the floor, Clyde supported the bill and called on his colleagues to settle labor problems in a "businesslike, man-fashioned" manner and not to combine "mystic deductions, with mythical delusions" in refutation.[33] Indicative of the importance the administration attached to the wage and hour legislation, Secretary of Labor Frances Perkins entertained the subcommittee with an unprecedented luncheon and met with them to discuss problems. Clyde faced conflicting concerns: his state's unions only grudgingly supported the reforms because they were aimed at unorganized labor, and the powerful lumber industry in Maine wanted its workers exempt.

The legislation eventually passed as the Fair Labor Standards Act and by 1940 provided raises for 12 million workers to forty cents an hour and a forty-hour workweek. Clyde honored his obligation to industry by persistently trying to exempt Maine's three thousand pulp and logging industry workers, but floor leader Sam Rayburn of Texas refused amendments.

Clyde's other committees were Public Buildings and Grounds and War Claims, but he did little more than put in an occasional appearance there.

Margaret had some problems of her own in organizing Clyde's home and office. Both Patten and a Skowhegan woman who worked as housekeeper lived with the Smiths. Clyde liked his meals on time, and frequently when he came home with Margaret and Patten, nothing was ready or what was ready was under- or overcooked.

Compounding the housekeeping problems, the Smiths welcomed visitors from Maine to Washington into their home for meals and frequently overnight. Right after they moved to the capital, two hundred Boy Scouts from Maine, twenty-six of them from Clyde's district, arrived for the National Jamboree. The Smiths met them at the train, escorted them to their camps, took them to an amusement park, and arranged rides on the Goodyear blimp. When Clyde learned that three scouts had left their parental permission forms for the blimp ride at their camp, he put them in a taxi and got them back in time for the ride. Margaret cooked fried chicken for the *Waterville Sentinel* newspaper boys who followed the scouts, and later she made gallons of ice cream for the Colby College baseball team of twenty-one boys. A senior class came next, then members of the local Daughters of the American Revolution, and a group of eleven who settled into the house just as the plumbing broke down. Future governor of Maine John Reed arrived in Washington in 1938 with four other students and a teacher from Monmouth Academy and considered it "remarkable" that Margaret watched "all these boys piling out of the car," a Model-T Ford, let them "bunk out" at her house, and "the next morning got up and personally cooked a big bacon and egg breakfast for us."[34] The Smiths, of course, reported all this to the press back home and announced plans to locate a larger house in order to entertain more Maine visitors.

Early on, legislators lost their allure for Margaret. At first, she had been awed at being in the same building, down the hall, or in the presence of men about whom she read in the paper or heard extolled on the radio. Respectful of their power and experience, Margaret watched, as fascinated as a tourist, the House oligarchy conduct business on the floor. Her own responsibilities in managing Clyde's office, however, brought her into daily contact with the staff members who actually ran Congress. She saw assistants doing congressmen's research, speechwriting, correspondence, press releases, and, in many instances, determining his votes. Most of these assistants were young and female, which was a recent development. When her secretary, Bratchelder, arrived in Washington in 1912, there were only four women congressional secretaries. With a more jaundiced eye, as her transformation from being Skowhegan's girl about town to being Washington's woman about Congress took place, she visited, gossiped, and learned. Margaret concluded, as many other observers had, that there was more mediocrity than brilliance in the House membership and, indeed, that most of the fat, bald, old men were entrenched in sinecures and marking time to gain seniority. In pursuit of rank, determined only by the number of years served, she saw congressmen who had grown infirm, lost their hearing, or become senile. She turned her critical eye on Clyde as she watched him, not an educated man, sitting all evening laboriously trying to write a speech.

The women representatives particularly intrigued Margaret. In the Seventy-fifth Congress there were eight females, one of whom had been elected to take the seat of her deceased husband and another who had been appointed to fill an unexpired term. The two women with seniority were Edith Nourse Rogers of Massachusetts and Mary Norton, whom Margaret knew best because of her association with Clyde. In Congress since 1924, Norton had grown up Irish-poor; like Margaret, she had no college and only a secretarial background. Twenty-two years older than Margaret, Norton had to fight to obtain an office job at the turn of the century. "Won't have a woman in this office," one man told her. "We have never had women in this office, never will have women in this office."[35] After marriage, Norton decided she could not be a "Sitting Room Sarah" or "Kitchen Katie" and began to work in city politics and then served on her party's state committee, as Margaret had. In the House, with the advantage of Democratic majorities, Norton had worked hard, won a place on the Labor Committee, and, with the death of the chairman, became the first woman in Congress to chair a committee. Like many other congressional aides, and wives, Margaret concluded that she could do this work as well as most and better than many others in Congress.

For all Clyde's efforts, his only real success was in securing two new Coast Guard stations for his state, but Margaret kept voters back home informed of his efforts and sometimes typed until midnight to get the word out. Not until late each evening did Clyde close his office and go home with Margaret and Patten. On weekends they seldom socialized aside from constituent entertainment, and the only relaxation in which they indulged was croquet. As fiercely competitive in this game as in life, Clyde let his opponents establish a huge lead, then started to play, and invariably won.

Exhausted and suffering from the unending heat of summer in Washington, in August 1937 Clyde had a heart attack while working late at the office. The doctor restricted him to his house for six weeks while Margaret and Patten continued to run the office until the session ended a few weeks later. Clyde managed to keep his poor health out of the Washington and Maine newspapers.

The Smiths returned to Skowhegan in September 1937, and the Republican county committee organized a banquet in Clyde's honor at Lakewood Country Club, the biggest affair of its kind ever held in Somerset County. Governor Lewis O. Barrows, who had defeated Blin Page in the 1936 primary, Senator Wallace H. White, and Congressmen Ralph Owen Brewster and James C. Oliver were present with over four hundred others. Despite the social setting and well-wishing, the political undercurrent was palpable. Eloquent in his remarks as always, Clyde announced that he would seek reelection in the June primary and then, without advance warning to Barrows, stated that he would be a candidate for governor in 1940. The governor retaliated by commenting for the first time in public on Clyde's recent illness.

Clyde's medical records indicate that he had been treated for angina as early as 1933 but that his electrocardiogram had revealed no coronary occlusion. His physician had provided him with morphine tablets to use for his sharp chest pains and released him. Margaret said that "the doctors told him that he should not run again for any office. But he did and went through one of the hardest campaigns of his entire career."[36] Although press speculation began about his poor health in the 1938 reelection campaign, Clyde staunchly denied the rumors as political attacks. Running as a "Townsendite," he made the $200 monthly pension that Dr. Francis Townsend championed his main issue. "It is now seven years since Dr. Townsend announced his pension plan to the world," Clyde said, "and it is a tragedy that the Townsend Plan has not been adopted."[37] In 1923, he reminded voters, he had been called the "Most Dangerous Man in America" because he had called for old age relief; now he was called the "Father of the Old Age Movement in Maine."[38]

Although Margaret had learned in Washington that fewer than a dozen congressional wives actively campaigned for their husbands, much less were on their payroll, she purchased a silver fox hat and again toured the Second District with Clyde. She had updated their black book with maps of all the roads in the area along with the names and addresses of key people along each route. This time they brought Alice Betty along, and the tiny dog proved an added attraction for campaign crowds. Clyde's pro–New Deal opponent was Democratic National Committeeman F. Harold Dulord, and while Clyde maintained that the New Deal had not done enough for the elderly, Governor Barrows ran for reelection on an anti–New Deal platform. Suspicious that Clyde might have had a stroke, the press watched him carefully, but all they could point out was that he spoke "in a slow but distinct manner," in contrast to his dramatic style of the past.[39] The voters reelected Clyde handily, but exhausted, he went to see Dr. John A. Kolmer right after the campaign. Kolmer told Clyde that although he had had "some loss in sexual libido," his heart was "most likely in good condition." He advised Clyde "to abstain from sexual activity," "live abstemiously," and "decrease rather than increase his political activities."[40]

The Smiths returned to Washington and to a new house at 3028 Newark and resumed their former routine. Life was easier because the Smiths' Skowhegan friend, Blanche Bernier, became their live-in housekeeper at the suggestion of Margaret's mother. Blanche's brother, Joseph, had recently married Margaret's sister, Laura, and Carrie Chase thought the move to Washington would be good for Blanche and Margaret. Blanche had no experience in running a house that was always filled with guests, but she quickly learned and won Margaret's highest accolades of "a good worker" and "a perfectionist."[41]

Rumblings from Maine, however, led Clyde to issue a public announcement on 1 February 1939 in rebuttal to "various statements being circulated that I am seriously ill and unable to attend to duty."[42] He attributed the accusations to "political enemies" and maintained that he was, "and had been during the past year, on the job every day, including Sundays and evenings." If there had been an absence of headlines, it was because he served "without playing bands and marching parades."

To disprove the rumors, Clyde increased his already prodigious work schedule. More vigorously than ever, he championed higher tariffs to protect Maine industries. "Since boyhood," Clyde stated, "I have advocated a tariff so high that not a dollar's worth of goods that can be made in this country should reach our shores from foreign nations."[43] Forthrightly, he supported striking Skowhegan shoe workers in a factory he had brought to town and maintained publicly that the owner had accumulated more personal wealth than the total savings of all his employees. To prevent northern industry from moving South to take advantage of what he called "starvation wages," Clyde worked for an increase in the minimum wage.[44] He also continued his support for the Townsend Plan and won from Dr. Townsend acknowledgment that he was "one of the best friends of the Townsend Plan in Washington."[45]

Margaret's responsibilities increased as Clyde's health declined. She added research to her handling of the mail and provided Clyde with statistics to support his proposals of more aid to the elderly and a higher minimum wage. Margaret also accompanied Clyde on fact-finding tours and returned home to Maine to represent him at political gatherings. A seasoned campaigner by now, Margaret was at ease in informal settings but "had no desire to attract attention," she said, "and Clyde like most officeholders was not receptive to any staff member competing with him." When she accepted her first invitation to speak in her own right and asked Clyde to help her write a speech, "he was not entirely pleased that I had accepted the invitation and said that since I had committed myself, I should write my own speech." She did, but had difficulty because the Kennebec County Women's Republican Club wanted her to talk on her official Washington social life. Not having one aside from the Congressional Club's annual tea, Margaret decided, after noticing on her calendar that the day of her talk was Navy Day, to speak on the origins of the holiday. Her research turned up more information on the inadequacy of the navy than on the holiday, and so, Margaret said, "I wrote three double-spaced pages on the sad shape of our Navy which I included in the middle of my talk."[46]

In March Clyde placed an ad in district newspapers announcing a fifty-dollar reward "for the name of the person circulating insidious stories about me being ill and unable to attend to duty. My activities in Congress bespeak good health. Have attended all Congressional sessions and every committee meeting, working night and day for my constituency."[47]

The Smiths continued to avoid social Washington. Only once did Clyde accept an invitation to a White House reception but "didn't like it," he said, and never went again.[48] Only once did he attend one of the common large dinner parties, and then, in defiance of protocol that rigidly required other guests to wait for the departure of the highest ranking guests, loudly at 10:00 P.M. told Margaret, "Now, Sis, it is time for us to get home."

Margaret believed that Clyde was never comfortable in Washington and "never did like being in Congress where you can't be quite as close to people as you can back home."[49] "Clyde was a small-town boy," she said, "a big fish in a little pond, and he liked it that way. He liked to be surrounded by people wanting things. He liked to have people come in the office and ask him for various favors. He was always lending them a dollar or two dollars or something. That was his life." "He preferred Skowhegan and Maine" to Washington, Margaret said, and "would have preferred being Governor and working closely with the people."[50]

Clyde wrote the Maine press in mid-1939, "You may feel free to inform your readers that I am a candidate for Governor."[51] Then Dr. Paul F. Dickens wrote him after his August physical examination that although "I know that you have probably set your goal to be governor . . . then senator," his health would not allow it.[52] Dickens set Clyde's chances of taking part in any congressional activity at 20 percent and of recovery between 40 and 60 percent. The official physician of Congress, Dr. George W. Calver, agreed and ordered Clyde to take two weeks of bed rest in August. Margaret released a statement to the press that "heat and overwork" had exhausted Clyde.[53] In the seven months of the session, Clyde had taken off only two

Sundays, five evenings, and one afternoon while other congressmen commonly golfed or fished for relaxation. "He is confident that after a brief rest he will be able to resume his duties uninterrupted for the remainder of the session," she concluded. Publicly, Clyde made light about being put to bed for "repairs" and said that his "highly efficient helpmate" would take his dictation at home and keep his office open as usual, "never failing to give attention to every visitor and answering every letter within one day" of when it was received.[54] Clyde took care of voting by pairing his vote with a colleague voting opposite to him, and, reassured, the press back home reported that "Congressman Smith who worked himself sick, will continue to work." In November Clyde announced that he had decided not to run for governor in 1940 but would run for Congress instead. Clyde's primary petition, which Maine required to win a place on the ballot, secured over fifteen thousand signatures, more than seven times the number needed for renomination.

Clyde's health did not improve, and, at his request, Margaret returned to Maine in early April 1940 to represent him at the state Republican convention. While there, she received an emergency call that Clyde had had another heart attack and, with her parents, hastened back to Washington. On the Friday evening of the last weekend of Clyde's life, Dr. Dickens advised him "to swing his support to a candidate of his choice" and that issuing that statement was to "be his last political activity."[55] As Margaret understood the situation from Dr. Dickens and the other heart specialist who came to the house to examine Clyde, "worry was the worst thing for one in that condition," and if Clyde "didn't have that primary facing him," his chances of improvement would be better.[56] Margaret believed, however, that "there were several whom he might not like or might not want to take his place, who would jump into the race," and that that would upset Clyde more.

Dickens then suggested, Margaret maintained, that she should take out primary papers and, when she hesitated, insisted that she talk to both the Republican congressional leaders, Representative Joseph Martin of Massachusetts and Senator Wallace H. White of Maine. On Saturday, 7 April, after White listened to Margaret, he told her that "he understood completely" and for her not to worry about running herself because "he had a man all ready to run." When he told Margaret who his candidate was, she said, "Senator, that's just the man who I know would not be helpful to Clyde." Margaret fared better with Martin, who told her that he thought it was "wonderful" that she would run in Clyde's place. "Go ahead and do it," he said, "anything to save Clyde's life."[57]

On Sunday, 8 April, Margaret told Dickens that if he wanted to suggest to Clyde that she run, she "had no objection to that, and that if he agreed to it," she would run.[58] "I didn't seek it," she insisted. After talking to Clyde "through the afternoon," Dickens came out of the bedroom and asked Margaret "to come in and take a statement." Clyde sat up in bed and dictated,

My physician, Dr. Paul S. Dickens, informs me that I am a seriously ill man—that it is his opinion that even if I should survive I may be physically unable to take an active part in Congressional affairs for an indefinite time in the future. All that I can ask of my friends and supporters is that in the coming primary and general election, if unable to enter the campaign, they support the candidate of my choice, my wife and partner in public life. I know of no one else who has the full knowledge of my ideas and plans or is as well qualified as she is, to carry on those ideas and my unfinished work for the district.[59]

Then, Margaret said, he "read word for word the statement, signed it himself personally, and just sort of sighed." Clyde told Margaret to call the "group of eight," his most important supporters in Maine, and inform them before releasing the statement. She came back downstairs to the hall telephone, made the calls, and then instructed Roland Patten to inform the press of Clyde's "withdrawing in my favor." A few hours later, Clyde was dead. "We didn't expect him to die," Margaret said. "When he signed that paper, he couldn't have been better."[60]

With the Capitol flags lowered to half mast, the House and the Senate adjourned in respect, and Representative Martin told the press that Congress had lost "an extremely valuable member."[61] Margaret traveled by train to Waterville with Clyde's body and then by car to Skowhegan. On Water Street residents stood quietly in front of stores with their drapes closed and watched the funeral cortege pass. Skowhegan schools and businesses closed on the day of Clyde's funeral at the house on Fairview. Over four hundred people, including the governor, attended the service and viewed the body in a lighted glass-covered casket. "I'd never seen anything like that," photographer Lyndon Huff said, when he was called to photograph the service.[62] Margaret had wanted Reverend Merriam, who had officiated in her marriage ceremony, to conduct the funeral, but he was ill, and she asked Skowhegan's three other Protestant ministers instead. In eulogy, one minister observed that Clyde had been in politics since 1898 and that in his sixty-three years of life, he had engaged in forty-nine political campaigns. Astoundingly, he had never been defeated, "a matter of most forgiveable pride."[63] The brief service included, at Margaret's request, the reading of the Edgar A. Guest poem, "Let Me Live by the Side of the Road." As funeral approached campaign rally, the Reverend Thomas S. Cleaver characterized Clyde's relationship with his wife as "one of the finest examples of teamwork. His heartaches and disappointments, his joys and success have been hers," and he urged her to carry on Clyde's work.[64] Then the funeral party moved in a long line of cars with their headlights on to the cemetery at Hartland, where Margaret had Clyde's body interred in his family's plot. With no time or inclination for mourning, Margaret left the funeral for the campaign trail.

Chapter Three

THE WIDOW'S GAME

Exhausted and unable to remember the woman's name, Margaret nevertheless smiled warmly and concentrated on what she was saying. Both efforts required discipline because her mind kept flitting away to tonight's meeting and tomorrow's rally, and her lips joined her feet in silent competition as to which hurt the most.

"Have you seen Mr. Smith Goes to Washington?*" the woman asked.*

"No," Margaret responded, not wanting to admit that she did not know what the woman was talking about. She had learned from watching Clyde say too much that it was often better to say nothing.

"The James Stewart movie?" the woman persisted.

"No." Margaret forced her lips to keep smiling and her eyes not to turn to the other members of the Kennebec County Women's Republican Club who were waiting to speak to her. Her mind, however, estimated that it would take another thirty minutes to shake hands with each of them. "Should I?"

"Oh yes," the woman enthused. "Jean Arthur is wonderful in it, but the reason I ask is because it gave me this great idea for poor Clyde. I loved that man, but I never got to mention it to him, and I thought maybe you could use it."

Unexpectedly, Margaret felt the familiar stab of jealousy that had often hurt her in the past when women gushed over Clyde. She had thought that her competitive nature had overcome her possessive instincts. Easy, she silently warned herself; you need this silly woman's vote if you are to prove that you are as good a politician as Clyde.

"We want to form," the woman went on, gesturing toward the other women, "a Mrs. Smith Goes to Washington *Club."*

Margaret's smile suddenly became sincere, and her attention riveted on her supporter. "That is a wonderful idea, and you are kind to think of it."

The next half hour passed quickly as the women told of their plans to have a movie party when the film opened that weekend in Waterville. Margaret promised to come, asked who would call the Sentinel, *and did they plan to put up posters?*

When Blanche Bernier signaled her that it was time to leave for Smithfield, Margaret thanked the women for their help and assured them that she intended to carry on Clyde's work as he had asked her to do.

Blanche drove the big Maxwell while Margaret collapsed beside her. "How did I do?" Margaret asked with her eyes closed, shoes off, and head against the seat.

"They liked you," Blanche assured her, "and they want to help you. Most of them are married, and they wonder what they would do if their husbands died."

Blanche went on to point out that Margaret was still reading her speeches but that she was better at answering questions. "Mr. Smith goes to the Senate, not the House," Blanche added.

"Maybe Mrs. Smith will too," Margaret grinned and opened the black book to see who owned the filling station coming up. "Let's stop and fill up the gas tank."

Blanche said that they didn't need any gas, but Margaret told her that they did need the votes of the men sitting outside the station. "Don't fill up the tank next time. Just put in a dollar's worth so we can stop and buy more along the way. That's what Clyde always did."

Margaret introduced herself to the men as Clyde's widow and told them that he had asked her to finish his work. Most of them had known Clyde, and Margaret listened appreciatively while they repeated the stories about him that she had heard for years. She did not say much but asked what they thought about the war in Europe, how their crops were doing, and what Congress could do to help them.

Blanche came out with two cold drinks that she had bought, and she and Margaret continued on to Smithfield.

Whether motivated by self-discipline or ambition, Margaret returned to Washington immediately after the funeral to take up Clyde's work. She personally escorted a visiting group of high school seniors from Waterville to the Glen Echo amusement park and treated them to tickets for the fun house. Surprised, because he knew that she was recently widowed, their principal said, "You really shouldn't have gone to all this trouble." "Clyde would have wanted it this way," Margaret replied.[1]

Unlike when a senator died in office and the governor appointed a successor, the law required that a deceased congressman be replaced by the voters. With less than a week left to circulate nomination papers for signature and file them with Maine's secretary of state, Margaret entered the campaign for the regular election in 1940. Then she announced for the special election to complete Clyde's term. With the press sympathetically reporting that she was "carrying out her husband's death-bed wish," she had little difficulty securing the requisite signatures for the primary and support for the special election.[2]

In prim hat and white gloves, Margaret ran as a widow in the May election to fill Clyde's seat. Commonly shown ironing in her kitchen in campaign photographs, she frequently mentioned Clyde, his goals, and his unfinished work for the district in interviews. "I am not asking for sympathy," she insisted, "but instead for confidence . . . consideration," and the opportunity to complete what Clyde had begun.[3] Margaret stressed the Townsend legislation as her "paramount" concern and maintained that Clyde had "almost made his life work pensions."[4] Their office received hundreds of letters from needy, older people who required "little attentions like new teeth, glasses, pills. If we allow our older people to go to their deaths in unhappiness and privation," Margaret said, "we as a human race are a failure."[5] Margaret overwhelmed her one primary opponent, party regular Frederick P. Bonney of Augusta, with an eleven-to-one vote and, with no Democratic opponent in the 3 June general special election, officially became Clyde's successor. Speaker William B. Bankhead of Alabama, only months before his death in September, swore Margaret in on 10 June.

For the 17 June regular primary Margaret netted three more stalwarts of the party—John G. Marshall of Augusta, Arthur Lancaster of Gardiner, and Hodgden C. Buzzell of Belfast—and Bonney, who ran again. Drawing a deep breath but never considering not running, Margaret continued to campaign. She diligently worked in Clyde's office during the week and late each Friday commuted to Maine by plane to seek votes in her seven-county district over the weekend. Late Sunday she returned to Washington and took up Clyde's work again.

Clyde had largely ignored foreign affairs in his concentration on relief for the elderly and for labor, but events in Europe during Margaret's primary did not give her the same option. Although war had been declared in September 1939, the concept of the Phony War, which had developed after the German offensive stopped with the occupation of Poland, led many to believe a general war would not follow. Then, days after Clyde's death, the Germans invaded Denmark and Norway and, with Margaret's campaign underway, entered Holland, Luxembourg, Belgium, and France. As the depression had been the backdrop for Clyde's congressional career, the German blitzkrieg made war the focus of Margaret's campaign.

Like the seasoned campaigner she had become under Clyde's tutelage, Margaret made the transition to military issues with ease. She used the one speech she had made on her own as Clyde's wife to the Republican women of Waterville on Navy Day 1937 as evidence of her prescient concern for preparedness. She had observed then that the navy was "inadequate. It had been completely neglected: old ships—not painted, not kept in good shape. Those who oppose naval protection," she had gone on to say, "fail to perceive the attack, if any, will come from the sea."[6] Simultaneously reminding audiences of Maine's, if not the Second District's, 3,478-mile shoreline and shipbuilding industry, Margaret pointed to both vulnerability and advantage. The latter she stressed in promises to campaign in Congress for Maine's "proper proportion of national defense" contracts.[7] "A policy of national defense was advocated by me," she maintained with more hyperbole than fact, "before it became a popular issue." In a statement to the press on 24 May 1940, Margaret said that "money spent on the Navy is not extravagance. It is an insurance against involvement in war. Immediate and complete preparedness must be our goal."[8]

Preparedness won Margaret a valuable ally. When she solicited the support of the owner of Maine's only chain of newspapers, Guy P. Gannett, she was immediately asked about her views on national defense and, in particular, the navy. Again, she dusted off her Navy Day speech and sent him faded clippings reporting it from his *Waterville Sentinel* and *Kennebec Journal*. Convinced, Gannett gave Margaret editorial support.

Selling preparedness as an economic as well as military issue, Margaret announced on 2 June 1940 that she had requested that the army and navy consider Norridgewock as an army air base, Penobscot Bay as a naval air base, and Maine for several pilot training schools. She was careful, however, to add in a Farmington address that "our boys must not be sent into battle on foreign soil."[9] Successful in treading what was as late as 1940 the precarious political line between preparedness and noninvolvement, Margaret received high marks from the *Lewiston Journal*. Editorially the *Journal* said that she was "keenly alive to the preparedness need in this troublous hour," but a stinger was included in the commendation that she was "as intelligently active about it, as any man could be—more so, in fact, than some."[10] The *Journal* reported that Margaret stressed the military issue because it was a concern a woman might be expected to overlook, and "conservative Maine has a prejudice against women representing it in Congress."[11]

Although the twentieth anniversary of women's suffrage was celebrated in 1940, and feminist politicians had blazed trails into local, county, state, and federal bastions, government remained male dominated. Across the nation thirty women were running for Congress, including Jeannette Rankin who had won the first female seat in the House in 1916 and who was now competing for a second term. In the Seventy-seventh Congress, along with Margaret, there were ten women, five of whom had succeeded their husbands. Margaret commonly observed in her campaigning that two of these congresswomen had ties to Maine. Massachusetts representative Edith Nourse Rogers had been born in Maine, and Frances P. Bolton of Ohio had a summer home in Maine. The assistant chairman of the Republican National Committee, Margaret also mentioned frequently, was Marion Martin of Augusta.

Nonetheless, the *Lewiston Journal* reported that there was "a definite opposition to Mrs. Smith among women voters. This opposition is not a personal matter but comes from a very pronounced sentiment that the congressional place is a man's job, not a woman's."[12] Reporter Dorris A. Westall of the *Portland Telegram* wrote that even Margaret's opponents could "find no fault with her except that she's a woman."[13] In a polite and gentlemanly manner, her opponents complimented Margaret's amazing vitality, quiet sincerity, and vote-getting ability, acknowledged her as quick-witted and conservative in her dress, and allowed that she was "altogether the gentlewoman of 1940." But to a man they stressed that "these unsettled times meant Congress was a man's job," and the leading male candidate, John G. Marshall, added, "A flick of the wrist and a smile won't do it."[14]

Margaret's response was to campaign less as the widow and housewife, which had led to the *Boston Globe* headline following her special election, "Maine Is Sending a Housekeeper," and to present herself as the most qualified candidate.[15] "Had I been just a woman candidate," she said, "it is doubtful except on a sympathetic vote that I would have won."[16] After being sworn in as Clyde's successor on 10 June Margaret emphasized the seniority she would have in receiving committee assignments if she was reelected. She also maintained that she was the only candidate who would not need to serve an apprenticeship because she was already familiar with how Congress worked. To stress her experience, she stated that she had run Clyde's office and "did everything but go on the floor of the House" for him.[17] In substantiation, Colby College professor Herbert C. Libbey said that he "happened to know that Mr. Smith came to have profound respect for the business ability, the keen political judgement, quick grasp of details and the good sense of leadership of Mrs. Smith."[18]

Although the Republican party had endorsed the equal rights amendment, which feminist Alice Paul had introduced in 1923, at its 1940 national convention Margaret handled the woman issue gingerly. Originally she meekly said that since women had "met the responsibilities of citizenship, it might not seem inappropriate that they should have an effective part in determining the policies of our government and the legislation under which our people shall live."[19] In a handwritten statement Margaret wrote on being a woman candidate, she more forthrightly declared that since "Maine has five representatives in Congress, are not the women of our state entitled to one of these positions?"[20] Considering the statement provocative, she crossed it out of her speech. Libbey argued that women had characteristics men lacked: "an amazing sense of intuition," "indomitable courage and fortitude," and a "humanitarian view" as opposed to the male's "commercial approach."[21] "I am not a feminist," Mrs. C. E. Towns, the founder of the Mrs. Smith Goes to Washington Club said, and "I would not vote for Mrs. Smith simply because she is a woman. Nor will I vote against her for the same reason."[22] By the end of the primary, Margaret's "Vote for the one who will vote for you," earned her most effective rebuttal to being female, the endorsement of Clyde's support group, the State Federation of Labor.[23]

For insurance, the day before the 17 June primary she leaked to the press a story that Skowhegan might get an air training base. To the astonishment of party regulars, the press, and Margaret, she won without a run-off over her opponents. Margaret received a staggering 27,037 votes, Marshall 6,768, Bonney 2,578, and Lancaster 1,554. Well-wishers streamed into the house on Fairview, and Margaret stayed up all night in celebration.

In her fourth campaign in three months Margaret faced Democrat Edward J. Beauchamp in the September general election. From Lewiston, Beauchamp was the Androscoggin County attorney, and he saw gender as his best issue. Patronizingly, he "wished he had four women opponents" and quoted his supporters as urging Margaret to get "back to the pots and pans."[24] In contrast, the *Lewiston Journal* observed that "there is no reason why a woman shouldn't be elected to office, if she can get the votes."[25] The *Portland Telegram* added that if Margaret had "to be twice as smart and work twice as hard as a man to succeed," she was.[26] Youthful in appearance, Beauchamp used a theme song with the lyrics that "it no longer requires three chins and a fifty-seven inch waistline to be a representative and be heard in Washington." "Is This Gallantry?" headlines queried, and one reporter suggested that Beauchamp take a look at his opponent because "there are those who will assure you that Mrs. Smith is also slim, energetic, and, in the opinion of many, she is a beautiful woman."[27] Beauchamp's heavy-handed campaigning cost him the support of a traditionally Democratic group, the Boot and Shoe Workers Union, which under the leadership of Leo Goodman announced for Margaret.

Margaret's first political test came during the general election campaign. For the first time in American history the administration asked Congress to legislate a peacetime draft, which would mobilize some 900,000 men between the ages of twenty-one and thirty-five. A volatile issue that evoked memories of Americans in World War I trenches, the conscription bill aroused passions and motivated congressmen to hurl insults at each other. Two otherwise distinguished legislators exchanged physical, in addition to verbal, blows. The Republican leadership adamantly opposed the Selective Training and Service Act and expected members, especially the most junior of all representatives, to vote accordingly. Across the nation women, particularly those in peace organizations, lobbied against putting their sons in uniforms. In the middle of a campaign in a conservative Republican state, Margaret quietly defied all expectations and cast her first important vote resolutely in favor of preparedness with the president's majority.

Her vote received no special publicity, and Beauchamp failed to pick up on it. With the Republican machine behind the party candidates generally, if not her specifically, Margaret again won handily with 57,152 votes to Beauchamp's 31,334. "It wasn't even close," Margaret smugly observed, and she did not fail to notice that her tally was nearly three times larger than Clyde's highest vote had been.[28]

Although elected in her own right, Margaret's difficulties with the woman issue continued, as did her own ambivalence about the best response. Right after her election, she spoke at the national convention of the Federation of Women's Republican Clubs in Detroit. "I am not here today simply as a woman," she told the eight hundred women present, "but as one of the citizens elected last month."[29] Margaret urged the women to support Wendell Willkie, the party's candidate for president in the November election, because women might be able to make the difference in his election. Willkie was having his own difficulties with women because he had promised to replace President Franklin Roosevelt's longtime secretary of labor, Frances Perkins, with whom Clyde had worked well, with a man. Defensively, Willkie added that his mother was his father's law partner, his maternal grandmother had been a Presbyterian minister, and his aunt was a doctor, but he believed a man would do a better job as labor secretary.

Margaret announced to the press in Maine that she was leaving early for Washington because she wanted to attend Eleanor Roosevelt's Gridiron Widows dinner. For several years the president's wife had invited Washington's female press corps and women representatives in Congress to dine with her in protest at the White House on the same evening as the Gridiron Press Club held its male-only banquet for the president. In 1940 the dinner was on 14 December, Margaret's forty-third birthday, and when she disingenuously told this to Mrs. Roosevelt, the First Lady led her guests in singing "Happy Birthday." "Well, I never expected to have a birthday party in the White House," Margaret was quoted as saying in the considerable publicity she received along with the dinner.[30]

The birthday press coverage led to a *Washington Post* story the next week, but the *Post* photo had Margaret back in the kitchen in an apron with sifter in hand, making an apple pie. That photograph led to others depicting Margaret as what she had never been or become: a good cook. As a good politician, however, Margaret referred to her apple pie as "Maine Apple Pie" and to the baked beans that most of the later kitchen stories featured as "Maine Baked Beans."[31] She said that as a child the way she knew it was Saturday was that the aroma of baked beans filled the house. Her mother had prepared them for every Saturday night supper and had served the leftovers for Sunday morning and Monday noon meals. Baked beans became a part of Margaret's life, and she continued to cook them every Saturday evening after she and Clyde married.

According to Margaret's recipe, she soaked two pounds of State of Maine dry beans overnight in cold water and in the morning parboiled them until their skins cracked when she blew upon them. Then she cut an onion into quarters and placed it in the bottom of the bean pot, put the beans on top of the onion, and cut a half-pound of salt pork in small pieces to place on top of the beans. Over all of this she poured a mixture of a half cup of molasses, two teaspoons of dry mustard, one-fourth teaspoon of red pepper, one teaspoon of ginger, one and one-half tablespoons of salt, and a pint of boiling water. Margaret told reporters to bake the mixture at 300 degrees for six hours and to serve with steamed brown bread or hot johnny cake.

Margaret said later that she was desperate for name recognition and did not mind being photographed cooking and happily sent out copies of other Maine-oriented recipes upon request. This early she had no problem, as she did later, with whether the press referred to her as Mrs. Clyde Smith, Margaret Smith, or Maggie Smith. She simply wanted as much publicity as possible, and, as an attractive woman with a pleasing smile, she found herself in demand in the women's section of newspapers. But also desiring respect, Margaret eventually learned the denigration implicit in the publicity she received. She wanted serious attention but found herself grouped with women, not congressmen, and she was treated frivolously. "No one cares how a man walks across the floor," she complained, "but every step *we* take is noticed. Every move we women make is commented on."[32] By June Margaret had learned the liability of being grouped with the other congressional women and told the National Business and Professional Women's Club that she intended to "avoid any tendency to organize in an effort to stand as one sex against another." To be an effective legislator she had to work with the male majority, and Margaret confessed that she had "never felt more complimented than when included as 'we guys' or one of the congressmen."[33]

Margaret Chase Smith, as she decided to designate herself, was the twenty-fifth woman in congressional history to be sworn in as a member of the House of Representatives. In the Seventy-seventh Congress Smith was one of eight women. Hattie Carraway of Arkansas, who had succeeded her husband in 1931, was the lone female in the Senate, and of the seven women in the House, Smith, having been sworn in first in June, was senior only to Jeannette Rankin, who had succeeded in her reelection bid. Mary Norton of New Jersey, first elected in 1925, was senior among the women and, along with Edith Nourse Rogers of Massachusetts, in her eighth term; Caroline Goodwin O'Day of New York was third; fourth, Jessie Sumner of Illinois; and fifth, Frances P. Bolton of Ohio, ahead of Smith by four months. Rogers and Bolton, in addition to Smith, had replaced their husbands in office and then had been elected in their own right. Clara McMillan of South Carolina had also succeeded her husband in 1939 but had lost her 1940 reelection bid. Smith was the only one playing the widow's game who had also been her husband's secretary.

Smith used the two weeks before Congress convened to move from the house she and Clyde had shared to a two-bedroom apartment in the Delano, a small hotel used by several representatives. Of the old entourage, she kept only her dog Minnix, who had replaced Alice Betty, in the apartment and asked Bernier and Patten to locate quarters of their own but to continue as staff at the office. Smith stayed in Clyde's office, Room 131 on the main floor of the Old House Office Building across Independence Avenue from the Capitol. In the two-room suite of offices, Smith installed Bernier as receptionist, a position she maintained for twenty-five years. Surprisingly similar in appearance to Smith, Bernier was a small, blond woman with a quiet, ingratiating manner. At the office she presided not only over the waiting room with its constantly ringing telephone, number 1369, platter of Maine apples, and bowl of cigarettes but also over the combination kitchen–beauty parlor hidden behind bookcases. Bernier shopped for coffee, tea, and soups, which she prepared for Smith and the other staff members on a hot plate, and for Smith's household supplies. In the beauty parlor area the versatile and ever-willing Bernier cut, shampooed, and set Smith's prematurely graying hair. Becoming the indispensable person in Smith's life, Bernier also made most of Smith's clothes from brightly colored fabrics and simple suit patterns.

The remaining front office area had desks for Patten and a secretary, Lena B. Haskell from Mechanic Falls, and Smith had the other room as her province. There she had dark red velvet drapes, a leather couch, and more reminders of Maine: a large state flag, an aquarium, and two small spruce trees in window boxes. On her desk Smith kept several photographs of Clyde, a small American flag, a vase of fresh flowers, and a radio.

According to the *Washington Post,* all of the female representatives "showed up with a new Hair-Do, all prettied up" for the opening session of Congress.[34] For the second time Smith was sworn in as a member of Congress on 6 January 1941, this time with 434 other representatives and by the new Speaker of the House, Sam Rayburn of Texas. Smith was already fond of Mr. Sam, because, although divorced now, his wife had been his secretary, a fact Margaret had used in her earlier argument with Clyde. The House membership was 61 percent Democrat, and, perhaps in celebration of that continued majority, during the opening session the speaker slammed his new mesquite gavel, a gift from supporters in Brownwood, Texas, down so hard that it shattered in a shower of splinters.

Smith listened with the other members of the government when Franklin Roosevelt in his State of the Union address maintained that "at no previous time has American security been as seriously threatened from without as it is today."[35] The president asked Congress to approve a new program to lend and lease matériel to nations whose defense he decided was vital to American security. While inspiring many with his dramatic call for the United States to become the arsenal of democracy, Roosevelt infuriated others as he inched away from neutrality. The Republican leadership opposed the legislation, and the other representatives from Maine, to a man, announced their intention to vote against the lend-lease bill. Wallace H. White, with seniority dating back to 1930, chaired the congressional delegation from Maine. The state's junior senator was former governor Ralph Owen Brewster, who had moved up after three terms in the House in the 1940 elections, leaving James C. Oliver, senior among the other representatives, Frank Fellows and Smith. Again, with surprising independence in the face of a united state delegation, Smith neither sought their counsel nor responded in advance to their inquiries as to how she intended to vote. In March Smith shocked them by voting with the majority for lend-lease. In return, she said she received "some black looks,"[36] but informed the voters back home that "as long as British resistance is successful, we have little to fear."[37]

Later the administration asked for authority to arm ships carrying American trade, and again the isolationists in the Republican party organized in opposition. Smith voted for the legislation and against the majority of her party. When the Selective Service Act was up for extension during the summer of 1941, isolationists came within one vote in the House to defeating it. Consistently, but at greater odds with Maine's representatives and Republicans generally, Smith voted for the extension and claimed that her vote was the one that made passage possible.

She paid for her independence. The widow's game assumed compliance and rested on the certainty of the beneficiary's voting correctly. Wielding its formidable power, the party leadership denied Smith's claim to Clyde's seat on the prestigious Labor Committee and banished her to the political hinterland of Invalid Pensions, Post Offices and Post Roads, and Education. Unrepentant, Smith wrote in her biographical entry in the *Congressional Directory* that she had won election with a startling plurality of 25,181 votes.

Bravado aside, Smith believed she knew how Congress worked. She referred back to Clyde, "I knew everything he did, and through him I had been close to many of the Congressmen I had to work with now. So I just kept on doing what I had *been* doing. The only thing different was the voting."[38] She had difficulty with the voting. Once she rushed on to the floor to vote on a tax bill, heard her name called, and responded, "Yea," only to hear the next representative called answer, "Here."[39]

Not that Smith ever admitted it, but Clyde had walked the fine line between principle and politics more adroitly and had had the committee assignments and the productivity to prove it. The cumbersome 435-member House was an oligarchy, controlled by an entrenched 20 or so members who were bonded by party, gender, and the political sine qua non of seniority. As a member of the minority party, female, and a freshman, Smith had some lessons to learn, lessons that Clyde had learned at the turn of the century. Hamstrung by her voting, with no committees of benefit to her district, and on the record for her declaration that floor debates were for publicity value, Smith served her first term in political purgatory, more expendable from the party's perspective than most other widows.

She had not run for Congress, as many of her New Deal colleagues had, with a passion to reform the nation. Smith was in pursuit of no cause and motivated by no principle, aside from that she had pursued since childhood, a better job. As prosaic as her attitude was, she valued her position as more prestigious and remunerative than anything Skowhegan had to offer and wanted to hold on to it. Being a congresswoman had the cachet of being addressed as "The Honorable" and being set apart as unique, respected, and powerful—heady enticement for a small town girl.

In her office she continued the long hours she had worked with Clyde, and his practices of answering mail the day it arrived and holding open house for visitors from Maine became Smith's habits. The only difference was that without a wife and household staff, she entertained guests with lunch in the congressional dining room. Stymied elsewhere, Smith decided to reform the House restaurant and "talked darkly" with the other women about the "terribly heavy and greasy" food. Smith wanted a good dietician, variety, bright china, and, above all, a salad. Learning the improbability of reforming any Capitol institution, Smith reported that she had decided to restrain "this feminine impulse lest she offend her male colleagues."[40] Outside the office Smith sought opportunities for service to Maine to be reported back home. She visited Fort Meade and publicized that the army used Maine potatoes, and when the steel industry reported a shortage, Smith suggested the use of Maine granite. The congresswoman placed a basket of peonies at the foot of the Washington statue of Hannibal Hamlin, Abraham Lincoln's first vice president and Maine's only one. Smith introduced legislation to erect a memorial to the Revolutionary War general and first American secretary of war, Henry Knox, at Thomason, Maine. Regardless of her efforts to demonstrate benefits to the district, Smith received more publicity when she changed hats, which she did not do often. "I see Mrs. Congresswoman Smith has a new hat," a columnist observed, and then, around the state, photograph after photograph was printed of Smith in her new hat.[41]

Years later Smith could smile about her obscurity and tell the story of a distinguished senator's complimenting her at a political dinner. "We are all so proud of what you are doing, little lady," he said condescendingly, "and I can tell you confidentially, the party leaders are interested and are watching you carefully." A few minutes later he whispered to her, "I wonder if you could point out that new Maine Representative, Margaret Smith. I've been wanting to meet her."[42]

Although there is slight mention in the voluminous Margaret Chase Smith files about the work of her committees, true to her personal work ethic, Smith attended the meetings as reliably as she sat in on every House session. During the long hours of sitting, she observed the power of the chairmen, earned only by tenure, and watched the speaker, thinking "how wonderful it would be to be a public official of the standing he had. I learned a great deal from him."[43] In keeping with House protocol that freshmen representatives did not speak on the floor, Smith did not ask for recognition her first year or her second. Becoming self-conscious about her own reticence, Smith, seated next to Mr. Sam at a dinner party, said, "I suppose you think I couldn't make a speech." The formidable Rayburn replied, "To the contrary, Margaret, I think you could make a very effective speech, but let me give you just a word of caution. The unspoken word never defeats anyone."[44] Smith introduced one significant bill during her first term, an amendment to the Selective Service Act to defer the drafting of married men living with their wives, as men with dependents already were deferred during peacetime. Her purpose was to avoid the needless disruption of families as long as possible; although the legislation did not pass, it was enacted by a Department of War ruling.

Directly, Smith served her own cause by authoring a weekly newsletter, which she titled *Washington and You.* Before congressional newsletters became common and staff written, Smith's was unique, and she wrote it herself. Better, several state newspapers, both in and out of her district, printed it. In a forthright style, she recounted relevant events to the folks back home, educating as well as informing them on the workings of the government and quietly casting herself as both authority and principal actor.

Longer lived than *Washington and You* and of more political benefit was Smith's friendship with Elizabeth May Craig, a new reporter for the newspapers Guy Gannett owned in Maine. Craig's husband had been the Washington bureau chief for the *New York Herald,* and at a time when there were few women reporters in the capital, Craig had worked for him and had been a stringer for several other papers. A fixture in Washington before the Smiths had arrived, Craig had that crank reputation common to outspoken feminist pioneers. As a young woman during Woodrow Wilson's second inauguration, she had participated in the first protest march on suffrage that had resulted in violence, and she had attended Eleanor Roosevelt's first press conference in 1933. Unsuccessfully, she had lobbied Mrs. Roosevelt to invite male reporters to her press conferences, and she had asked the House and Senate Rules committees to install women's rest rooms in the press galleries. A diminutive and attractive woman who commonly wore blue to match her eyes, Craig as a widow lived with her son and daughter in a one-hundred-year-old house in Washington. She supported her family by representing as many out-of-town papers as she could attract until 1940 when Gannett, Maine's newspaper czar, employed her to write exclusively for him.

Smith and Craig met before Clyde's death. Indeed, Craig was at the house the night he died and said, "It was one of the strangest political events of my life. He was telling her how to run, the knowledge he had gained in his years in politics, advising her how to take his seat and handle politicians."[45] In her columns, titled "Inside Washington," Craig championed Smith's election to a full term in Congress. With little pretense of objectivity, Craig expressed her "great admiration" and "affection" for Smith and in almost every press release mentioned in personal terms Smith's clothes, hair, smile, apartment, and office.[46] Eventually there were references to Smith's congressional committees, but initially the female minutiae predominated. Craig covered all of Maine's representatives, but her special relationship with Smith became obvious. Don Larrabee, who wrote for the *Bangor Daily News* before succeeding Craig in 1966 for the Gannett papers in Portland, Augusta, and Waterville, observed her walking into Smith's office, opening a file, and reading everything in it. "She had complete access," Larrabee said a little enviously as her rival, and she "covered Smith morning 'til night." In Larrabee's view Craig became Smith's "Boswell."[47]

John Murphy, another Gannett reporter, had as one of his first assignments in the Portland office rewriting the copy Craig sent from Washington. With a curt "see if you can turn this crap into English," his editor would hand over Craig's columns, which commonly began, "Well, . . ."[48] Other "old-timers," columnist Bill Caldwell remembered, complained about editing copy from Craig that was "garbled and messed up" and which they "had a bitch of a time rewriting." "Christ, will she ever learn to put a period in a sentence," they would mutter.[49]

At the same time, Craig, who shortened her byline to simply May Craig, was becoming the star among Gannett reporters. Because she was from Virginia and had never been to Maine, Craig began accompanying Smith on her trips home in order to learn about her new audience. She stayed with Smith, first at Clyde's huge old mansion and then at the Chases's small frame house where Smith had been born, after Smith sold Clyde's house. She sold it at a reduced price in order to induce the osteopaths purchasing it to convert it into a hospital named after Clyde. Smith's father, George Chase, had died in 1946, and her mother, Carrie, enjoyed the company of the two women. During Smith's campaign for the general election, she and Craig traveled to Quoddy Village, Westport, and Pittfield. Craig always brought along her little Olivetti, one of the earliest portable, folding typewriters reporters in Maine had seen, and she spoke to journalism classes and visited newspaper offices, with Smith in tow. Smith spoke to Republican groups, union assemblies, and Townsend Clubs, with Craig along. Alone, each woman was effective; together they were memorable. Soon John Murphy's parents, and much of Maine, "couldn't start the day without reading May Craig's Washington column," and in the column they read about Smith.[50] Larrabee believed Craig "made" Smith by "really building her up, giving her a lot of attention, and bringing everything she did to people's attention."[51]

The two women were about the same age, both widowed, and earning their own way in a man's town in male fields. Craig was the more experienced of the two and became Smith's mentor, and as a feminist she enjoyed championing Smith. In exchange, Smith was good copy and a better news source. The result was a mutually profitable friendship and numerous columns, invitations, and thank-you notes, all collected by Patten and put into scrapbooks by Bernier. During oral history interviews about the Smith-Craig friendship, several people asked that the tape recorder be turned off in order to pass on some half-remembered, never substantiated rumor that the relationship was lesbian. "The only grandmother who was a virgin" was the comment reporter Liz Carpenter remembered about May Craig. Alleged lesbianism about Smith also appears in her papers in the statement Bill Lewis prepared for her on Marion Martin, founder of the National Federation of Republican Women's Clubs. Martin had heard from Selma Wagg, who was under consideration as a national committee woman from Maine, that Smith "was a lesbian." The gossip reached Smith through Owen Brewster, and she immediately called both women "to find out exactly who was talking and smearing her."[52] There is no evidence to support the allegations and what was almost certainly her long-lived premarital affair with Clyde to suggest otherwise.

"Hats off to Margaret Smith," Craig enthused in her column the day after the Japanese attack on Pearl Harbor. Contrasting Smith's courageous votes for preparedness with Montana representative Jeannette Rankin's pacifism, Craig reported that Rankin had tried to speak before casting her sole vote against war but was told, "Sit down, sister."[53] Possibly alone among those living on "the day of infamy," 7 December 1941, Smith had no memory of where she was when she learned of the sneak attack. With the other members of Congress, the cabinet, and the Supreme Court, she crowded into the House chamber with its jammed galleries and listened to President Roosevelt's brief, five-hundred-word call for war. After joining in the thunderous applause for the president and casting her vote for war, Smith triumphantly issued a press statement: "I am satisfied that I have done right in following the Administration's foreign policy and voting for all defense measures."[54] As isolationists scurried for cover, internationalists like Smith seized the moment to announce for reelection.

Senator White convened the Maine delegation to discuss the state's "hot-corner" geography that placed it, he said, in the "front line trenches" of aerial defense for the nation.[55] While the delegates agreed that West Coast defenses had priority, they considered the possibility that threats there might be a diversion for an East Coast attack. White divided oversight responsibility for state wartime industries and assigned Smith the woolen industry and coordination of Canadian-American production of potatoes, fish, lumber, and pulp.

Although providing for national defense was undoubtedly a delegation concern, securing wartime contracts and advantages was of immediate priority. Smith's first service to Maine involved saving from seizure by the navy the steamboat *North Haven,* which provided mail, passenger, and freight service to four outlying islands. According to the press coverage, Smith "passed a sleepless night" using the machinery at her command on behalf of the steamboat. Because she knew "the wheels, the ropes, and the wires" to pull, she was able to send "a victory telegram" home that the boat would be spared.[56]

The war necessitated a change in Smith's campaign style. Along with the other members of Congress, she had an X gas ration card that entitled her to an unlimited supply, but she announced that she would leave her car in Washington and travel home by train. She placed an ad in the papers, titled "Mrs. Smith's Invitation," which stated, "I expect to attend the Republican Convention. Drop in and see me."[57] While home, Smith gave up her practice of driving all over the Second District and used the bus and train to locate herself in a central area of each county at a specified time and asked interested voters to come to her. "Politics should be out for the duration," she said. "I am depending on my record as your representative." Republican candidates began traveling together and speaking before the same audiences, a practice Smith referred to as "taking the Republican tour."[58]

Smith had uncontested primaries in 1942, 1944, and 1946, and she won easily over Democratic opponents: Bradford Redonnet, David Staples, and Edward Beauchamp, respectively. Better, her seat proved a cheap one to maintain, with campaign expenditures averaging two thousand dollars. Her success was in part related to Republican dominance in the state during the war that placed Sumner Sewall in the governor's mansion, kept White and Brewster in the Senate, and made Smith senior in the House over Fellows and newcomer Robert Hale. The better explanation for Smith's longevity was her securing an invaluable seat on the House Naval Affairs Committee.

As Smith told the story, she had "outwitted" the Republican Committee on Committees by using "feminine shrewdness."[59] She asked for appointment to the House Appropriations Committee, which was the political equivalent of requesting admission to heaven while listing Naval Affairs as a presumably reluctant second choice. Part of this ruse involved Connecticut's new congresswoman, the famous Clare Boothe Luce, wife of *Time* and *Life* publisher Henry Luce. Representative Luce, ignoring the House's hoary rules of seniority, campaigned publicly for assignment to Foreign Affairs but listed the Military Affairs Committee second. Smith convinced the credulous that she reasoned that Luce, because of her husband's clout, would be pacified with her second choice, which somehow would require that Smith receive Naval Affairs. Minority leader Joseph W. Martin of Massachusetts who assigned Smith to Naval Affairs and Luce to the Military Affairs Committee said only, "I made two women happy in one day which is more than most men can say."[60] The more likely explanation had to do with tradition, second only to seniority as an operating principle in the House, and with Carl Vinson, second to no one where naval affairs were concerned. Given Maine's extensive shoreline, naval yards, and shipbuilding industry, the state had long had a representative on the Naval Affairs Committee. Owen Brewster was on the committee before he moved to the Senate and that body's Naval Affairs Committee, and Smith was now Maine's senior congresswoman.

More important in Smith's appointment was the approval of committee chairman Vinson, who had the power to ignore tradition if he chose.

The "Admiral," as it was Vinson's pleasure to be called, arrogantly ran his committee, as all of the other powerful standing committees were run, as a "tight ship." He commissioned his freshmen members "Ensigns" and publicly addressed them as such. More ponderously than the navy, which he referred to as "my Navy," he promoted "Ensigns" to "Commanders," and "Commanders," after years of swabbing his decks by voting correctly, to "Captains." From Milledgeville, a backwoods Georgia town of Skowhegan dimensions, Vinson had been in the House since 1914. By 1931 endurance had won for him an impregnable position of power from which he vanquished all challengers, whether they were admirals whose names he pretended to forget, senators whom he scathingly denounced as being from the "quote Upper house unquote," or committee members with whom he spoke at his pleasure or not at all. Certainly no one received appointment to Naval Affairs without the prior approval of Vinson.[61]

Smith's alternate story to outwitting the Republican Committee on Committees was that she took Vinson her much-used Navy Day speech of 1937. Glaring at the seemingly demure Smith through glasses that perpetually and precariously sat at the end of his long nose, Vinson read the "proof" that she was a longtime supporter of preparedness, not a Pearl Harbor convert. He remembered that at the same time as Smith was speaking in the late 1930s, he had failed to secure the votes to build fortifications at Guam. Whether taken in or not by Smith's speech to the Waterville women Republicans, the wily Vinson knew that she had consistently voted as an internationalist since 1940. He asked her why his committee needed a woman, and Smith replied that "women were mothers, sisters, wives and who was more affected by the military than those women."[62] Vinson's answer might have been WAVES, WACS, and WAFS or the tens of millions of women workers in military industries, but Smith, more feminine than feminist, chose what she considered the more politic response. With unrealized patronization, he announced that "because of the thousands of women in military services," Smith would join his committee "to provide a woman's point of view."[63] Wary of the denigration that commonly accompanied female type-casting, Smith retorted that she was "interested in the WAVES, SPARS, and women generally" but the reason that she had asked for appointment to Naval Affairs was "Maine's long coastline, shipbuilding and navy-yard interests. I have always been interested in the navy."[64]

Smith realized that she had now achieved what all representatives seek: a seat on an important committee that could provide benefits to their home state. That Smith was on Naval Affairs during wartime increased her stature tenfold and potentially gave her a voice outside her district and beyond Maine. On this committee, in closed sessions, she would be privy to military intelligence and a participant in the planning of naval strategy. She was separate now from the anonymity of most of the 435 members of Congress and distinct among the seven women members. Of course, first Smith had to get along with Carl Vinson.

Fastidious in her hat and gloves and punctilious in arriving before the 10:00 A.M. scheduled time, Smith faithfully attended the Naval Affairs meetings in Room 313 of the House Office Building. The room had two tiers of committee seats in a horseshoe arrangement, and since Smith was the junior Republican "Ensign," she sat on the chairman's right in the last seat on the lower tier. Possibly Vinson mistook Smith's New England reticence for deference, but certainly he approved of her silence at meetings. As was her habit, she prepared for each meeting, sat erect and attentive, and was pleasant in her manner. Vinson was the first of many southern legislators to respond as he had been trained as a boy by treating Smith with gallant courtesy, if not respect.

In sharp counterpoint to Smith's fastidiousness, the tall, stooped Vinson slouched into meetings in rumpled navy blue suits, mismatched with brown and white striped shirts. Noted for his oversized collars, ankle-high shoes, and food-stained ties, Vinson appalled Smith by publicly chewing the end of a long-dead cigar and frequently spitting into, or only near, a stained spittoon. Vinson sat, slumped down, in the center of the upper tier of his twenty-six committee members and struck reporters alternately as a "country lawyer . . . once removed from the cracker barrel" and as a "dictator."[65]

The Admiral's chivalrous attitude toward Smith did not extend to the male members of Naval Affairs. Once, when junior members Lyndon Johnson and Warren Magnuson began barraging a witness with questions, Vinson stopped the meeting and, according to Magnuson, said, "I want to see you two boys in the back room." Like naughty students, the two congressmen stood with lowered heads in Vinson's small, private office behind the committee room while "he let us have it." "We have a rule in this committee," meaning that he had a dictate, Vinson told them, that first-year members asked one question, second-year two, "and so on."[66]

Congresswoman Frances Bolton, who became Smith's closest friend among the women members, maintained that Smith quickly learned how to work successfully with the Vinsons of the House. "She knew these men up there," Bolton smiled. "Oh, how she knew them. In minutes she could tell me what to watch out for, whether he could be trusted."[67]

The first plum Smith received from Vinson was appointment to a six-member subcommittee to investigate congestion at naval bases. She had been on Naval Affairs for only a few weeks when she suggested the importance of improving living conditions in coastal areas near naval facilities in order to increase worker morale and efficiency. As was customary when a member suggested a study with which the chairman agreed, Vinson created a subcommittee but hesitated in naming the members. Tradition also dictated that the person requesting the study be appointed as a member, and the Admiral looked long and hard at Smith. "I could see Mr. Vinson was in a quandary, you know, just what to do," Smith remembered, but then he quietly said, "Mrs. Smith."[68] The first woman representative to be sent on an inspection trip, a well-publicized first, Smith traveled in April 1943 with six members of the subcommittee to Norfolk, San Diego, San Francisco, Portland, and Newport. Moving across the country on overcrowded and overheated, slow-moving and ever-dirty trains, the trip was hardly a junket. Smith observed that there were almost no other women traveling and learned, as every professional woman on the road with male colleagues has had to learn, the difficulties of maintaining dignity while tending to bodily functions and hygiene. Never varying her uniform of homemade suit, hat, gloves, high heels, hose, and girdle, Smith did the best she could with her short, gray hair and eschewed makeup altogether. The men found her an inconvenience at best, and because she did not drink, smoke, or gamble, they sought sanctuary away from her in club cars and late-night card games. To her credit, Smith asked for no special treatment as a woman, retired early to give the men their privacy, then lay awake listening to drunken soldiers, reeling down the aisles, laughing and singing.

Arrival brought more difficulties. The chairman stepped aside to allow Smith, the lady, to exit first, but she refused. "I told him then and there that I must be considered a member of the committee," she said, and took her place, as seniority dictated, at the end of the line.[69] The representatives put in long days with public hearings and inspection tours at each base and learned first-hand the ramifications of overcrowding on defense production. During the war some 9 million people packed up and moved to military camps, munition plants, aircraft factories, and shipyards. There they inundated housing, city services, and medical facilities, and the personal problems resulting from being unable to find a place to live, a ride to work, or a doctor for a sick child led to massive absenteeism from work.

In San Francisco Smith visited stores converted to housing facilities through construction of stalls furnished with cots that rented for a dollar a night. In one building twenty-eight families lived on the first floor and fourteen on the second with one toilet for all. Smith became increasingly concerned about the large numbers of young women moving away from home to good-paying jobs near naval bases and the thousands of males stationed there. With surprising, near shocking, frankness she documented the rise in venereal disease among these "young girls, not professionals" in excess of the national average.[70]

In city after city as April turned into May the representatives saw the same problems. Smith considered the waterfront areas "highly dangerous" and noted that drunkenness accounted for 35 percent of the arrests of servicemen.[71] She believed indoor recreational facilities like bowling and skating would help and deplored the lack of discounts for servicemen at movies and restaurants. Instead, both civilian and military officials testified to price gouging, with inflated charges for food, rent, and services.

The tour had two significant dividends for Smith. The first was national publicity, because the hearings attracted large crowds of spectators and reporters. With her ready smile and uniqueness as the only female representative along, Smith became the favored subject of photographers and received from them the title of "Vice-Admiral." Although she was snapped primping before a mirror once and often compared for best-dressed congresswoman with former model Luce, Smith received serious press attention as a hard-working representative. She could also disarm hardened reporters, as she did once when she was walking to a meeting and discovered a flock of reporters. Looking behind her, she asked them if a celebrity was coming. "You" was their chorused reply.[72]

Smith's other dividend was William Chesley Lewis, Jr. He was on loan from the Department of Navy as counsel to the House Naval Affairs Committee and was the advance man for the subcommittee's tour. A small, slim man, thirty years old to Smith's forty-five, Lewis was a master of organization and efficiency and in his quiet and unobtrusive manner had his diverse group of congressmen under military discipline. Smith first remembered Lewis's seeking her out in California to ascertain her interests in their investigation. She simply told him that she wanted to make it possible for people "to live decently" on naval bases and to prevent "young women from going to the fleet and getting themselves in trouble."[73]

The subcommittee made it a habit to have dinner together, but then the men quickly left Smith for pleasures they did not mention to her. Lewis began asking Smith if "she would like to walk around the block," probably, she thought, "to keep her out of the men's way" but maybe because she was "very lonely with nobody to associate with. The men were all very nice to me but I never went out with them on their outside excursions." Smith and Lewis liked each other and were immensely similar in their hard-working, spartan habits. After their evening walks, Smith said that she would "go to her room and I don't know where he would go but that was the end of that."[74]

Smith changed the routine once when she decided she needed to see the hot spots where trouble commonly occurred at night. Lewis told her that he could not take her, but Smith said that she "could dress differently and make-up differently" to avoid recognition. Reluctantly, Lewis arranged Smith's "night out on the town," but when she appeared in her "disguise," the other committee members were waiting to go along. Lewis had sanitized the excursion, but Smith said that she "made up for it the next day" by visiting the jail and asking the large number of women arrested the night before what had happened.[75]

At hearings Lewis started passing the usually silent Smith a question for the witness. "I would hesitate about asking it because this was new ground for me, and I knew that they might come back at me and get me involved in a discussion I couldn't handle." More important, though, Smith believed that "if I did not ask that question, this young man who had been so kind to me would not give me another question. He impressed me as being of that temperament."[76] Smith asked his questions and secured more headlines, and Lewis received a congressional conduit whom he could influence and use to voice his own concerns.

At the culmination of the tour, the subcommittee took an official ride from Bath to Boston on the destroyer *Erban,* which made Smith the first woman to do so. Although some women workers in war industries had resisted the safety precaution of wearing coveralls and tying their hair back, Smith cheerfully donned the too-large, white canvas coveralls that the president of Bath Iron Works, builder of the ship, selected for her, and she tied up her hair. "Just can't go on a ship in skirts," she said and added that she had been warned that she might get seasick and was quietly given the key to a room.[77] She did not, she bragged, although some of the men did.

The Republican leadership treated Smith more cordially after her nationally publicized tour. Candidly, she told a Washington audience that she had been "really afraid of Mr. Martin when I first arrived . . . but it wasn't long before he made me feel like we were colleagues." Smith began introducing the minority leader as "my boss."[78] Jubilant over the navy contracts pouring into Maine and aware that the navy was the nation's largest industrial employer, state Republican leaders invited Smith to be the first woman to chair their annual convention.

In Smith's long-term memory it was Vinson who became her "mentor" and "idol," and from all accounts the old curmudgeon was pleased with her.[79] He encouraged her, at Lewis's suggestion, to participate in the examination of committee witnesses and observed that Smith wrote out her questions in longhand, brought statistical evidence to support her position, and refused to be put off with pleasantries by admirals, company presidents, or administration spokesmen who showed up without doing their homework. "Purring," Vinson "just sat there," a colleague noted, "with his hands folded as if in prayer. He was pleased and proud that anyone could be tougher than he was."[80] He saw Smith as a schoolmarm, despite her disastrous and brief months as a teacher, whose superiority could reduce grown men to little boys. Observing Clare Boothe Luce in her designer clothes and little-girl hair bows, Vinson had to be pleased that he had drawn Smith as his token woman. When Luce finally bullied Military Affairs into sending her on an inspection tour of the European theater of the war, Vinson responded by putting Smith on a subcommittee to inspect Pacific bases. By no means the first male to encourage what reporters called a "cat fight," the chairman laughed when he heard that the press had asked Smith if she intended to travel with an aide as Luce planned, and Smith "snorted," "What for?" Encouraged, Smith added that Luce "was in too big a hurry" and that "dressing doesn't make a Congresswoman."[81] According to Smith, "women should be shown no favors in Congress because of their sex," and, not thinking to aim higher, should work to be "as good as a man."[82] Before Smith and Luce, unheralded by the press, representatives Frances Bolton and Edith Nourse Rogers had quietly and productively visited the European front as members of the House Foreign Affairs Committee.

Complaints of other women on various inspection tours that they had not been allowed to confer with male officials led to Vinson's being asked if Smith would be allowed to talk on her Pacific tour. In his usual blunt manner, Vinson replied that Smith could "talk anytime, anywhere about anything. I have complete confidence in her."[83] At the time, Smith did not feel well enough to talk to anyone because she had just received in one day five injections for typhus, smallpox, typhoid, yellow fever, and tetanus.

The ten-member Naval Affairs Subcommittee left on a twenty-five-thousand-mile, three-week trip in December 1944. Limited to one small suitcase, Smith traveled in a borrowed WAVES (Women Accepted for Voluntary Emergency Service) seersucker uniform. For security reasons their itinerary was not announced in advance. The representatives first visited Pearl Harbor, where they received more inoculations, and then Guam, Samoa, and Australia. Although they got no closer to the front than Saipan in the Marianas, which had been liberated from the Japanese during the summer of 1944, the committee met with enlisted men, officers, and Admiral Chester Nimitz. The commander-in-chief of the U.S. Pacific Fleet and Pacific Ocean Area, Nimitz took his visitors on board an aircraft carrier for a day of battle practice at sea. Clad in coveralls and smiling, Smith struck political gold again when the press photographed her in a gun emplacement with Nimitz. The group received national attention because their inspection tour was the first by a congressional delegation since the war began, but Smith garnered most of the publicity. To the pleasure of the press, she celebrated her birthday while at sea, but during the night they entered an earlier time zone and Smith announced that it was her birthday all over again. She refused to say which birthday to the reporters or in the *Congressional Directory,* but it was her forty-seventh.

Smith's interest in the trip was to see what was being done and what should be done for the health and morale of the men. "You can not imagine it unless you see it," she said about one base. "Ten thousand men on an island a couple of miles in diameter with not a tree, just sea and sky and water." She saw a need for rest homes for the wounded and battle fatigued and for more hospital provisions. Her comments educated the people back home to the military belief that while the war in Europe was ending, the war in the Pacific was just beginning. Because of the enormous distances, "ships, ships, ships are needed for everything," she said. "And everybody must write and write and write, whether they get letters from their men or not. Mail from home is what they want more than you will ever know." Smith took the names of the men she met from Maine to call their parents on Christmas Day with their messages "as her Christmas gift" to them.[84]

Upon her return after twenty-one days, the press heralded Smith as an expert on naval affairs and reported rumors that she was being touted as a possible undersecretary of the navy. A vacancy existed because Undersecretary James Forrestal had recently been named to replace the deceased secretary of the navy, Frank Knox. Smith did not become the first female undersecretary—no one has—but she did receive as a member of the congested areas subcommittee a Presidential Commendation. Reading "For outstanding contribution to the prosecution of the war," the tribute was the first received by a subcommittee. She also had the satisfaction of seeing several of her recommendations to the Department of the Navy enacted, but not her suggestion that bell-bottomed pants be redesigned to include pockets. Only Helen of Troy, Smith believed, could have launched more ships than she did in the aftermath of her tour.

For all of Smith's efforts to be treated as a congressman and not as a congresswoman, she found herself increasingly involved with women's issues. While denying that she ever "separated the issues between men and women," Smith learned that both women's groups and individual females with problems assumed her sympathy and sought her out for remedy.[85] "My mail is full of the troubles caused by war," she wrote in her *Washington and You* newsletter.[86] She learned that girls under the age of sixteen, unlike boys, were prohibited from working in war industries and introduced legislation to equalize access to the lucrative jobs. The legislation did not succeed, but the Department of War enacted Smith's recommendation by independent ruling. She also championed housing on military bases for the families of commissioned officers in long-term residence and more efficient delivery of allotment checks to the wives of enlisted men. She succeeded in securing, again by Department of War ruling, maternity and infant care for military dependents at base hospitals. By March 1944, over 2,000 women in Maine had benefited from the care, and nationally over 250,000 mothers and babies had been helped.

Always low key in her approach, Smith was in the House over four years before she spoke on the floor, and her maiden speech was in support of public nurseries and day care centers. During her first tour of congested areas, she had become aware of the large numbers of dependent-age children who were left unattended by working mothers. "Latchkey children," "eight-hour orphans," and "juvenile delinquency" were new phrases in common use during the war. All of the references were in relation to both the increased numbers of children and the inadequate number of day care facilities available. Mothers simultaneously were propagandized that it was their patriotic duty to work in defense industries and condemned for not staying home to care for their children. The public debate, like most others involving varying interpretations on women's roles as citizens and mothers, was loud to shrill and rancorous to hateful. Under the guise of legitimate reporting but also reflective of a vested interest in controversy, the press printed frequent stories of hundreds of babies left in parked cars at defense industries, numerous children hurt in accidents in unsupervised homes, and common acts of vandalism by teenagers roaming the streets.

Although Smith extolled "woman's mother instinct," with no explanation of her own lack of desire for children, she appreciated both the practical and patriotic necessity of women war workers and spoke out in favor of public support for child care.[87] The bill Smith championed on the floor was the Lanham Act, which provided matching funds for locally controlled day care facilities. The act called for some $40 million to aid 65,772 children in 2,243 projects, most of them after-school programs at public schools. Smith argued that since the War Manpower Commission wanted 600,000 more women workers, there was no choice but to provide day care centers.

When the Taber Amendment to the Lanham Act proposed cutting the funding in half, Smith joined with six other women representatives to argue against it. The amendment failed by five votes, and more, if not adequate, day care facilities resulted. Insisting that the lack of child care facilities was "sowing a whirlwind of juvenile delinquency," Smith called for more funding, not less, as an "investment, not a short-term expenditure." Adequate facilities, Smith believed, would increase worker productivity, decrease absenteeism, and mitigate labor turnover.[88]

"I am not a feminist," Smith said over and over during her public career, and added that she was "particularly conscious of, and perhaps sensitive to, the general criticism that women selfishly seek equal rights without agreeing to give up their feminine privileges." She took as her slogan, "Women are people," and criticized feminists for being only for women. On the most controversial feminist issue of her day, the equal rights amendment, Smith gave limited support with the proviso that women accept equal responsibilities.[89] The militant suffrage leader, Alice Paul, who had founded the National Woman's party to promote full equality under the law for women, had first proposed the ERA. The amendment, introduced in Congress in 1923, stated that "men and women shall have equal rights throughout the United States and every place subject to its jurisdiction." Congress had taken no action on the ERA in 1923, and Paul had continued to introduce it at each subsequent session. During the 1930s and early 1940s the bill had received some favorable, if sporadic, committee action, and in 1938 had made it to the Senate floor, albeit unsuccessfully. In 1940 the Republican party had put the ERA in its platform, and in 1944 both the Democratic and Republican parties had endorsed the amendment.

The 1944 elections returned ten women to the House of Representatives, the largest number in congressional history, but cost Hattie Carraway her Senate seat in a contest with J. William Fulbright. Possibly because of their war work, women had more government influence than ever before, and for the Seventy-ninth Congress Alice Paul put together an ERA sponsor list that for the first time included all of the female representatives plus one hundred congressmen. Smith knew Paul "quite well," she said. "I used to go over there" to the National Woman's party headquarters, and "she used to come to the office often"—too often, as Smith recalled, because she considered Paul "aggressive in taking her petitions around and securing sponsors" and believed the ERA campaign failed because of her militant "approach of male legislators."[90]

Paul's plan, with the able leadership of Congressman Louis Ludlow of Indiana, got the ERA out of the House Judiciary Committee, after twenty-two years of feminist effort, and onto the the floor. The language of the amendment had been changed in 1943 to read: "Equality of rights under the law shall not be denied or abridged by the United States or by any State on account of sex." Also reported to the floor of the Senate in 1945, the bill had the endorsement of thirty governors and thirty-three national women's organizations. The widespread expectation was that the legislation would pass as a vote of thanks for women's war work. When the amendment came up for vote first in the Senate, it received a majority but failed for lack of the two-thirds vote required for amendments.

Aside from agreeing to be a sponsor for the first time, Smith did not promote the equal rights amendment during committee hearings, in the *Congressional Record,* or in public statements and speeches. "I was always a co-sponsor," she said, "but I was always a co-sponsor feeling that they would know that I was for women and that they should get a man or two to head the list."[91]

Smith fared better, according to feminist criteria, in the battle for rights for women in the military. Since the American Revolution and the legend of Molly Pitcher, inspired by Mary Ludwig Hayes at Monmouth Courthouse or, possibly, Margaret Corbin at the battle at Fort Washington, women have fought in the wars of the United States. Disguised as male soldiers, women have been unmasked as participants in the War of 1812, the Mexican War, and the Civil War before being officially organized as nurses first during the Civil War and then the Spanish-American War. During World War I Smith could have enlisted as a Naval Reserve yeomanette when Secretary of Navy Josephus Daniels enrolled women for the first time as clerical assistants, or she could have joined some thirty-four thousand women who served in an expanded Army and Navy Nurses Corps in both the United States and abroad.

Before American entry into World War II, Smith wrote in her 30 January 1941 *Washington and You* column that "half of the population can not be left out if the defense effort is to be effective." Her interest on behalf of women was "not so much shouldering guns, or driving tanks or wearing uniforms" but in serving. She participated in a White House conference with Mrs. Roosevelt "to discuss fundamentals of women's participation in defense" and wrote Secretary of War Henry Stimson to ask that women be appointed to defense boards.[92]

After Pearl Harbor Smith applauded the proliferation of military options for women in the Women's Army Corps, Coast Guard Women, Women's Marine Corps Reserve, and in each branch's nurse corps. Because of her position on Naval Affairs, she became particularly involved with the WAVES, SPARS, and women marines, and on her inspection tours Vinson asked that she specifically visit facilities for women. By 1944 Smith had toured training schools and assignment areas for women in fourteen states and the District of Columbia. In liaison with Captain Mildred McAfee, director of the WAVES, Captain Dorothy Stratton, director of the SPARS, and Captain Ruth Cheney Streeter of the women marines, Smith "went through the paces" with the inductees. She stayed in their quarters, ate in their mess halls, attended their classes, participated in their physical training exercises, which included taking a parachute jump, and, after graduation, visited them on their assignments. She watched graduates working as weather forecasters, air controllers, communications officers, "repair women," and varied medical personnel. From this practical vantage point, the congresswoman successfully championed the woman's request to wear "dungarees" as work uniform, to have "hair-dressing facilities," laundry and ironing rooms, and both private lounges and public ones for dates as part of their housing, and to end the 2:00 A.M. curfew imposed on women but not on men.[93]

At the suggestion of the Department of Navy, Smith introduced legislation in 1944 both to permit higher rank and better benefits for women and to allow them to serve overseas. Although WACs were already serving abroad in noncombat roles, Smith's bill ran into what she called "a little prejudice by those who feel the women's place is in the home." One congressman argued that the WAVES would "find hardships overseas that no American woman should have to endure." "Bring all the nurses home" then, Smith retorted.[94]

Smith's original proposal was to allow women to serve anywhere except on board ships and in combat areas, and she secured House passage twice, but both times her bill died in the Senate Naval Affairs Committee. Reluctantly she limited her request to the "American area" of North and South America, Hawaii, Alaska, the Canal Zone, and the Caribbean.[95] She still had to request a statement of need from Admiral Nimitz for 5,000 WAVES, 1,535 marine women, and 150 SPARS immediately in Hawaii to release men for combat duty before she broke the Senate logjam.

The Department of Navy in late 1945 asked the Naval Affairs Committee to propose legislation establishing both permanent and reserve status for women in the navy, but Carl Vinson, more powerful than ever, favored only reserve service for the time being. Smith's carefully balanced response was that while she did not believe women in the army, navy, and air force should be kept on as reservists on inactive duty indefinitely, she also did not want permanent status "merely as a noble gesture for their splendid war service." As Smith succinctly put it, "Either there was a permanent need or there wasn't." If there was need, she would fight for regular as well as reserve status. If there was no need, she favored reserve service only when there was another war. To ascertain need, Smith used a tactic she would later employ frequently with the military in the future. She presented the navy with an "Interrogation on Women's Reserve Legislation" and, according to her account in *Declaration of Conscience,* concluded that their answers were not satisfactory, and that, accordingly, "the legislation did not pass." In the official marine history, however, Smith attempted in committee to amend Vinson's bill to provide regular service despite Vinson's warning that her amendment would kill the whole bill. A warning from Vinson, Smith knew, had a way of becoming fact, and the bill died in committee.[96]

In 1947 the Senate combined the navy and army bills to make women part of the regular armed forces as well as the reserves. In favor of "woman power," both General of the Army Dwight D. Eisenhower and Fleet Admiral Chester W. Nimitz testified before the Armed Services Committee, newly created by combining the Naval and Military Affairs committees. The legislation passed the Senate in July 1947 and was sent to the House. No longer chairman but still dominant, Carl Vinson not only made a virtue of skepticism toward senators, generals, and admirals but was also offended that the Senate had not waited, as was customary, for the House to act first on personnel matters. The bill languished for eight months in subcommittee before the new Republican chairman of Armed Services, W. G. (Ham) Andrews of New York, with Vinson's encouragement decided to bring it before the committee with permanent status eliminated.[97]

Smith learned that statements from representatives of the navy in an off-the-record executive session of the committee had motivated the change in the bill. The statements, which Smith ascertained were unauthorized, were to the effect that regular status would lead to a draft for women in another war, West Point's becoming coed, and women on board navy ships. Furious and "ready to fight," Smith fired off a letter to Andrews that she released to the press reiterating her position that "either the Armed Services have a *permanent* need of women officers and enlisted women or they don't." Instead of a "dodging 'maybe,' " Smith called for a "forthright" response like the Senate's and opposed reserve status only "because there is no such thing as a service career for a Reservist."[98] Although unmentioned in *Declaration of Conscience,* attached to the file copy of Smith's letter was a memo from her secretary indicating that Bill Lewis, now a colonel, was advising her. If there was no need for women in the services, Lewis said, then "they couldn't have them in any capacity." He added that if Smith were asked to identify "naval representatives" who made the unauthorized statements, she should respond that "the issues are above personalities."[99] Compounding the greatest controversy of her political career to date, Smith heard from military women that they opposed her position because they preferred to forgo regular status in order to hold on to their reserve standing. The committee vote went against Smith twenty-six to one. "I got my ears pinned back," she said.[100]

Because of what she called a "tactical error" of the navy's legislative counsel, Smith learned that Andrews and Vinson "in a surprising defiance of normal parliamentary procedure" had placed the women's bill on the consent calendar. Ordinarily bills put on the consent calendar are not controversial because once there they cannot be debated or amended. Furious because the leadership was "steamrolling" her opposition and "utterly disregarding" the Senate bill, Smith decided to use the one rule that would keep them from "getting away with it." Bills on the consent calendar had to pass unanimously, and Smith's one objection could prevent that. "They must have felt that in the final crunch, I wouldn't dare to object," Smith said, but they "kept a steady eye on me, some of them coming up to me to plead or argue, a few almost threatening reprisals." Their repeated point was that she would kill the entire bill, and Andrews added, "You'll be making a fool of yourself, Margaret." All of this Smith stubbornly, courageously, and/or foolhardedly ignored when the new Speaker, Joseph Martin asked if there were objections; she responded "in a firm voice 'I object.' "[101]

In the ensuing firestorm of criticism, Smith garnered an unlikely champion, Democratic minority leader John W. McCormack of Massachusetts. "The gentlewoman from Maine did the right thing," McCormack said on the floor. If her opponents had "taken a little look" at her chin, they would have seen that she "is not the type that can be bluffed." McCormack added his congratulations and admiration, but the issue was stalemated, not settled.[102]

When Ham Andrews brought the bill to the floor for debate, Smith amended it to give women regular status. Bill Lewis wrote the amendment for her as a substitute for the lengthy and technical one written by the staff counsel, criticized by Smith as "a patronage appointee of my adversary Dewey Short," Republican representative from Missouri. In the debate, opponents of regular service used "biological differences between the sexes" that inexplicably made the female "more deadly than the male." In a blatant reference to Smith, Short misquoted, "Hell hath no fury like a woman's scorn," and argued that 8 percent of women in the services became illegitimately pregnant. Those who "reach the age of menopause or go through the change of life," he added, would have "stupendous if not prohibitive" medical expenses.[103] At age fifty, Smith was probably menopausal and offended, but her amendment garnered enough support that a "frantic call" went out from the leadership to get the bill's supporters to the floor for the vote.[104] Smith lost for the third time.

Lewis said that by this time the issue "had literally become a crusade" with Smith. She wrote Secretary of Defense James V. Forrestal about the "duplicity" of official representatives of the armed services opposing regular status for women "behind closed doors" while the public position of the Defense Department was in favor. She told Forrestal that it was "imperative" that he take "immediate action" while the legislation was before a conference committee. The secretary complied, the House conferees gave way, and the Women's Armed Services Integration Act gave women regular as well as reserve standing. "I lost all the battles," Smith said, "except the last one."[105]

The press heralded Smith's success and commonly referred to her as the mother of the WAVES in recounting her wartime efforts on the Naval Affairs Committee. Ired, Representative Melvin Maas of Minnesota who had sponsored the legislation establishing the WAVES said, "Well, I don't know Mrs. Smith, and if she is the mother of the WAVES, there must be some mistake, because I'm the father."[106]

Smith's last battle in the House secured for her as significant a support group as military women, the Air Reserve Association. The conflict concerned unification of the Departments of War and Navy and the proposed Department of the Air Force. In retrospect, Smith claimed to have supported these issues since 1941 but remained silent for years on learning that her Naval Affairs Committee was a "hotbed of anti-Unification forces." Observing Carl Vinson's "unrivaled Congressional cunning" in preventing merger bills from getting out of committee, Smith waited until the Republicans achieved their 1947 majority in Congress before announcing her position and making "the first break" in "that strongest of all Navy strongholds." Merger of the Naval Affairs and Military Affairs committees in Congress strengthened Smith's position, but the leadership bypassed the resulting Armed Services Committee and sent the unification bill, House resolution 4214, to the Executive Expenditures Committee. Chairman Clare Hoffman of Michigan, according to Smith, borrowed "a leaf from 'Admiral' Vinson's log" and tried to "bottle up" the bill in his committee until Congress adjourned.[107]

Smith's involvement with unification began in May 1947 while she and her friend from naval inspection tours, Bill Lewis, were visiting his parents in Oklahoma City. Lewis's father, Army Air Corps Reserve Colonel William C. Lewis, Sr., was executive director of the Air Reserve Association. An urgent call from the association brought Smith, father, and son back to Washington to try to "resurrect" the near-moribund bill. While the Lewises organized the air reservists in a "letter bomb" campaign to convince Speaker Joe Martin to order the legislation out of committee, Smith began quietly lobbying committee members. She reminded them that the Republican party had promised in the 1946 election to unify the services and that to fail to do so now that the party had majority control would be a "betrayal."[108]

Smith achieved a position of leadership in the fight when she was asked to appear with famous air force ace Jimmy Doolittle on the radio debate program, "American Forum of the Air." The two argued for unification against "the father of the WAVES," Melvin Maas, and Congressman Harry R. Sheppard, former Naval Affairs committeeman. By no means a debater, Smith was invited to participate only after two other representatives had refused. "There was some question," Smith said frankly, "as to whether I could hold my own." Bill Lewis helped her prepare an opening and closing statement and advised her to let Doolittle carry the brunt of the exchange. The debate went well, but Smith maintained that the air force supplied Doolittle with the information she had requested after telling her that they did not have it. Aside from the national exposure, Smith had the pleasure of hearing Doolittle tell others that after her closing statement Maas leaned across the table and said, "Maggie, you made a God-damned fool out of me." Undoubtedly due to many other initiatives also, the unification bill came out of committee eight days later and passed the House eleven days later. The Senate concurred, and President Truman signed the legislation on 26 July 1947.[109]

A final inspection tour for the House Military Affairs Committee further enhanced Smith's national presence. As chair of the Medical Subcommittee, Smith left in September 1947 with eight other congressmen for a five-week tour of American occupation zones in sixteen nations in Europe, the Middle East, and North Africa. Over 150 legislators were abroad at the time because of the debate over the Marshall Plan to reconstruct war-torn nations. Because she was again the only woman along, the press singled her out with comments about her long hemlines, which servicemen did not like, the five hundred lollipops she brought along to give to children, and her being the first woman to address the Iranian legislature. The trip home on a Douglas C-54 generated the most headlines, however, when the number 3 engine went out and number 2 began sputtering over the Atlantic eight hundred miles and four hours away from Azores. The twenty-five people on board put on inflatable Mae West life preservers and an Air Rescue B-1 intercepted the crippled plane on its way back to the Azores to give a position report in case it "ditched." "It was a bit of a sweat," the committee's military aide said, "but Mrs. Smith was the coolest person on the plane." She opened a box of souvenir harmonicas she had purchased in Switzerland and suggested a song fest, if not specifically "Nearer My God to Thee."[110]

Despite her triumphs, Smith lamented that "it left the impression, I'm afraid, that I was a feminist. And if there is any one thing I have attempted to avoid it is being a feminist. I definitely resent being called a feminist."[111]

Smith did not resent being called ambitious, because she had decided to use her success as a springboard to the U.S. Senate.

Chapter Four

AMERICA'S HEROINE

"Bill, I need your help. Something awful has happened."

"Calm down, Margaret."

Bill Lewis had never before heard the note of panic he heard now in Margaret's voice, and he found it unsettling.

"Hildreth has put out an analysis of my voting record that accuses me of being 'pro-communist, a traitor to the Republican Party, a tool of the CIO [Congress of Industrial Organizations] and a political companion of Representative Vito Marcantonio.' "[1]

"It that all?"

Ignoring his quiet attempt at humor, Margaret wailed, "What am I going to do?"

"You are going to get control of yourself," Bill said sternly, "and tell me why the governor is making these accusations. What is he offering as proof? Did he issue this as a press release?"

"No," Margaret explained. "A friend sent me a copy of an anonymous mailing she received with the understanding that Hildreth's people sent it." With voice rising again, "Bill, this is very serious. People can be fooled about this."

"Margaret, I am not going to talk to you if you insist on hysterics." Silence. "All right, now are any of the charges true?"

"Of course not, but that doesn't matter."

"It matters, and you must conduct yourself as though it matters a great deal. You have been falsely attacked; that is your position. Better, you are a lady who has been maliciously attacked by a swaggering bully."

"Bill, you don't understand. This is not your typical campaign smear.

What I am looking at purports to be a factual analysis of my voting record. It's impressive."

"I like that word smear."

"I don't like it at all, and you wouldn't either if you were in my place."

"Is your voting record accurately represented?"

"I guess so. He refers to hundreds of my votes, and then he uses comparisons and percentages."

After a long pause, "I'll tell you what I'll do, Margaret. I'll come by your office in the morning to get the smear sheet and check it against your votes in the Congressional Record. *First, we will document the inaccuracy of these smears."*

"Stop using that ugly word."

"No, you start using that word. We are going to make being smeared your campaign. You are going to stand before every Grange and woman's club in Maine, looking like everybody's fragile, white-haired grandmother and say that you are being smeared by those rich bullies in the party machine. People are going to rush to your defense."

"I don't know, Bill."

"I do, Margaret, trust me, but first I need the facts. Nothing is more effective than the truth."

After sipping the rare wine of the Republican sweep of 1946, Smith began "casting longing glances at the upper house," the *Lewiston Journal* reported.[2] If she decided to run, the editorial continued, she would "be fighting for keeps" and probably against former governor Sumner Sewall and incumbent governor Horace Hildreth.[3] According to May Craig, Smith had already met with publisher Guy Gannett in his Washington hotel room, and he had encouraged her to run. In contrast, Craig did not, and said, "This time I was faint-hearted. You can stay in the House, forever, so why risk it with the Senate." "I will never know, unless I try," Smith responded.[4] Although Smith had received her smallest vote in the 1946 election, she confirmed for many the early rumor that she intended to run for the Senate in 1948 when she announced plans to drive all over Maine to campaign in fisheries, lumber camps, woolen mills, and canneries.

In going to the people, Smith applied to the state the campaign style she had developed in the Second District. Never a member of the Republican establishment as her husband had been, over the years Smith had built a loose network of supporters: small town postmasters, service station and grocery store owners, housewives, a sprinkling of professionals, and local chapters of the Business and Professional Women's Clubs. Between elections she had maintained contact with these people through steady correspondence and visits, both of which commonly began with her asking, "What can I do for you?" When election time came around again, as it seemed increasingly to do more often, Smith, working only with her Washington staff, asked her supporters to circulate primary papers, arrange meetings where she could speak, and get out the vote on election day. She had never employed a campaign staff, solicited campaign funds, or spent more than a few hundred dollars on campaign paraphernalia like buttons, ribbons, car stickers, and newspaper and radio ads. This was laid-back, down-home, grass-roots campaigning even for the 1940s, but for Smith it worked. It also indicated that she remained outside the Maine Republican party apparatus, fourth-term congresswoman or not.

Governor John Reed who as a young veteran was starting out in business and politics in Fort Fairfield observed Smith's 1948 campaign as chairman of the Republican town committee. He saw her as an "outsider" "bucking" the Republican party "inner circle" against Sewall and Hildreth who had come "up through the ranks." To Reed, Smith was a "pioneer in developing a personal organization" of "loyal, enthusiastic, strong supporters"; "no question in my mind that she was the first one to do this." Traditionally, Republican dominance of Maine depended on a network that began at the local level with the town committee, spread to the county committee, and was dominated by the state committee, of which Smith, interestingly, had one time been a member, but more as Clyde's wife than a future political contender. "If the word filtered down from the top that Mr. X was the one the party favored," Reed continued, "then you got the whole party apparatus behind that candidate." In contrast, Smith "had these key people everywhere"; "she had a chairperson in every hamlet, every city and town and plantation in the whole state," Reed said. "She picked people very carefully," and "they believed in her." "They were for Margaret Smith, and they weren't going to worry about other candidates."[5]

The person whom Smith was most interested in recruiting for her Senate campaign was William Chesley Lewis, Jr., whom she had first met on the Naval Affairs Committee. Their friendship had grown over the years, and Smith, alone in Washington, increasingly visited Lewis, a bachelor, and his parents, Nelle and William Lewis, with whom he lived. The Lewis family was from Oklahoma where Bill had been born in 1912 in Wilburton. Both parents were attorneys, and after Bill had graduated from the University of Oklahoma with a bachelor of arts and a doctor of jurisprudence degree, his father had sponsored him and his mother, who also had a law degree, for admission to practice before the U.S. Supreme Court. Chief Justice Charles Evans Hughes had observed upon their acceptance that the Lewises were the first family in the history of the Court to be admitted. An only child, Lewis was particularly close to his mother, and Smith believed that "he saw in her what he would have liked for his mother to have done."[6]

Before Smith announced for the Senate on 1 June 1947, she traveled to Oklahoma with Lewis to visit his retired parents. Their mutual concern was as much to secure Bill's appointment as assistant secretary of the new Department of Air Force as to assess Smith's chances for the Senate. Upon their return, Smith immediately followed Maine's senior senator Wallace White's announcement of his intention to retire after thirty years in Congress with a statement of her candidacy. Affirming confidence in her experience and ability, she declared that she desired "a wider opportunity to serve" because "such service is my sole mission in political life."[7]

Then on 30 July 1947, Smith wrote both President Harry Truman and his aide Dave Niles to request consideration of Lewis for the air force appointment. Referring to Lewis as a "young man" who "was the most important single factor in resurrecting unification and getting it passed," Smith assured the president that Lewis "knows Congress and how it works." Although Smith received assurances that her nomination would receive "careful consideration," Lewis did not receive the appointment. Instead, Smith secured Lewis, the astute political pro from Oklahoma, to manage her politically risky campaign in xenophobic Maine.[8]

Maintaining a profile so low that he was barely mentioned in the Maine press until Smith's 1972 campaign, Lewis set up headquarters in Carrie Chase's home in Skowhegan. Working with only two secretaries from the Washington office, who also moved into the little house on North Avenue, Lewis organized like a military commander. The seventy-two-year-old Carrie enjoyed having the house in which she and Margaret had been born "vibrating" again and "mothered" the campaign staff.[9]

Confirming press speculation, Governor Hildreth announced in September, and Sewall followed a few weeks later. In addition to being party regulars, Smith's two formidable opponents were both well liked and respected, well heeled and connected. Hildreth at forty-eight had the résumé of an all-American politician. Born in Gardiner and educated at Bowdoin where he had been both a varsity athlete and varsity debater, Hildreth had a Harvard Law School degree and had served in both the Maine House and Senate before his two terms as governor. He had not only the power of incumbency in Augusta but also the prestige of being chairman of both the New England Governors Association and the National Governors Association. Former Governor Sewall of Bath had recently returned to Maine from a term as military governor of the German Province of Württemburg-Baden. A veteran of World Wars I and II, Sewall had flown in the first war with Eddie Rickenbacker and in the second with Jimmy Doolittle. He had been decorated by both France and the United States and had never lost an election. Albion P. Beverage also entered the Republican primary, although he was an unknown from Dresden.

Immediately after the entry of the party luminaries, the press reported suggestions to Smith that she withdraw from the campaign "to save yourself from defeat."[10] "Why should I?" was the Smith retort that Lewis publicized. "I was there first."[11] Feisty became the first characteristic of the Margaret Chase Smith whom Bill Lewis created. Smith's campaign began the day after Christmas 1947, when she barnstormed the state, snow, ice, and blizzards notwithstanding. "Making political hay while the snow flies," Smith, campaigning in Bangor in February, slipped on ice and fractured her right arm in falling.[12] Lewis informed the press that after receiving a cast, Smith gamely drove sixty miles to Rockland to keep her next appointment and then on another hundred miles to Portland for her next speech. When she received praise for continuing to campaign with her arm in a sling, made from a bright silk scarf she had purchased in Paris on her last junket, the press wrote about her lucky "political break."[13] A disgruntled critic, C. F. Gilliland of Dryden, charged that the break was a "phoney [sic]" to get publicity.[14]

Lewis's Smith was not only feisty, she was also a responsible, hardworking representative who did not shirk her duties in Washington. Campaigning only on weekends, Smith made the arduous trip back and forth to Washington in the same 1945 Dodge that she drove around Maine. "Been everyplace just about in that car," she said.[15] Unlike her opponents, Smith did not attend the state Republican convention in March but had it announced that she was in Washington voting for a tax cut, the Marshall Plan, and a bill to restore the Veterans Administration. Smith's battle to secure regular as well as reserve status for women in the armed services overlapped the campaign and was extensively reported in the Maine papers. On the day she won that fight, the *Sentinel* headline read, "Today Was Margaret Chase Smith Day in the House." "Don't trade a record for a promise" became Smith's campaign slogan, and Lewis had posters with "The Can-Do Candidate with the Can-Did Record" printed.[16]

In Lewis's hands frugality also became a Smith trademark. The public learned that her mother's home was her only campaign headquarters and her two secretaries her only paid workers. Altogether in the primary Smith spent only $3,800 to Hildreth's $7,500 and Sewall's $16,600. Her largest contribution was $1,000 and came from the New York cosmetic firm Elizabeth Arden, but Lewis emphasized the "little woman in the Worumbo Mills who contributed $2.00 even though she had been threatened with the loss of her job for doing so."[17] Smith chastised one of her well-advertised unpaid campaign workers for purchasing unbudgeted matches and pencils and refused to reimburse her. Unpublicized was the fact that when Roland Patten left her office staff on 1 July 1948, during the campaign, another of Smith's frugal practices was to write the House disbursing office: "Please change to Carrie Chase, listing her at the same rate. Checks should be mailed to Mrs. Chase at Skowhegan, Maine."[18]

Female but not feminist was another Smith characteristic Lewis publicized. Noting that 64 percent of the registered voters in Maine were women and that 40 percent of those who signed Smith's nomination papers were also female, Lewis emphasized every sexist remark made against Smith in the context that all women were the objects of the slur. Most frequently quoted was the comment attributed only to "a Maine politician," who may have been Lewis, that "the little lady has simply stepped out of her class."[19]

"The Senate is big-league stuff," the criticism continued. "Nobody in Maine can get into the Senate without a political machine, fat campaign funds, the right business connections, and the help of the powers that be. Margaret hasn't got any of these things."[20] Mrs. Sewall's slam, "Why take a woman to Washington when you can get a man," also received considerable attention.[21] When asked if she would be excluded from representing Maine when men gathered in all-male bars and clubs to make laws, Smith replied that "people don't want their laws made that way. They want them made out in the open."[22] Another whisper reported by the press was that the "Senate was no place for a woman,"[23] and Smith's response was that the slur "was a direct challenge to every woman in Maine."[24]

In a much publicized speech, titled "What Is Woman's Place?" Smith answered, "Everywhere," and elaborated, "(1) in the home as wives and mothers; (2) in organized civic, business and professional groups; (3) in industry and business; and (4) in Government and politics." "Citizenship," Smith said, "is without sex," and "the inescapable fact is that women hold the control of public offices with their majority voting power."[25] Since Smith was Maine's first female candidate for the Senate, whether women would vote as a bloc for her became a public issue. Opposition papers like the *Bangor Daily News* editorialized against voting "for a woman candidate just because she is a woman."[26] Opponents did not comment on the propriety of voting for a male candidate just because he was a male. Smith insisted that she was "not asking for support as a woman but as a qualified candidate."[27]

The state's senior senator, Owen Brewster, who favored a male colleague, referred to Smith as "the girl,"[28] and a columnist described her as "a modest, grey-haired little person."[29] A source Lewis characterized as "a prominent Maine Republican" in a release he prepared for the press called Smith a "member of the weaker sex" who could not withstand the rigors of the office.[30] In response, campaigning at the Clark Shoe Company, Smith turned up the bottom of her shoe to show photographers the hole she had worn in the sole with her "strenuous campaigning."[31] The company gave her two pairs of shoes, both with the high heels she favored to boost her height. An article surveying Skowhegan opinion on Smith elicited comments that she was "just plain sensible," "never one for gallivanting around," "did a lot of the things Mr. Smith got credit for," and that the "worse thing anyone can say about her is that she is a woman."[32]

The Margaret Chase Smith whom Lewis projected was undeniably feminine and invariably referred to as a "lady" in campaign ads. A typical poster read, "One of Seven Lady Members of the U.S. House of Representatives Aspires to Be the Only Lady Member of the U.S. Senate."[33] Earlier she had on occasion worn corsages, and more recently she had received as a gift a tiny glass tube with a pin attached in which she could put water and keep a flower fresh all day. During the campaign, at Lewis's insistence, she began wearing a fresh rose in the tube every day and, once the press acknowledged the rose as her trademark, for the rest of her life. Smith's campaign demeanor continued to be quiet, lady-like, and unthreatening to males and females alike, but her campaign photographs showed more flair: a toss of her head, lovely smile, and uplifted chin. Her hair was completely gray, forever untouched with artificial color, and her invariable suits brightly colored but demure. Never forward, overbearing, or argumentative, Smith ingratiated herself as a political anomaly, and people just plain liked her. She was one of them, a typical Mainer on the hustings.

In one respect Smith was atypical as a New Englander and as a Republican. Lewis ran her as a liberal. Separating herself from the "false liberals" of the New Deal who "misused public power and public funds for the selfish ends of an intolerant majority," Smith redefined liberalism. A "true liberal" was "practical" and did not advocate "huge expenditures for every conceivable social purpose." In a speech almost certainly written by Lewis, Smith maintained that the purpose of government was "to insist upon self-reliance" and "local self-government." She saw "governmental aid as a supplement to responsible individualism," not a substitute.[34]

As a liberal Republican, Smith made national security her primary issue, "because without national security there is no hope." Stressing her leadership role as a member of the Armed Services Committee, Smith affirmed her support for continuing universal military training, thus maintaining the nation on peacetime war status for the first time in American history. Second only to national defense, Smith championed veterans as Congress's "highest priority" and unabashedly maintained that reserve organizations rated her their "best friend and champion."[35] On the controversial domestic issues of the 1948 campaign, Smith called the housing shortage the nation's "number one national disgrace."[36] She opposed a return to wartime price controls, favored federal aid to education, and opposed socialized medicine. Predictably if inconsistently, Smith called for a substantial reduction in taxes and an increase in social security benefits.

Considering each other the principal opponent while dividing the traditional Republican base, Hildreth and Sewall at first ignored Smith as they did Beverage. By April, however, Owen Brewster, whom columnist Drew Pearson referred to as Hildreth's "mouthpiece," told "the boys" that "they best concern themselves" with Smith.[37] At Brewster's suggestion, the candidates attacked Smith as a maverick Republican who was not respected by the party leadership in Congress and therefore would not be an effective representative for Maine. Party regular Burton M. Cross initiated the attack by telling the press that he wished Smith "was more of a Republican."[38] Another critic referred to Smith as a "traitor to the party."[39] A widely circulated "Dear State of Maine" letter from Dorothy Sabin Winslow asserted that, although eligible, Smith had been kept off the Appropriations and Agriculture committees by the Republican leadership "as punishment."[40]

Smith's rebuttal brought national attention to the campaign, because she secured endorsements from congressional leaders. Speaker Joseph Martin praised Smith's loyalty to the Republican party, and majority whip Leslie Arends said that "our party benefitted by your ready response to every call for action." Armed Services chairman Ham Andrews sent his "personal compliments," and California congressman Leroy Johnsons said that "no one in the House has greater good will among the members."[41] After interviewing dozens of legislators in Washington, *Maine Sunday Telegram* reporter Edward D. Talberth wrote that Congress was "pulling to a man" for Smith to win.[42]

By the end of April the campaign had turned ugly. Cora E. Edgerly of Portland put out an extensive mailing titled "Why I Shall Not Vote for Margaret Chase Smith." Edgerly's fourteen reasons varied from the scurrilous to the malevolent, which was not to say to the inaccurate. She considered Smith "lacking in education," a Catholic, and out to get Joe Martin as a husband. Edgerly "didn't like the way Smith got her first husband" and believed that Smith "slipped into Congress on the coat-tails of her dead husband."[43]

In addition to Edgerly, whom Lewis deemed "the primary smear tactician," Smith supporter Mildred Childs reported a "whispering campaign" that the congresswoman "was really French" and had changed her name to Chase from "Chasse." Another rumor held that Smith was supporting her late husband's illegitimate child, Rita Quinn. The person spreading the rumors, Childs maintained, was a paid employee of Governor Hildreth, and his "express purpose was to travel around and spread ugly rumors" about Smith.[44]

Of more concern to Smith and Lewis was an anonymously printed and distributed circular purporting to be a factual analysis of her voting record in the Seventy-sixth through the Eightieth congresses. With impressive detail and sober tone the report, titled "Voting Record of Representative Margaret Chase Smith," implied that she was a traitor to the Republican party, pro-Communist, a CIO operative, and a sympathizer of the radical New York congressman Vito Marcantonio.[45] Specifically, the report alleged that on 242 measures, Smith's votes had been in opposition to the majority of the party 29.3 percent of the time. She had voted with Marcantonio on 44.2 percent of those votes, had supported the CIO eleven out of twelve votes, and had consistently voted against the House Un-American Activities Committee.

Smith and Lewis were not successful at ascertaining the origins of the attack, but they believed that Governor Hildreth was responsible. The *Chicago Daily Tribune* alleged as much,[46] and the *Portland Sunday Telegram* reported that the analysis was "presumably sent out from Hildreth's campaign headquarters."[47] Hildreth neither disavowed the charge nor deplored the anonymous attack. Later Smith said that Brewster and "the woman who organized the Republican women of the country . . . got that smear sheet out."[48]

Smith was frightened because this was the first serious attack of her political career, but Lewis calmly went to the *Congressional Record* to determine the accuracy of the accusations. What he found was not so much inaccuracy as different explanations for Smith's votes. When Lewis reported to Smith that he could prepare an effective refutation, she was somewhat mollified but wanted his rebuttal distributed immediately. "That's not the way to handle this," Lewis told her. "If you answer it now, the smear artists will simply jump to some other form." Instead, Lewis wanted silence from Smith to assure her attackers that she had no response. He wanted to gamble that they would "saturate the state" with these few charges; then right before the vote she could effectively answer. "But that's very risky," she protested. Lewis agreed but prevailed, as he increasingly did, and added to Smith's consternation by marking with colored pins on a large wall map of Maine where each "smear sheet" was reported. Soon Lewis had the map ablaze with color and Smith near prostrate with anxiety.[49]

On 21 May, one month to the day before the primary election, Lewis allowed Smith to respond. With martial thoroughness he chose a friendly audience, the Somerset County Women's Republican Club, which was the only women's group in the state to endorse her besides the Federation of Business and Professional Women. Then he wrote seven typed, single-spaced pages for her to read with some thirty-seven references to smear: "smear tactic," "smear charges," "smear sheet," "smear writer."[50] She worried about the length of the speech, but Lewis again convinced her that thoroughness was essential, and "after all," he insisted, "a home county audience will love to hear their daughter defend herself and rip into the smearers."[51]

The rebuttal was impressive. Although she had cast over 1,500 record votes in her congressional career, her anonymous attacker had selected only 242 for consideration. Since the "smearer's" total votes considered was "inaccurate and misrepresentative," Smith used the 1,500 figure as her standard of comparison for the votes her attacker criticized. Comparing his "71 handpicked votes" against the Republican party to the 1,500 total, Smith concluded with accuracy as debatable as her opponent's that she had failed to vote Republican only 4.7 percent of the time. Using the same math, her votes with Marcantonio were 7 percent, but dropping her own standard of comparison and using only the 12 votes taken in reference to the CIO in 1947, Smith concluded that she had voted against the CIO ten times. In the same manner, she had voted to support the House Un-American Activities Committee in sixteen votes of twenty.[52]

For good measure, Smith concluded that her unknown accuser must have had "communist training" from his evident adeptness at "fabricating lies and spinning half-truths." With righteous fervor she added that the "smear charges" were "ridiculous and . . . a pack of lies." As Lewis had predicted, her audience loved the sight of their feisty, gray-haired Margaret taking on the unnamed, low-down Goliath whom they generalized as all of her political adversaries combined.[53]

The next day Lewis mailed "Margaret Smith's Answer" kits to every city, town, and plantation that had a Smith-for-Senate committee. Affirming in her cover letter that she could not match "the machines and money" of her opponents, she enclosed postcards, costing just a penny and already addressed by Lewis's parents to supporters, to be used for meeting notices, three-by-five sheets on which to get volunteers to pledge work, a few printed pamphlets summarizing her voting record, and, most important, her "answer to the Smear Smith Sheets . . . so you will be prepared to refute the smears." Smith signed her letter, "Gratefully."[54]

Guy Gannett's newspapers, supportive of Smith since 1940, printed the spin Lewis put on Smith's "hard-hitting answer." "Small fires of organized support for Smith," the Portland Sunday Telegram wrote, "started lighting up all over the state from Fort Kent in the north on the Canadian border to Kittery in the south on the New Hampshire border."[55]

During the last weeks of the campaign, Smith's rhetoric became increasingly bold and nearly strident. She challenged President Truman's denigration of the "do-nothing" Republican Eightieth Congress by enumerating enacted legislation: unification of the armed services, aid to Greece and Turkey, the Taft-Hartley Act, the presidential succession bill, the Marshall Plan, the federal housing program, and revival of the draft. Reversing the president's own "give-'em-hell" tactics, Smith castigated Truman for being "soft" on communism. She saw history repeating itself with Soviet postwar "aggression" replicating Nazi conquest and believed the United States should wage "economic warfare" against the Soviet Union. In keeping with the growing Cold War hysteria, Smith accepted that the Soviet Union was "threatening to take over the world through Communism" and considered it essential for the United States "to weaken" the Soviet "war machine."[56] Smith flatly advocated use of the "Atomic Bomb if necessary," as the events leading to the Berlin blockade in June 1948 became the fearful backdrop of the campaign.[57]

Possibly out of desperation, Smith sailed close to the winds of feminism as she began associating herself with the press's darling, Clare Boothe Luce. In prepared statements answering anticipated questions, Smith repeatedly pointed out that Luce had voted the same way Smith had. More telling, Smith invited her good friend, Representative Frances Bolton of Ohio, to campaign for her in Maine. Liz Carpenter, just starting out in Washington as a young reporter, remembered the Smith-Bolton cooperation as the first evidence of "political sisterhood" she had seen.[58] Independently wealthy, Bolton contributed financially to Smith's campaign, traveled with her during the primary, and spoke for her on the radio. "Quiet, gracious, always charming" was Bolton's description of Smith. "Liked by everyone who knows her," Bolton continued, but "what is far more important . . . she is respected as few members of Congress are respected." Bolton maintained that Smith's influence in Washington was "very real." "Don't underestimate this," she cautioned, "because it is an asset no newcomer can possibly bring to this Senate job." Bolton's speech was one Lewis would have been proud to have written but probably did not, because Bolton characterized Smith's work as feminist, "successful pioneering for women in a new field."[59]

Merton Henry, an undergraduate at Bowdoin, worked as a volunteer gofer for Smith in the Portland campaign headquarters under Cumberland County chairman Raymond Oakes and office manager Ruth Morrison. A "shoestring operation," as Henry characterized it, the office did not have the funds or people on Election Day to transport the large number of Smith supporters who called for rides to the polls. They did, however, have the telephone numbers Hildreth's headquarters had run in an ad telling people to call if they needed transportation. The numbers were for taxi service, and Henry said, "So when we had surplus people to be hauled to the polls, we just simply called those numbers and the taxis picked them up and hauled Smith supporters to the polls, and Governor Hildreth paid the bill." Henry added, Hildreth "never knew it and we never dared tell Senator Smith until about thirty or forty years later."[60]

Smith and Lewis waited out the vote at Carrie Chase's house. Although election results were broadcast on television for the first time, Smith listened to the tally on Carrie's radio because she did not own a television set and was vaguely uncomfortable with the new medium. When the earliest returns showed Smith ahead, visitors started coming by. Eventually over two hundred people crowded into the little house on North Avenue to be greeted by Carrie and to observe that Smith remained calm as her lead held. Carrie's telephone, number 660, and the second one Lewis had installed rang constantly with well-wishers, reporters wanting interviews, and supporters urging Smith to predict an early victory. "It's amazing" was her only comment as her lead increased, but she gave a happy sigh of relief when she heard that Hildreth had called to concede. "Sorry it had to be you, Horace," Smith said graciously, "and please give my regards to Katherine." Smith stayed up all night as she had once done with Clyde on election nights, but this time she was to observers very much with Bill Lewis. "I'm happy. I'm honored. I'm humble," Smith told the press while Lyndon Huff snapped her photograph sitting at a telegram-covered desk, talking on the telephone, and smiling triumphantly.[61]

The Associated Press carried the photo over the headline, "Thumping Victory," while other newspapers used verbs like "trounces," "drubs," and "sweeps."[62] When the votes were counted, Smith's 63,786 total was more than Hildreth's 30,949, Sewall's 21,768, and Beverage's 6,399 combined. She carried sixteen of Maine's twenty-one cities including Hildreth's stronghold, Augusta, and his birthplace, Gardiner, and fourteen of the state's sixteen counties.

In a masterful political stroke, Smith flew to Philadelphia for the Republican National Convention. There she was feted by the Maine delegation at a reception for over 250 in Owen Brewster's suite, although the senior senator had vigorously opposed her candidacy. Columnist Lowell Mellett reported that when a reporter told Brewster at the convention that Smith had won, the senator had startled him with his profane response. Brewster's only printable comment had been that he "did not know what the people of Maine were thinking, because Smith had been a New Dealer since she arrived in Washington." The Republican leadership had given her "the silent treatment" as a result.[63] The convention's powerful presiding officer, Speaker Joe Martin introduced Smith to the convention and referred to her as an "exceptional talent" who would reach the Senate "under her own power." Smiling radiantly, Smith spoke briefly from notes Lewis had typed for her on blue cards about her victory's being an augury for a Republican victory in November if the party became one of the rank and file. Certainly, Smith maintained, her success would mean thousands of female votes for the party in the general election and a "political home for women in the future."[64] For a heady moment Smith stood in the national spotlight and felt right at home.

Republicans immediately added a new item to their political wardrobe, skirttails, and firmly latched on to Smith's. The party publicized that 113 women were delegates at the convention, a 12 percent increase over 1944, and that 240 women were alternates. Further, the platform committee had equal male-female representation, Mrs. Dudley Hay was the convention's first female secretary, Mary Donlon was the first woman to chair a convention subcommittee, and Francis Burke Redick was the first of her gender to nominate a presidential candidate. In this frenzy of feminist expediency, almost all of the party's candidates had women second their nominations, including Governor Earl Warren of California, who had the actress Irene Dunne as his supporter. Thomas Dewey, again the party's nominee, promised to name a woman to his cabinet if he were victorious.

Adrian H. Scolten, a physician, was Smith's Democratic opponent, and in the campaign he was both the forgotten man and the invisible candidate. Most newspapers failed to publish his photograph, much less his views. Vaguely, he opposed the Taft-Hartley Act, which outlawed unfair labor union practices and which Smith had supported. Simultaneously other papers insisted that the AFL-CIO supported Smith, although she saw this as a slur and heatedly denied it. The old rumors that Smith broke up Clyde's marriage continued, and to them was added a photograph from the European tour of Smith sitting at a table covered with beer bottles in Trieste with American sailors. Democrats distributed the photo in dry areas of the state with the caption, "Look at her boozing with a gang of sailors."[65]

Aside from the Republican tour, Smith attended small, informal gatherings in parlors, at libraries, and increasingly at schools where she felt comfortable, although she received criticism for campaigning among those too young to vote. Smith believed the schoolchildren would not only remember her when they grew up but that they would go home and tell their parents about her visit. She felt vindicated when a parent reported his son's saying that Smith spent her time in Washington on the floor of the House and asked why she did not have a chair on which to sit.

Bill Lewis was less evident during the general campaign, and Smith went so far as to deny that she had a campaign manager; in another instance she claimed that she was her own campaign manager. Lewis managed one political coup at the end of the campaign, an article on Smith in the *Saturday Evening Post,* titled "The Senator from the Five and Ten Cent Store."[66] Indicative of the Republican confidence that would produce in November the *Chicago Daily Tribune* headline, "Dewey Defeats Truman," the *Post* article assumed Smith's victory. The story also put into national circulation Lewis's favorite Margaret Chase Smith anecdotes, all with a kernel of truth surrounded by a confectionery mass. As the title implied that she was leaving her job at Green Brothers Five-and-Ten-Cent Store for the U.S. Senate, so the article established her as an excellent student, a responsible worker in her father's barber shop giving customers shaves and haircuts, and a model homemaker with her recipe for blueberry muffins as proof.[67] Lewis papered the state with the magazine, and Mainers realized that Smith was a national celebrity.

Thomas Dewey called Smith at her mother's house the night before the election on 13 September to wish her well, and the next morning well-wishers started coming by. Again, Smith sat by the radio in Carrie's parlor and listened to returns that were even more gratifying than before. She received 159,182 votes to Scolten's 64,074, and her total, 71.4 percent, was the largest vote that any candidate in Maine history had received. Although Scolten said that "for the Republicans to have won Maine again is like the Dutch taking Holland . . . they have always had it," the Republican party publicized, "As Maine goes, so goes the nation."[68]

To exploit the symbolism, Thomas Dewey asked Smith to make six campaign speeches for him in October, and the party's "Wonder Girl," as the press referred to her, agreed.[69] Before she departed for appearances in New Mexico, Colorado, New Jersey, and Pennsylvania, the rumor of a cabinet appointment made the rounds in Maine. As Drew Pearson later reported it, state Republican leaders promised Smith a position in Dewey's cabinet if he were elected. Their interest was in her resignation and Hildreth's taking her place by appointment, but Smith said that although she was flattered, the people of Maine had elected her to the Senate, not the cabinet. Smith became uneasy in her campaigning for Dewey because of the emphasis on the "as Maine goes . . ." expectation and somewhat perversely, if prophetically, refuted the expectation. "After sober reflection and careful analysis of the Maine vote," she said in a Boston speech, "I feel we must guard against misrepresentation."[70] The presumed wisdom of the Maine vote as a political barometer began in 1880 when Mainers voted for James Garfield over Winfield Scott Hancock and the nation followed Maine's lead. In every presidential election that followed, the precedent held. In 1936, however, Mainers voted for Alf Landon, while the rest of the nation, excluding Vermont, voted for Franklin Roosevelt. The replacement wisdom suggested was that as Maine goes, so goes Vermont. In 1940 and 1944 national voters elected the Democratic nominee despite Maine's remaining faithful to the Republicans. Instead of relying on dubious precedent, Smith advised Republicans "to roll up our sleeves and start ringing doorbells."[71]

After the infamous defeat of the national Republican ticket in November, Smith's position was stronger than ever. She tried to persuade retiring Senator Wallace White to resign early in order to allow her to be sworn in and gain the seniority with which she had started in the House. Unsuccessful in that effort, Smith nonetheless triumphed over other elected officials in publicity. As America's heroine, she appeared on the cover of *U.S. News and World Report,* had articles about herself in *Redbook* and *Reader's Digest,* spoke at the Altrusa National Convention, the National Federation of Women's Republican Clubs, and the New York League of Business and Professional Women's Clubs. "Because I am an oddity," Smith said with a smile before she appeared on "Meet the Press," "I am deluged with radio, TV, and speaking requests."[72] As much as she enjoyed the limelight, especially the dinner the Women's National Press Club held in her honor, she feared that she was the "window dressing" of the Republican party.[73] Liz Carpenter, president of the press club, wanting "to show off a woman politician," arranged with Lewis for Smith to speak. With about five hundred newspaper editors from around the country present, Carpenter was disappointed with Smith's coming with her "speech cards," written by Lewis, which she "followed to the letter" and "just bored the editors to death."[74] Smith's fame spread to Hollywood with the 1949 movie *Adam's Rib,* starring Katharine Hepburn and Spencer Tracy, showing a photograph of the new senator on an office wall. More optimistically, May Craig who had long promoted Smith believed that she was "swamped with fame."[75] Craig, probably at Lewis's suggestion, also brought the trademark rose on Smith's lapel to the attention of the national press.

On 3 January 1949, Smith stepped into the Senate chamber for the first time, gingerly took the arm of her old adversary, Owen Brewster, and walked down the aisle to swear, if not to love, honor, and obey, to support and defend the Constitution. To her surprise a gallery filled with women applauded her historic entrance, and, in violation of Senate rules, her colleagues joined in, acknowledging Smith's uniqueness among the seventeen other new senators. Those who went unapplauded included Lyndon Baines

Johnson and Hubert H. Humphrey. "I'm nervous, I'm walking on air, and I'm all choked up," Smith jubilantly told a Business and Professional Women's audience of five hundred, her mother among them, a few hours later at a luncheon in her honor. "I'm naive enough to admit to you that I can hardly realize I am not in a wonderful dream," she said. In her most feminist address Smith went on to pledge herself "women's Senator at Large," "the voice of America's women on the floor of the Senate." "I was elected in spite of being a woman," she said with more candor than in Maine, "and that in itself was a victory for all women for it smashed the unwritten tradition that the Senate is no place for a woman."[76] In her first statement as a senator, Smith said that on behalf of women she would fight for domestic security, affordable homes, reasonable prices for food, better schools, and peace. In illustration Smith used her national podium to call on an undoubtedly startled Queen Juliana of Holland to stop the fighting in her rebelling colony, Indonesia. Smith maintained that the "women of the world are on trial" and that Juliana had an "unprecedented opportunity for a woman" to advance peace. If Juliana did not act, Smith threatened to cut off Marshall Plan aid to Holland.[77] For her efforts Smith received, if not peace in Indonesia, a bouquet of the first 225 congratulatory telegrams assembled by the Business and Professional Women, then a bouquet of headlines—"Voice of US Women," "Champion Women," "Serve Women," "Represent US Women"—and finally dozens of bouquets of flowers at her new office.[78]

The next day began with Brewster's asserting his leadership over the Maine congressional delegation. Charles P. Nelson of Augusta had won Smith's seat in the House and was present with Robert Hale of Portland and Frank Fellows of Bangor. Not so much to heal their differences as to step into Smith's spotlight, Brewster successfully championed Smith for an unheard-of place for a freshman senator on the Republican Policy Committee. The powerful Policy Committee had only eleven members, and for Smith to receive appointment was for her to take on the appearance, if not the reality, of a leadership role for the party. As unprecedented as her appointment, the committee issued a press statement that to have Smith as a member was evidence that the Republican party stood for "full and equal participation by women in political affairs."[79] Smith immediately paid her dues by voting under Brewster's lead for Robert A. Taft of Ohio as committee chairman over liberal Henry Cabot Lodge of Massachusetts.

Lest the leadership think they had tamed Smith, she asserted her independence from the party the next week in a speech before the Women's National Press Corps. In explaining why the Republicans had lost five consecutive presidential elections, Smith criticized the leadership's claim that the government should not intervene in the economic affairs of the people. The "little people" want protection, she maintained, and the Republicans "failed to protect the little guy."[80] In case the party failure headlines did not register with the leadership, a few weeks later on a Lincoln Day program

Smith said that the GOP was "dead as a pigeon" unless it stopped trying to lead the nation back to the nineteenth century. Compounding her treason, Smith repeated Truman's 1948 charge that the Republicans had become a "party of special interests."[81] Whether connected or not, the leadership appointed Smith to the purgatory of the District of Columbia Committee, probably making her the only senator ever to serve on Policy and District of Columbia simultaneously. With her usual forthrightness, she had requested Armed Services and Appropriations and believed her unique position in the Senate might obtain them for her. Only senators from nearby states desired appointment on the District of Columbia Committee, because the work was both hard and thankless from voters in distant states. The district citizens had no vote and no city government; the president appointed three commissioners to govern them, and the congressional committees handled their fiscal affairs. Democrats demonstrated that they could also play the female card by appointing Smith chairman of a District of Columbia subcommittee on health and public welfare. The appointment made her the only Republican to chair a subcommittee or committee.

A political Midas, Smith turned everything she touched in 1949 into headlines. Overnight the moribund D.C. Committee became controversial, and Smith's subcommittee was the hot spot. J. Howard McGrath of Rhode Island, the chairman of the full committee, introduced legislation to allow the D.C. pound to turn over unclaimed animals to "educational, scientific and governmental institutions . . . for scientific purposes." He "specially appointed" Smith's subcommittee to handle the proposal, whether to defuse the issue with a "lady chairman" or to have a Republican superstar in the hot seat, he did not specify.[82] The two days of hearings Smith conducted attracted national attention as more than two hundred angry opponents of the legislation jammed the chamber. The antivivisectionists, mostly women, outnumbered proponents of the legislation four to one. Shrilly, they presented bloody evidence of the thousands of dogs and cats killed at the pound each year, and passionately they described the dying agonies of animals experimented on by scientists. When proponents introduced evidence of vivisection's leading to procedures to save blue babies, opponents interrupted them with jeers, prayers, scornful laughter, and tears. Not to be upstaged, supporters brought in emotional mothers of blue babies to testify and introduced three surviving babies: a five-year-old boy, a six-year-old girl, and a fifteen-year-old boy. With the chamber fused to explode emotionally, Smith had difficulty maintaining order and threatened to hold closed sessions, but throughout she remained calm and detached. But the bill Smith directed from subcommittee to the floor failed to pass because of its "ambiguity."[83]

Smith's other committee was Expenditures, which controlled spending by executive departments and had both Joseph McCarthy of Wisconsin and Karl Mundt of South Dakota as freshman members with Smith. The three also were members of the Expenditures Investigations Subcommittee, which had brought national prominence to Harry Truman during the war.

Smith's golden touch involved the subcommittee in over three weeks of highly publicized hearings on "5 percenters," middlemen who took 5 percent of the contract fee they secured from the government for a firm. This was the first federal bribery investigation since Albert B. Fall and Teapot Dome, and congressional investigators targeted Major General Harry H. Vaughan, a friend of Truman for over thirty years and now a White House military aide. Senator Clyde Hoey of North Carolina, fearing embarrassment for the president, wanted to hold closed sessions, but Smith joined McCarthy and Mundt in insisting on hearings open to the public. Smith said that the subcommittee's role was "semi-judicial" and supported executive sessions "only to avoid smearing innocent people."[84] This public use of the fateful word *smear,* which had become as much her trademark as the rose on her lapel, was her first since the 1948 campaign.

Like many other committee investigations, these became part sideshow with Hoey as tintype southern politician—snow-white hair and pink flower on Palm Beach suit—and Vaughan—bluff backslapper explaining seven deep freezers as gifts, one to Mrs. Truman. Inadvertently, Smith became part of the fun when newspapers released a photograph of the office wall of James V. Hunt, one of the influence peddlers under investigation. Covered with autographed photos, the wall displayed Smith, McCarthy, and Mundt along with Truman and other Democrats. Foolishly, Smith tried to explain her photo, which had been routinely mailed and involved no association with Hunt. In gallant putdown, Hoey responded that "any man would be glad to have the picture of the lady from Maine. I am going to ask her for one myself."[85] The subcommittee's report, characterized by the *Washington Post* as surprisingly thoughtful and illuminating, accepted the necessity of middlemen. Recognizing that corruption was complex and not likely to be eradicated, the senators contented themselves with rebuking Vaughan.

Smith lived alone in a room at the Statler Hotel for which she paid five dollars a day. The price included maid service and the most sought-after luxury of all in postwar America, air conditioning. Smith got up early in the morning, dressed in a plain suit, and arrived at her office before her staff. Formerly the office of J. William Fulbright of Arkansas, Suite 329 had little besides fresh paint and a fine view of the Capitol to commend it. On the door Smith hung a welcome sign with the surf breaking on the rocky coast of Maine and a lighthouse in the distance. Inside there were three small offices and the only television set in the whole building. Blanche Bernier continued at the front desk as receptionist but now had Bill Lewis in the same room as administrative assistant. Since the reception area was small and public, Lewis attempted to gain privacy by placing his desk behind a tall bookcase by the window. Reporters and constituents were still only a foot away, so Lewis obtained a telephone amplifier that allowed him to speak quietly and still be heard, hopefully only by the person to whom he was speaking. Lewis wrote his parents that he had also installed a "radio-phonograph wire recorder so that the office is almost like an apartment. We can see the television at night and I have the soft, deep tone radio on low during the day. It gives the reception room a very quiet, and restful atmosphere. Even Margaret approves. This together with the refrigerator and my bar just about completes the home atmosphere." Lena Haskell and Helen Wing had made the move from the House to the Senate with Smith and worked in the second room as secretaries with three assistants. Their space was also limited, and the only solution was to place their desks against each other and joke that the only people in the federal system who had less space than congressmen were prisoners. The third room was Smith's office, her morning sanctuary, "since it's quiet then and I have to think," she said.[86]

Smith had an office allowance of $23,880 for salaries. Bill Lewis received the bulk of the allowance with his $10,000 salary as administrative assistant, a position recently created in the 1946 Legislative Reorganization Act. The salary constituted a severe financial loss for Lewis, but he recognized the influence he had on Smith and through her on the Senate. Familiar with the workings of Congress, Lewis understood the potential power of his position, a position that might allow a dominant congressional aide to become an "assistant senator" and maybe a few to be senator in all but title. As the administrative aide for a female senator, Lewis's position was already enhanced, because in the congressional male bastion, many of Smith's peers were more at ease in dealing with him on business while being charming toward her. He had bypassed the usual dreary route of first working as an intern, then being promoted to legislative assistant and finally to committee staffer. Those menial jobs involved endless typing, duplicating, stapling, and filing in offices that were a crowded maze of desks, chairs, bookcases, and filing cabinets. Congressional offices were sweatshops with similar wages but worse hours. A contemplative man, Lewis knew what he was doing in signing on with Smith, but, like her, he had no vision or goal to pursue through his office for the good of the people, the nation, and certainly not for the state. As with many others on Capitol Hill, power and influence were ends themselves.

Overwhelmed herself by her new position, Smith accepted her dependence on Lewis and worried that she would not be able to retain him. She announced that his title was executive assistant and gave him complete control of the office, control he used to build a wall around Smith so that he alone determined access to her. As reporter Don Larrabee saw it, "People didn't get to see Margaret Chase Smith or talk to her or gain entrée to the office to get much information unless Bill wanted them to." From longtime observation, Larrabee believed that a "dependency" developed between Lewis and Smith. She "needed him," but he "needed her too." Larrabee became one of the first to refer to Lewis as "the power behind the throne," "a Pygmalion," and "Machiavellian" in his considered acquisition and use of power.[87] Liz Carpenter was not far behind Larrabee and believed that "if you wanted Margaret Smith to vote a certain way, you had to go to Bill Lewis first. Clear it with Bill."[88]

Commonly Smith worked in her office each morning until her 10:00 A.M. committee meeting. In addition to preparing for her committees and meeting visitors, she had been asked to write a five-day-a-week column for distribution to thirty-five newspapers in nineteen states. The only columnist in the Senate, Smith received envy for her national forum, gossip that Lewis was her ghost writer, and speculation that the column would lead to a vice presidential nomination in 1952. The speculation about a nomination led CBS reporter Bob Trout to ask Smith what she would do if she woke up one morning and found herself in the White House. "I'd go right to Mrs. Truman," she responded, "apologize and go home."[89] Never noted for humor, Smith saw many repetitions of this story in print but admitted in 1988 that Bob Trout had given her the response before asking her the question on the air. She continued her habit of regular attendance at committee meetings and of keeping a low profile on the floor.

The seat she drew in the Senate chamber was number one to the far left of the presiding officer, on the front row side aisle, and formerly the desk of the father of the Tennessee Valley Authority, George Norris of Nebraska. Colleagues scorned the distant location, but Smith saw immediate benefit in being able to visit with senators as they walked in and out. Wayne Morse of Oregon had the adjoining seat and found it frequently occupied by Smith's old friend, Vice President Alben Barkley. Morse joked that he was going to charge rent on his popular seat, and once Barkley handed over twenty-five cents. House members did not have assigned desks, and Smith took particular pleasure in the fact that her Senate desk had been built in 1819, the year Maine had applied for statehood. Indicative of its age, Smith's mahogany desk had an inkwell, a penholder, and a glass shaker of blotting sand. At the vice president's rostrum there were two old snuffboxes, one on each side, and a time-honored tradition required a senior senator to take each newcomer, even if female, up for a dip. Senator Ralph Flanders of Vermont escorted Smith. Senatorial dress was gradually changing from the custom of cutaway coats and shaped trousers to conservative business suits. Smith gave up the hat she had worn in the House chamber but continued to wear gloves from her office to the Senate chamber.

In the Eighty-first Congress, tradition required members to address each other as "the Senator from" and then add the state to indicate that members represent states and the House represents people. If a senator failed to use the correct terminology, a reprimand came from the chair. Smith corrected colleagues who called her Mrs. Smith off the floor by replying, "Senator Smith." During the first quorum call, the clerk hesitated over two Smiths being present, and Margaret Chase Smith braced for a Mrs. Smith, but the clerk called, "Smith of Maine" for Margaret and "Smith of New Jersey" for Alexander Smith.[90]

Although Smith reliably attended Senate sessions, with Lewis commonly escorting her from the office and standing in the rear, she rarely spoke. She boasted that she was the most silent member of the Senate to "disprove the slander that women talk incessantly."[91] Her first floor debate was in April 1949 when she favored extension of disability coverage given to regular armed forces personnel to reserves and National Guardsmen killed or injured in training. The legislation passed unanimously, which indicated that Smith's effort was gratuitous. Perceiving her support differently, the Air Reserve Association in October commended Smith as the "foremost champion in Congress of the Reservists."[92]

Smith also championed her other constituency, women, by sponsoring with Guy Gillett of Iowa the seemingly annual equal rights amendment effort. "Women are people," she argued in a second floor speech, and "it is high time we stop thinking of them as second class citizens." As she had in the House, Smith asked women to give up "feminine privileges" for equal rights.[93] The opposition was formidable and included Eleanor Roosevelt, Frances Perkins, the National League of Women Voters, the YWCA, the American Association of University Women, and the AFL-CIO. During three days of debate as emotional as always on this subject, Estes Kefauver of Tennessee claimed that the ERA would "eliminate rape as a crime" and lead to joint bathroom facilities.[94] Carl Hayden of Arizona attached an amendment retaining "all rights, benefits or exemptions" already conferred on women.[95] Smith failed in the few minutes left for debate to explain to supporters that ERA proponents did not want the amendment. Senators happily seized the opportunity to vote for special privileges and equal rights and sent both on to the House, where House Judiciary chairman Emanuel Celler of New York never reported the bill to the floor.

ERA opponents having kept the world safe for separate rest rooms, Smith set out to secure one, still referred to as retiring rooms in the Capitol, and garnered more headlines than with her legislative battles. The only women's rest room near the Senate chamber was the crowded public one by the visitors' gallery. At first Smith waited until she could return to the Senate Office Building, but during long sessions and on roll calls she did not have time to make the trip back and forth. The public facility had lines outside and involved undignified contact with female reporters and visitors. Finally Smith wrote Carl Hayden, who chaired the Committee on Rules and Administration, to request a private "women's lavatory" in the Capitol.[96] Hayden refused and cited as precedent Hattie Carraway who had not secured a facility of her own until she earned the privilege as a committee chair. Smith did not press the issue but leaked the story to Drew Pearson and through him to the national press. A public discussion followed in reference to Smith's being discriminated against in areas other than rest rooms. The Senate steam room, massage tables, and swimming pool were off-limits because the men used these facilities while naked, and the free Senate barber shop did not cut women's hair. A few months later Hayden informed Smith that he had located a "ladies' room" for her.[97]

Committee chairman or not, Smith's predecessor, Hattie Carraway, had not been taken seriously as a senator. Considered a pawn of Arkansas political bosses, Carraway became an in-house joke because she spent her time in the Senate chamber knitting. She also had a bottle of milk delivered to her office door each morning and put her empties back out for pickup. Her one legislative initiative was to secure passage of a law requiring parachutes for every airline passenger. She secured laughter instead but fared better than her predecessor, Rebecca Latimer Felton. Felton, known in the Senate as Mother Felton, was eighty-seven and not steady on her feet when the governor of Georgia appointed her to fill the unexpired term of Thomas Watson. A tiny, gray-haired woman, Felton came to her swearing-in dressed in a floor-length gown and was kept waiting while the senators discussed how she could be refused entry to the gentlemen's club. Irate Capitol Hill women began filling the gallery, and the men reluctantly ushered Felton in on a wave of female applause. Smith did not intend to become a joke, and she meant to be taken seriously.

By Smith's second year in the Senate, her colleagues had ceased their self-conscious rising when she entered and departed the chamber and accepted her as a senator. They never adjusted to her unpredictability on votes and demeaned her lack of consistency as female and not, as Smith insisted, independence. Smith championed the creation of a department of welfare and wrote the minority report in favor, although Brewster led the fight against and won. Voting first with the Republicans to slash foreign aid, Smith then voted with the Democrats to exempt Point 4 technical aid from the cut. In another contradiction Smith first voted against aid to Francisco Franco's Spain but, convinced by the military that the United States needed Spanish military bases, changed her vote. She was also one of the few Republicans to vote for a seventy-group air force. She voted against Taft, Brewster, and most Republicans and in favor of the North Atlantic Treaty Organization (NATO), but on an amendment to the Taft-Hartley Act that would eliminate the injunction clause, labor leaders believed they had her vote until emissaries from Taft turned her around.

Sensitive to the speculation that Lewis told her how to vote, Senator Smith came across a letter decades later that Lewis had written his parents about her vote against labor. Triumphantly, Smith attached a note to the letter to say that "it indicates clearly that William C. Lewis, Jr., DID NOT control my votes. My votes came from my own personal decisions. This is very essential in any research that is done on me." As Lewis explained the situation to his parents, the other senators had previously committed themselves forty-five to forty-six for labor, and "if Margaret had voted against Taft and for Labor it would have been a tie vote 45 to 45 in which event Vice President Barkley would have had to vote . . . for Labor and against Taft." Speculation was that losing the vote would have meant "the political death of Taft." Smith voted for Taft, and "I would have voted the other way," Lewis added, "but in the long run Margaret's labor votes have always been better decisions than my own."[98] This one letter is the only evidence that Smith voted against Lewis's advice, and at the time what was learned was not independence from her assistant but the independence Smith believed would come from not announcing her vote ahead of time.

Party leaders moved from their assessment of a woman's changing her mind, to considering Smith a liberal, to labeling her finally a Young Turk. The last occurred over a "Statement of Principles" the Republican leadership authored and expected their members to endorse. Smith complained publicly that the statement was too long, some twenty-five hundred words, vague, and "filled with generalities."[99] She, along with only Henry Cabot Lodge, refused to sign, but alone wrote her own eighty-nine word statement of Republican objectives. Her ten party goals were to reduce taxes, balance the budget, end government waste, fight communism, develop a bipartisan foreign policy, oppose socialized medicine, maintain a balance between labor and management, provide social security, retain veteran benefits, and "smash" the civil rights filibuster.[100]

Smith had demonstrated in the House that she was her own woman, but defiance of the leadership in the Senate was more serious. At first she received little discipline because of her unique position and the honors she brought to the party. The Associated Press named Smith Woman of the Year in Politics, and the Mutual Broadcasting System chose her as one of ten Americans who did the most for the welfare of the United States. The Gallup Poll put Smith on their ten Most Admired Women list, which had Eleanor Roosevelt as number one and Madame Chiang Kai-shek as number two. Smith was the only Republican Alben Barkley trusted with the gavel in the Senate, and the Senate itself honored Smith with appointment to UNESCO as its representative.

Smith also gained some immunity because from her election on, she had been touted for the 1952 vice presidential nomination. Previously a woman had not been nominated for either president or vice president by a major party's convention, and Smith had developed an interest in being the first woman to do a great many things. Despite the growing political wisdom among pundits that the party clever enough to nominate a woman as vice president would win in 1952, public sentiment was largely negative, even among women. A poll by *Cosmopolitan* magazine elicited comments such as "aghast," "shudder," and the "thought of a Commandress-in-Chief."[101] In Maine Peter Mills reported that, as opposed to drafting Smith as a favorite daughter nominee, "you can depend on the Maine women politicians to dig each others eyes out."[102] Guy Gannett felt differently and began promoting

Smith's candidacy editorially, and Owen Brewster told Smith that she could "easily be the popular vice presidential candidate in 1952."[103]

Before the Republican convention in Chicago the summer of 1952, Smith's longtime support group, the Business and Professional Women's Club, organized a campaign on her behalf. Led by Dorothy Tichener, president of the New York chapter, and Isabella Jones of the Pennsylvania group, the women claimed about 250 pledged delegates at the convention. Working from a Smith for Vice President headquarters at the Conrad Hilton Hotel, supporters advertised that half the delegates at the convention were women. They secured Clare Boothe Luce to nominate Smith, and about twenty others wanted to second her nomination. All of this was accomplished before Dwight David Eisenhower received the party's presidential nomination over Robert Taft. Eisenhower's nomination seemingly strengthened Smith's chances because she had championed him the year before in Maine. Smith had made a statewide broadcast in opposition to what she characterized as a "scurrilous smear sheet," distributed by the state Republican chairman, Ralph Masterman. The sheet claimed that Eisenhower was "pro-communist and a stooge of the Communists." When the Maine Republican convention voted to support Eisenhower's nomination, Smith received the credit.[104]

Smith was absent from both the vice presidential campaign and the convention. Her mother, seventy-six-year-old Carrie Chase, had surgery for abdominal cancer at the Thayer Medical Center in Waterville, Maine, and was there during the convention with a terminal diagnosis. Smith stayed at her mother's bedside, although the chairman of the convention, Joe Martin, offered her the opportunity to speak at the convention. The way Drew Pearson reported it was that when Martin offered her twenty-five minutes to speak, Smith said she would do it, and when he called back to change it to fifteen minutes, she still said yes. But when he called a third time to say five minutes and she would have to represent a minority, Smith asked, "What do you mean, a minority? Are we dividing the Republican Party up into the Irish, the Greeks, the Jews, the Italians, and the Negroes?" "No," Martin replied. "You represent the women." "Under the circumstances, you can give the five minutes to someone else," Smith decided.[105] The convention was a slugfest between supporters of Robert Taft and the Eisenhower forces. When Eisenhower won, the question was whether to open the convention for vice presidential nominations. Taft threatened to support Smith, which would have made her nomination a near certainty, but according to Smith, Eisenhower did not want a woman on the ballot.

Bill Lewis said that Isabella Jones called him from the convention to report that Eisenhower had chosen Richard Nixon, an earlier Taft supporter, for the vice presidential nomination in order to heal the breach in the party. "The question was," she said, "what we should do at that point—that they had gone so far they hated to drop it." Lewis outlined alternatives to her of going ahead with the nomination or of making the nomination and then withdrawing it. "The one thing he knew Senator Smith would not want to happen," Lewis said, was to say that "Margaret Smith had requested that her name not be placed in nomination." "Unfortunately," Lewis wrote later, "that was exactly what they did—the very thing I told them not to do."[106] Clare Boothe Luce from the floor read a statement, written by May Craig, "It is the desire of 200 women of this convention and of millions of women throughout the country, that I should place in nomination the name of Senator Margaret Chase Smith of Maine." Then, after a roar of applause that Lewis believed might have stopped Nixon's nomination with the support of the Taft forces, Luce continued, "In these circumstances, she wishes her name withdrawn because she does not wish to create divisions of loyalties on the floor of this convention."[107] Smith issued no denial at the time, made some campaign speeches for Eisenhower, but managed to be out of town when Nixon came to Skowhegan to speak. Her mother died a few months later, and the family held the funeral service, as she had asked, in her North Avenue home with Lewis as a pallbearer. Then she was buried at the Southside Cemetery.

Women at the Democratic convention made much of Smith's being denied the nomination for vice president. Judge Sarah Hughes of Texas, national president of the Business and Professional Women, said the Republican leadership had "blocked" the effort to nominate Smith and "barred" anyone from doing so. This action showed, Hughes maintained, "the difference in the attitude between Democrats and Republicans toward women." Several Republicans urged Smith to repudiate Hughes's statement, but Smith replied that "I cannot in good conscience" do so because "the truth is that I did not participate in the decision" to withdraw my nomination.[108] Both Hughes and India Edwards had their names placed in nomination by the Democrats and then immediately withdrawn in favor of John Sparkman of Alabama. Once again Smith was in the familiar role of victim. Nationally women believed that she was in need of their protection and began to champion her for a future presidential nomination.

Chapter Five

DECLARATION OF CONSCIENCE

She had never before felt so alone and frightened. Trembling slightly, she looked over her shoulder to be certain that Bill Lewis was standing a few feet away with the stack of blue-inked mimeographs in his hands. She could still change her mind.

Bill would be disappointed because he was certain she should take a stand. Ramrod stiff, forever standing as if at attention, Bill always wanted her to be stronger than she was, and she wanted to please him. This time he was asking too much. If he wanted someone to speak out, he could do it himself.

All her political instincts told her that she should not do this. She was a freshman senator from a conservative Republican state. She had never made a major speech on the floor of the Senate, and, smiling wryly, she admitted privately that she was not an orator. Worse, as the lone female among ninety-five men, she might appear to be a nagging, whining woman.

Nearly convinced, she glanced around the almost empty chamber and flinched as she unexpectedly met the baleful glare of Joseph R. McCarthy. Seated behind her, he threatened with his hulking presence, and she knew with certainty that he would punish her if she spoke.

Good sense might have changed her mind, but she would not be intimidated. With stiffened Yankee backbone and chin defiantly raised, she rose and said, "Mr. President." In so doing, Margaret Chase Smith separated herself forever from the thousands of faceless and forgotten U.S. senators and became a courageous defender of the democratic process.

Mr. President, I speak as a Republican. I speak as a woman. I speak as United States Senator. I speak as an American.

The United States Senate has long enjoyed world-wide respect as the greatest de-
liberative body in the world. But recently that deliberative character has too often
been debased to the level of a forum of hate and character assassination sheltered
by the shield of congressional immunity.

I think it is high time that we remembered that we have sworn to uphold and
defend the Constitution. I think it is high time that we remembered that the Consti-
tution, as amended, speaks not only of the freedom of speech but also of trial by jury
instead of trial by accusation.

Those of us who shout the loudest about Americanism in making character as-
sassinations are all too frequently those who, by our own words and acts, ignore
some of the basic principles of Americanism—

The right to criticize.
The right to hold unpopular beliefs.
The right of independent thought.[1]

In the sudden postwar about-face from the Soviet Union as ally to enemy,
Margaret Chase Smith had been on the ramparts. She had accepted without
question the assumptions of the early cold warriors that history was repeating itself with "Russia's Stalin retracing Hitler's early path to aggressive
domination of the world."[2] Consistently she voted for increased defense
appropriations "to intensify economic warfare against Russia and to weaken
her war machine."[3] Smith was an early champion of the Marshall Plan,
without which she believed Europe would "fall into Communism as one
falls into a hole in the ground. Every minute we delay is a minute of progress
for the Communists."[4] She believed that the House Un-American Activities
Committee could "perform a real service by publicizing the techniques and
methods of Communists," and she voted for contempt citations against the
"Hollywood 10" writers, directors, and producers who refused to answer
as to whether they were Communists.[5] Smith also supported the McCarran
Act to regulate the Communist party.

Like many other Americans, Smith grew increasingly concerned about
Soviet espionage in the United States. Disclosures by the Canadian government in 1946 of a Soviet spy network alerted already wary Americans. Then
the House Un-American Activities Committee began hearings into Communist activity in the Departments of Treasury and Agriculture during the
1930s. Responding to political pressure, the Truman administration established the Loyalty Review Board in 1947 for government employees but
exacerbated fears instead of reassuring citizens by firing thousands of sus-
pected security risks. Next came the sensational spy charges in 1948 of the
reformed Communist Whittaker Chambers against State Department official
Alger Hiss and justice department charges against eleven American Communist party officials for advocating overthrow of the government. Add a
1949 backdrop of the triumph of Mao Zedong in China, attributed to fellow
travelers in the Department of State, and the Soviet testing of an atomic
bomb, assisted by agents Klaus Fuchs and Julius and Ethel Rosenberg, and
America was primed for a demagogic savior.

Smith met Joseph R. McCarthy at an informal dinner May Craig hosted. Craig had told her that McCarthy was "a comer with a great future," but while Smith considered him "pleasant," she was "not as impressed with him as May obviously was."[6] Her after-the-fact skepticism notwithstanding, Smith benefited immediately on the Committee on Expenditures in Executive Departments by knowing McCarthy socially. He was the committee's senior Republican and made party assignments on subcommittees. She asked for and received his permanent Investigations Subcommittee and "was sure that May Craig's friendship had been an important factor."[7]

Then came 12 February 1950 when McCarthy went to Wheeling, West Virginia, and donned the crusader's cape. In an otherwise unmemorable speech to the Women's Republican Club, he waved his ticket to infamy and declared, "I have here in my hand a list of 205—a list of names that were made known to the Secretary of State as being members of the Communist party and who nevertheless are still working and shaping policy in the State Department."[8] Over the next four months McCarthy repeated his charges, changing the number to fifty-seven and then eighty-one, and never producing proof. Without facts to refute, the administration's defense was as ineffective as McCarthy's headlines were shrill and his supporters numerous.

Like many other Americans, Smith was frightened about possible Communist infiltration of the government and "impressed" with what McCarthy was doing. She said that his " 'I hold in my hand a photostatic copy' had a most impressive tone and a ring of authenticity."[9] But she was discerning enough to notice that McCarthy's often-promised documentation was never forthcoming. After one of his harangues on the Senate floor, again waving purported affidavits, Smith, seated in front of him, turned and said, "Joe, let me see those." But, according to Smith, "he'd say, 'Why? Don't you believe me?' I'd say, 'I'd just like to take a look at them.' But he never would let anyone see them." On several other occasions Smith "in a friendly manner," she maintained, indicated to McCarthy her concern that he was not producing promised evidence.[10] Finally, he responded, "Margaret, you seem to be worried about what I am doing," and she said, "Yes, Joe. I want to see the proof. I have been waiting a long time now for you to produce proof."[11] He told her, "I will," and a while later gave Smith several photostatic copies, but she concluded that while "they appeared to be authentic," she could not see "how they clearly proved his charges." At first, she believed that this was because of her own "deficiency," meaning that she was not a lawyer, and "any lawyer Senator will tell you that lawyer Senators are superior to non-lawyer Senators."[12]

Then, too, as a good Republican, Smith enjoyed the damage McCarthy did to the Democrats and wanted "Democratic Senators speaking in defense of a Democratic Administration, a Democratic President, and a Democratic Secretary of State" to insist that McCarthy prove his charges.[13] The Democrats attempted to do just that by appointing the distinguished senator from

Maryland, Millard Tydings, chairman of a Foreign Relations subcommittee to investigate the validity of McCarthy's accusations against the State Department. Unfortunately, Tydings was up for reelection in 1950, and although he was assumed a sure winner, McCarthy and his supporters entered the campaign against him. By nature politicians are vulnerable, worried individuals who always have an eye on their next election, and McCarthy's power increased dramatically overnight. Fearful colleagues refused to criticize his guilt-by-association tactics, and, Smith said, "Lyndon Johnson was telling the people on his side to stay out of the fight."[14] Protected by congressional immunity from those he accused of Communist sympathies and by political intimidation from congressmen whom he outraged, McCarthy accelerated his intolerant, hysterical, red-hunting campaign. "Joe began to get publicity crazy," Smith said, "and the other Senators were now afraid to speak their minds, to take issue with him. It got to the point where some of us refused to be seen with people he disapproved of. A wave of fear had struck Washington."[15] The U.S. Senate, that shrine of democracy, became a thriving black petri dish of fear, silence, and accusation.

Unleashed, McCarthyism was as fearsome a threat to the democratic process as Americans have had in U.S. history, and Smith began to wonder less "whether I was as stupid as I had thought" and "to wonder about the validity, accuracy, credibility, and fairness" of the charges.[16] At the same time, from March through May, Smith said that "earnest liberals" singled her out as the "ideal person to rebut McCarthy."[17] First, Ed Hart, a member of the Senate Radio Correspondents' Gallery, and newspaper columnist Doris Fleeson urged Smith to challenge McCarthy. Hart arranged for Smith to visit columnist Walter Lippmann at his home, and Lippmann added his considerable influence to the others. May Craig did not. Smith believed that Craig "continued to admire and support" McCarthy and was convinced that he was performing "a great patriotic service to the country."[18] Their difference of opinion led to a "serious, if not irreparable, rupture," Smith said. Privately, Smith called Craig "a little dictator" who convinced people in Maine who were against McCarthy that she was also, while those who were pro-McCarthy knew she was one of them. To Lewis's ire, Craig had been telling people that she was Smith's "mentor" and that she wrote Smith's speeches, although Smith denied the allegation.[19]

Finally, Smith stormed into her office after listening to McCarthy accuse still more government employees of increasing prominence of being Communists and told Lewis that "something has to be done about that man." "Why don't you make a speech," Lewis responded, but Smith hesitated, "I couldn't get away with it." "Well, then, stop talking abut it," Lewis retorted and walked away in a rare display of temper with Smith.[20] More dependent on Lewis than ever now that he managed her office, Smith chose to risk political disaster rather than disappoint him. She asked Lewis to prepare a brief statement for her to invite several Republicans to join her in issuing.

Acting quickly, Lewis called Ed Hart for his suggestions and soon had a draft, which Smith considered "too wordy and too grandiose."[21] Over coffee in the Senate dining room, Smith showed a revised statement, which she had titled Declaration of Conscience, to the senator whom she considered her closest ally, George Aiken of Vermont. He "thought it was good" and not only agreed to be a sponsor but also joined Smith in working on a list of others to ask.[22] They agreed on Wayne L. Morse of Oregon, Robert C. Hendrickson of New Jersey, Irving M. Ives of New York, Edward J. Thye of Minnesota, and Charles W. Tobey of New Hampshire. Leverett Saltonstall of Massachusetts was initially listed, but on the original copy, his name was later scratched through. He, along with Henry Cabot Lodge and Ralph Flanders of Vermont, had earlier criticized McCarthy, but for varying reasons— "a tendency to nit-pick on language," to reveal confidences, to give in to criticism, and to defer to party leaders—they were eliminated by Smith and Aiken.[23] Smith and Lewis were particularly concerned about the Republican leadership, because Taft, William F. Knowland of California, Kenneth Wherry of Nebraska, and Owen Brewster were all McCarthy supporters. Whether or not they believed McCarthy's accusations, they saw political dividends to be gained and had the power to stop Smith and her sponsors if word leaked. Asking for "strict confidence," Smith called all five and read the statement over the telephone to them. They all agreed to be sponsors, and only one, Ives, asked that only one word be changed: the word *tactics* in the last sentence to *techniques.* Smith acquiesced.[24]

On Friday, 26 May 1950, Lewis drove Smith to Maine for some Memorial Day speeches and a visit to the house she had built in Skowhegan high on a hill overlooking the Kennebec River. The house-building project had been exciting for Smith. She had personally sketched on an envelope a modest, one-story ranch-style house of white clapboard with dark green shutters and a green slate roof. Then she had given her design to an architect with instructions to have two guest rooms and baths at one end, a long living room–dining room combination in the center, and her bedroom, bath, and kitchen at the other end. The front door was to open into a large entrance hall, which would be used as an office. By November she, Lewis, and Craig had been able to use the house, but from now on her return trips would be only with Lewis.

On the long drive to Maine, Smith and Lewis talked about McCarthy, and Smith began to make notes for a possible speech to accompany her statement. Then she took over the driving, and Lewis wrote down their ideas. At the house Lewis settled down in the back guest area, which had a small sitting room, bedroom, and bath and continued to put his thoughts on paper. Smith made a speech in each congressional district and visited with friends along the road, as was her habit. The evening before their return to Washington, she and Lewis sat down at Smith's dining room table overlooking the log-choked river below and wrote the speech they now agreed she should give to introduce the Declaration of Conscience. One would read a statement from the notes they had made, the other would change a word or phrase, and within a few hours they had a first draft. Lewis made a clean copy, which Smith edited on the drive back to Washington. The senator and her aide made one more decision on the way back to Washington, and it concerned timing. As the Senate's representative to UNESCO, Smith planned to depart on 2 June for a conference in Florence, Italy. Accordingly, they decided that Smith should deliver the speech on 1 June and leave Washington for ten days.

Maintaining what she referred to as "tight security," Smith had her trusted secretary cut a mimeograph stencil in the office and walk it to the Senate Service Department to make two hundred copies.[25] Smith's concern was, in part, that the leadership would hear about her initiative and prevent her from being recognized on the floor; she also worried that her nerve might fail and she would not follow through. No one else was informed of her intentions—not her family, staff, Maine supporters, or May Craig, especially not May Craig. More surprising, the six senators who had signed her statement honored her request for confidence. Smith was not given to nervousness and certainly not to tears or emotional outbursts, but she was as near her breaking point as she had ever been. Not Lewis; he was as disciplined as ever, and he stayed close to Smith. They had a quiet lunch in the office, but, as they prepared to leave for the Senate chamber, Smith said, "Bill, I may not have the courage to do this." "Of course, you do, Margaret," Bill replied. "You know the subject, and it has to be done."[26]

Just after lunch they left for the Senate. Ordinarily, Lewis escorted Smith to the floor and remained in the aisle next to the wall in case she needed him. This time he carried the stack of mimeographs with strict instructions from her not to distribute them to the press until she was on her feet and speaking. With that order, Lewis finally perceived the depth of her fear and sobered himself. "I was young. I was a woman. I worried that it was presumptuous of me to tell everyone else they were wrong," Smith said. "After all, I was facing many experienced legislators, many of whom supported McCarthy. I needed Bill there."[27] They waited in somber silence for the little subway train that would transport them from the Senate Office Building to the Capitol. Then, startlingly, Joseph McCarthy appeared beside them and, with instinct a python might envy, inquired, "Margaret, you look very serious. Are you going to make a speech?"[28] McCarthy did not know what Smith intended, but she was not sure of that and, given his network of informers, to assume that he had heard something of her plans was logical. She could have dissembled in responding, but forthrightness was her bedrock. "Yes, and you will not like it," she replied.

Again instinctively, "Is it about me?"

"Yes, but I'm not going to mention your name."

McCarthy frowned in contemplation, but the best threat he could come up with was, "Remember, Margaret, I control Wisconsin's twenty-seven convention votes!"

"For what?" Smith asked in confusion but received no response.[29] She concluded later that McCarthy was one of the few Republicans around who took seriously the speculation of a vice presidential bid from her.

On this day, Thursday, 1 June 1950, the Senate convened at noon, with chaplain Frederick Brown Harris praying that the members "with clear heads and pure hearts, worthy of the trust the Nation has committed to our hands,"[30] would do their work. Acting president pro tempore Carl Hayden of Arizona presided and had the roll called by assistant journal clerk James Anton. Smith noted that of her allies only Tobey, Ives, and Hendrickson were present, and she fought to still the panic that threatened to send her running from the room. Aiding her effort at self-control and bringing a grim smile to her face, she noticed that her adversary and McCarthy's friend, Owen Brewster, was also absent. With a quorum present, Hayden proceeded with the transaction of routine business and then recognized Senator William F. Knowland of California, who delivered a speech on the Amerasia spy case. The 1945 case had involved the publication of classified government documents in the "Communist-connected" *Amerasia* magazine, and Knowland wanted further investigation.[31] He feared that some of the government employees who were "transmission belts" in the case were still employed.[32] Knowland quoted at length from the earlier hearings of the Judiciary Committee into the case and elicited from McCarthy a request to yield. Always handy with a number, McCarthy maintained that in secret testimony to the committee it had been revealed that there were "seventeen Communist writers who wrote for both the American Council of the Institute of Pacific Relations and *Amerasia*." In a refrain that was already familiar, McCarthy in a second interruption drew attention to "documents which I hold in my hand at this time. None of them have ever before been made public," but all presumably proved the guilt of another Communist by association.[33] In still another request to yield, McCarthy demonstrated the final step in his frightening song and dance of alleged names, numbers and documents: an attack on Fifth Amendment protection. In her account of the session, Smith did not mention McCarthy's participation but said that to avoid the impression that she was rebutting Knowland, she quickly added to her speech the statement that "there have been enough proven cases, such as the Amerasia case, the Hiss case, the Coplon case, and the Gold case, to cause nationwide distrust and strong suspicion that there may be something to the unproved, sensational accusations."[34]

Bill Lewis had asked Hayden to call on Smith as soon as possible, before her nerve failed, but by the time Knowland finished, Senator Ives, Smith's cohort, had replaced Hayden as presiding officer. Ives suggested the absence of a quorum and asked for a roll call, but either anxious to get it over with or not desiring a larger audience, Smith asked that the order for a quorum be rescinded, and there were no objections.

Ives then recognized Smith, who, trembling, rose and began to read her declaration so quietly that Senator Alexander Smith of New Jersey left his desk and moved over to hear her. At the same time Bill Lewis distributed the mimeographed copies to the press gallery. "I still remember Bill coming to the press gallery with that speech just as she came up on the floor," reporter Don Larrabee said. "There was no advance copy out anywhere. It was a big surprise."[35] Within minutes reporters were leaning over the balcony railing to hear Smith and asking May Craig what Maggie was up to.[36] Lewis later referred to this time as "the moment of truth" between Smith and Craig because Craig's ignorance of Smith's most important speech in her career ended the speculation that "May was Margaret Chase Smith's mentor."[37] Haltingly, Smith pressed on but "had butterflies in my stomach. I was so nervous I didn't think I could actually go through to the end with it."[38]

Smith did make it through to the end of her fifteen minute speech and then more forthrightly read the Declaration of Conscience:

1. We are Republicans. But we are Americans first. It is as Americans that we express our concern with the growing confusion that threatens the security and stability of our country. Democrats and Republicans alike have contributed to that confusion.

2. The Democratic administration has initially created the confusion by its lack of effective leadership, by its contradictory grave warnings and optimistic assurances, by its complacency to the threat of communism here at home, by its oversensitiveness to rightful criticism, by its petty bitterness against its critics.

3. Certain elements of the Republican Party have materially added to this confusion in the hopes of riding the Republican Party to victory through the selfish political exploitation of fear, bigotry, ignorance, and intolerance. There are enough mistakes of the Democrats for Republicans to criticize constructively without resorting to political smears.

4. To this extent, Democrats and Republicans alike have unwittingly, but undeniably, played directly into the Communist design of "confuse, divide, and conquer."

5. It is high time that we stopped thinking politically as Republicans and Democrats about elections and started thinking patriotically as Americans about national security based on individual freedom. It is high time that we all stopped being tools and victims of totalitarian techniques—techniques that, if continued here unchecked, will surely end what we have come to cherish as the American way of life.[39]

Smith fell back in her seat, relieved that the deed was done, but still fearful because Lewis had warned her to expect an angry blast from McCarthy. All eyes except hers were on him, but McCarthy kept everyone waiting while he glared at the back of Smith's head. Then he lumbered to his feet and abruptly left the chamber. Amid a collective sigh of relief led by Smith, Senator Alexander Smith of New Jersey rose to congratulate Smith and state his whole-hearted agreement. Declaration signatory Robert Hendrickson of New Jersey followed with the adjectives "inspiring and thought-provoking" and the "best" he had heard in the Senate, "a clarion warning to which every one of us should pay heed."[40] Despite the blasting Smith had given the Democrats in their mishandling of McCarthy, both Millard Tydings of Maryland and Herbert Lehman of New York praised her remarks. Tydings, although referring peculiarly to Smith's having "entertained us," said that she had been "temperate, constructive, imaginative . . . and fair." Her "magnificent address" was an example of, he coined extemporaneously, "stateswoman-ship." Lehman quoted so exactly from Smith in his congratulations that he must have taken notes or had an advance copy of her remarks. He managed to use the Smith-Lewis trademark word *smear* three times in his brief state-ment, while the speech itself only used it five times.[41]

After these brief comments, the Senate moved on to other business, but a third Democrat, Paul Douglas of Illinois, walked over to Smith, grasped her hand warmly, and tried to speak. His eyes filled with tears, his voice choked up, and he walked away instead. A few others shook her hand, and Alexander Smith, still seated by her, said that he would like his name added as a signatory. Smith left the chamber for Maine and then Italy for the UNESCO conference in Florence. As planned ahead, Lewis stayed behind to monitor the furor the speech caused.

Smith received nationwide headlines on 2 June, and the press coverage continued for months. The initial response was positive on the day following the speech with references to a "voice of decency," "a worthy act," and "calm reasoning."[42] The *Washington Star* ran a cartoon of a battered ele-phant saying that the Democrats had not beaten him up; "my sweetheart from Maine did."[43] The *Hartford Courant* called the speech "an appeal for national honesty and decency,"[44] while the *Washington Post* said that Smith's were "words that desperately needed to be said for the salvation of the country."[45] Philip L. Graham, *Washington Post* publisher, called the declaration "magnificent."[46] "There was nothing in it with which any decent person could quarrel,"[47] the *Washington News* added, and the *St. Augustine Record* referred to Smith as a "statesman."[48] The *Chicago Sun Times* pre-ferred "Woman of the Hour,"[49] and the *Christian Science Monitor* editori-alized that Smith had performed a public service for a nation that was foundering in a "miasma of confusion, suspicion, and fear."[50] To the point, the *Kansas City Times* recalled no other issue in memory that had frightened senators from taking a stand and hoped that Smith spoke for the majority of her colleagues and that their tolerance of McCarthy would end. Reporter Martin Agronsky sent Senator Smith a bouquet of roses.

During the flurry of pro-Smith headlines McCarthy immediately took to the floor of the Senate to demand a more vigorous investigation of his alle-gations than the one being conducted by Millard Tydings's subcommittee.

"Let me make it clear," McCarthy shouted, "that this fight against Communism . . . shall not stop regardless of what any individual or group in this Senate" might say or do.[51] In support, Malcolm W. Bingay, in a *Houston Chronicle* column, wrote, "Now that the Communist columnists, the Truman politicians, and the thoughtless do-gooders have applauded . . . let's be sensible about it."[52]

The negative headlines followed: "A Darling Stumbles," "A Shock to Maine," "Hamstringing the Investigation," and "Maine Is Disappointed."[53] McCarthy's choleric supporter, Westbrook Pegler, wrote a blistering denunciation of Smith, calling her "a Moses in nylons," who was only a "nominal Republican" and "took advantage . . . of her sex" in her "selfish harmful criticism."[54] Others asserted that she was under Democratic influence and would "qualify as a 100% Fair Dealer" who immediately received as reward a "pleasant junket to Italy."[55] The criticism that must have pleased Lewis was that Smith had "smeared" McCarthy.[56] The *Saturday Evening Post* referred to the signers of the declaration as "the Soft Underbelly of the Republican Party," while *Life* magazine settled for "quixotic."[57] There was also the scurrilous innuendo bandied about that Smith's attack on McCarthy was "personal revenge" in that she had taken "his flattery too seriously" and considered them "close friends" until he scorned her.[58] The National Society of New England Women called the declaration "a Republican as well as national tragedy."[59]

By contrast, May Craig was generous and wrote that Smith had given a "terrific speech," which placed her "in the Big League." She gave the government "a good talking to," which it needed, Craig wrote, because it had been "eating political red herrings for breakfast, dinner, and supper." Craig saw Smith's motivation as political and believed the senator was after a vice presidential nomination or leadership of Republican liberals.[60] In agreement, *Newsweek* put Smith on its cover as a vice presidential possibility. Writing for the *Washington Post,* Walter Lippmann called the Declaration of Conscience "noble" and sent Smith a congratulatory telegram.[61] Smith provided Lippmann a copy of her statements the day she spoke with the note attached that "this came out of our little chat the other morning."[62] The senator also told Lippmann that Bill Lewis would be calling on him while she was abroad, and "I want to assure you that I rely upon him as literally my alter ego in my work."[63] Of the five thousand plus letters that Smith received, eight to one were positive. Best of all, Bernard Baruch said that if a male had been responsible for the declaration, he would be the next president of the United States.

The current president, Harry Truman, at first joked "that he wouldn't want to say anything that bad about the Republican Party" and then several days later sat by Smith at a luncheon. He told her then that her "Declaration of Conscience was one of the finest things that has happened here in Washington in all my years in the Senate and the White House."[64]

When pressed as to why he had not replied to Smith's charges, McCarthy said, "I don't fight with women Senators." He did apparently make jokes about them, because he referred to "Snow White and the Six Dwarfs," and accused Senator Charles Tobey of "speaking through a petticoat."[65] Tobey was up for reelection, and McCarthy campaigned in New Hampshire against him, calling him a "coddler of Communism" and a "fuzzy thinker."[66] McCarthy did not defeat Tobey, but in November he was successful in bringing down a more important foe, Tydings of Maryland. Overnight the criticism of McCarthy that Smith had generated in the Senate ended, and as colleagues became fearful, they left her vulnerable to retaliation. The press began to speculate that the signers of the declaration had asked Smith to remove their names. Responding that "none of the six Senators have withdrawn their names," Smith nervously added, "at least they haven't said anything to me about doing so."[67]

Unwittingly, Smith and Lewis augmented her vulnerability by making no plans past the declaration and the anticipated publicity. They appeared to believe naively that public opinion on McCarthy would change and Smith would be credited. Smith and her co-signers, none of whom were party leaders, made no attempt to enlist supporters, organize active opposition to McCarthy, or continue the effort in any manner. Moderates all, they chose the high, and politically ineffective, ground of criticizing McCarthy's excesses, not his sincerity or even his premise that the government was overrun by Communists. They made no effort to maintain their own unity, in which there was at least some influence, if not power. The problem was largely one of leadership, or the absence thereof, because Smith, who had initiated their action, chose to step aside while no one else stepped forward. Instead, the momentarily brave senators fell prey to the overtures of party leaders who were McCarthy's supporters.

Irving Ives was the first to succumb. "I've had occasion to be slightly critical of you in the past," he shamelessly told McCarthy publicly, "but I feel very strongly that all subversives must be weeded out of the government. I offer my full cooperation." Shortly afterward, Alexander Smith, who had asked that he be added as a declaration signatory, decided to "try to convert McCarthy rather than get him reprimanded publicly." Charles Tobey joined the ship jumpers when he responded to a critical constituent, "I have not disavowed Senator McCarthy. Many senators feel that his objectives are good, and I share that feeling." When McCarthy accused General George Marshall of participating in a "conspiracy of infamy," Robert C. Hendrickson commended the Wisconsin senator. With increasing bitterness, Smith watched each of her co-signers betray her with the single exception of Wayne Morse, who, she believed, remained loyal.[68] William Jenner of Indiana inflicted the first of a series of "chats" on her from McCarthy's cohorts, and Styles Bridges, whom Smith respected, spent nearly three hours with her. Bridges insisted that "China had fallen" as a result of State Department treachery and accepted "Joe's charges" as "serious." Unpersuaded, Smith remained friends with Bridges but said that "this was not the case with Mrs. Bridges, who really admired McCarthy. She was very cold to me after the speech, and she would remain so throughout my years in Washington."[69]

Smith's challenge to McCarthy was still being debated by the press and her colleagues when on 25 June an event occurred that immediately gave McCarthy an advantage. Without warning, the Communist North Korean army invaded South Korea, and in less than five years since World War II ended, the United States found itself at war again. This time the nation was fighting a Soviet satellite, and McCarthy's campaign to rid the government of Communists assumed the mantle of protecting national security. McCarthyism became Republican policy as the leadership saw the heightened possibility of victory in 1952.

Morally right and politically wrong, Smith appeared to have made a serious mistake, and when the new Congress organized in January 1951, McCarthy retaliated. That he had waited seven months was as surprising as it was inexplicable, but when he punished Smith, he chose the same context in which he had earlier rewarded her. As ranking Republican on the Executive Expenditures Committee, McCarthy, in Smith's words, "kicked" her off the permanent Investigations Subcommittee on which he had originally placed her, and he did so in a particularly low manner.[70] He waited until her office had closed on the evening before the full committee was to meet on subcommittee appointments. Then he had an aide slide under her door his appointments list with her name eliminated. But Smith and Lewis were in the office and immediately read the memo, which McCarthy had not intended her to have until immediately before the committee meeting. Angry at what was a violation of Senate procedure, Smith called McCarthy but said that she was told by the "girl" answering the telephone that he was not available. "Then give him this message," Smith said. "Tell him that I fully realize that kicking me off the Investigations Subcommittee is an act of vengeance to retaliate for my Declaration of Conscience."[71] "I take about so much," Smith wrote in a memo dated 27 November 1950, "but when I get tired of being kicked around, I explode." Now Smith decided, "I have been kicked around on committee assignments," and she exploded.[72]

Accompanied by Lewis, Smith appealed to the executive committee of the Executive Expenditures Committee the next morning. McCarthy was present and said that his action was not an "unfriendly" one toward Smith. He simply wanted experienced investigators on the committee and was replacing Smith with the newly elected California senator, Richard Nixon, who had extensive experience on the House Un-American Activities Committee. McCarthy added that the other Republican on the subcommittee, Karl Mundt, also had more experience than Smith. Smith responded but, she said, McCarthy "butted in" and she told him, "Joe, you keep quiet for a minute. I haven't said anything while you were talking—now I am going to have my say and you keep quiet." Reminding her colleagues that her investigative work went back to 1943 and the House Naval Affairs Committee, Smith established that she had more experience than Nixon, Mundt, and McCarthy. Heatedly, in the manner the press referred to as "schoolmarm," she told McCarthy that he had "not only disregarded custom, precedent, and common courtesy . . . you have even disregarded experience." As valid as her arguments were, John McClellan of Arkansas, the Democratic chairman of the committee, refused to become embroiled in a Republican fight, and McCarthy won.[73]

Republican leader Robert A. Taft of Ohio wrote Smith after the fact to deny that he had anything "whatever to do about this action and was never consulted." He "saw it in the paper," he said, and although Smith believed him, she was hardly consoled.[74] In contrast, when Owen Brewster was asked to champion Smith, he referred to an earlier episode when Smith had complained that her chair in the Senate chamber snagged her stockings. "We can't demand too much in the name of fair womanhood," he said. "After all, we got Senator Smith a new chair that doesn't hurt her nylons."[75] Nixon's response was that "when Margaret gets upset, she stays upset," but he saw her as "fearless in expressing her views" about McCarthy.[76] When the leadership also removed Smith from the Republican Policy Committee, she understood, as did the press, that they had given McCarthy a green light on her. Drew Pearson referred to the "kicking around"[77] given Smith, and reporter Doris Fleeson said that there was a "studied attempt to humiliate" Smith. Her "neck was on the block," Fleeson wrote, because of her "deviationism" from the party's support of McCarthyism.[78] In the *Denver Post*, Roscoe Fleming bluntly maintained that "in the new Congress, Mrs. Smith has been degraded, demoted, and insulted."[79]

In an unrelated action, the Republican leadership promoted Smith from the District of Columbia Committee to the Rules Committee, albeit to the least desired Rules subcommittee, Privileges and Elections. Unfortunately for the leadership, the subcommittee named Smith and Senator Mike Monroney of Oklahoma to investigate the Maryland "smear campaign," as Smith called it, in which McCarthy had secured the defeat of Millard Tydings.[80] Tydings did not dispute the results of the campaign but wanted "scandalous, scurrilous, libelous, and unlawful" conduct investigated.[81] Immediately recognizing his mistake, the ranking Rules Republican, Kenneth Wherry of Nebraska, called to say he was transferring Smith to a different subcommittee. Surprisingly complaisant about being booted from another subcommittee after fighting to hold on to her position on another, Smith told Wherry he "could do as he pleased" since "she had not asked for nor been consulted" about her assignment.[82] This time the Democratic subcommittee chairman, Guy Gillette of Iowa, refused to move Smith and simply increased the Maryland election investigators to four by adding Hendrickson and Thomas Hennings of Missouri.

An Associated Press report maintained that "all but open warfare was declared" by McCarthy and Smith with the investigation.[83] "McCarthy Doesn't Like Mrs. Smith" headlined a May Craig column on the Maryland inquiry and referred to "bad blood" between the two "personally."[84] Senator Charles Potter said McCarthy had an "obsession with destroying" Smith, and he was not sure she would "survive."[85] Other reports referred to Smith's questioning of witnesses during the February through May hearings as "intense" and noted that she refused to be "intimidated" by McCarthy and his "backstreet campaign."[86] Ralph Becker, assistant counsel to the subcommittee, believed Senator Smith was "outstanding in her interrogation of the witnesses" and altogether "most impressive" in her participation.[87] After the hearings Monroney despaired of writing the subcommittee report and told Smith at the end of June 1951 that "he was nearly going crazy" over it and asked her to have Lewis write it. Lewis wrote a scathing denunciation of McCarthy's manipulation of the election and "without anyone but Monroney, Smith, and Lewis knowing who had written it," the report went to the subcommittee.[88] Weeks passed while the subcommittee delayed release of its findings until, finally, Smith introduced a report of her own and threatened to inform the press that she had done so unless the committee acted. Faced with this ultimatum, the subcommittee issued in August a report that was largely hers, that is to say, Lewis's.

The thirty-nine-page report concluded that McCarthy was responsible for a composite photograph printed in a "smear tabloid," purportedly showing Tydings consulting with Earl Browder, chairman of the Communist Party U.S.A. The report characterized McCarthy's action as "false, malicious, devoid of simple decency and common honesty." The unusually strong language blasted the campaign as destructive "of our system of free elections" and "unreservedly denounces, condemns, and censures these tactics."[89] McCarthy, also a member of the Rules Committee, was furious about the report and publicly referred to Smith and Hendrickson as "puny politicians."[90] By a nine-to-three vote the Rules Committee accepted the report, but McCarthy wrote a minority report, which, Smith said, he could not get anyone else, including the two who had voted with him against the subcommittee report, Kenneth Wherry of Nebraska and William Jensen of Indiana, to sign. McCarthy then maintained that he did not ask them to join him in order to spare them "left-wing smear and character assassinations."[91] For two hours in the Senate on 20 August 1951, McCarthy attacked the Maryland report and called on Smith and Hendrickson to disqualify themselves because of their bias against him. Smith sat in front of McCarthy during his tirade and then in a two-minute rebuttal said that apparently McCarthy's "basis for disqualification was disagreement with Senator McCarthy."[92] Defiantly, she entered the Declaration of Conscience once again into the *Congressional Record* and earned a cartoon showing McCarthy nailing a sign on the Senate door saying that no consciences were wanted.[93] More isolated than ever,

Smith was alone in rebuttal to McCarthy, because Hendrickson chose to appease in his response. Not a single Democrat defended the Maryland report, but W. McNeil Lowry, Washington bureau chief for the Cox newspapers, commented on Smith's "courage," which he believed surpassed that she had demonstrated the year before.[94]

After this confrontation, the battle over committees turned murky. McCarthy did not pursue the removal of Smith from the Elections Subcommittee, saying, "Hell no, I am not going to waste my time on that mental midget." It was Smith who pursued the issue, saying, "I am not going to let either Senator McCarthy or the Democrats push me around."[95] On 24 September she asked the Rules chairman, Carl Hayden of Arizona, to have the committee decide whether she should be disqualified from the Elections Subcommittee. McCarthy left the meeting before Hayden acted on Smith's request but left behind a letter asking the committee not to disqualify her. McCarthy wanted Smith to disqualify herself. The committee voted unanimously that Smith was qualified for the subcommittee.

Then, in response to the Maryland election report, William Benton of Connecticut introduced a resolution to expel McCarthy from the Senate. The resolution went to the Elections Subcommittee, and Smith found herself again in a position to judge McCarthy. She startled her colleagues, and McCarthy, by saying about the Benton resolution that she both "disapproved . . . and resented it." She disapproved Benton's use of the Maryland report "to punish for the past instead of preventing in the future." Not only did Smith consider McCarthy redeemable, but she resented Benton's "tactical and strategic error" in asking for expulsion instead of censure. Expulsion required a two-thirds vote, which Smith did not believe was possible, while censure required only a simple majority.[96]

McCarthy next attacked Senator Hennings for having a law partner who was counsel for the editor of the *Daily Worker* and called on Hennings to remove himself from hearings on the Benton resolution. Hennings responded that his partner was a court-appointed attorney for the Communist editor and refused to resign from the Elections Committee. Smith was the only Republican to cross the aisle after the session ended to congratulate Hennings for standing up to McCarthy.

As the furor built over the Benton resolution, Kenneth Wherry died in December 1951 and left a Republican vacancy on both the Rules and the Appropriations committees. Senators, including Smith, quickly put aside principle in favor of personal advantage. McCarthy left Rules for Appropriations but had his supporters Everett Dirksen of Illinois and Herman Welker of Idaho named to replace him and Wherry. Smith requested to move from the Elections Subcommittee to the Rules Subcommittee, where she would be the ranking Republican and, if the Republicans became the majority party in 1952, chair. "Odd promotion," Hayden observed, to be transferred to a subcommittee that never meets, but added that "as a matter of cold practical politics, it's a good thing for Mrs. Smith to get out of the line of fire on McCarthy." Publicly, Smith rationalized that if she became chair of the subcommittee, she would champion the release of legislation now "bottled up."[97] The bills she wanted reported to the floor included repealing the poll tax, reporting of congressional income, broadcasting of congressional sessions, and establishing fair rules of Senate investigations. The other Republican on Elections, Hendrickson, also requested promotion to the Library Subcommittee. Smith's assumption was that the new Rules members, Dirksen and Welker, would be named to the Elections Subcommittee. That McCarthy's cronies would be sitting in judgment of him over the Benton resolution did not bother her. She had learned from her colleagues that in the Senate nothing was more important than seniority.

Smith's departure from the Elections Subcommittee bothered Republicans, Democrats, and press. "Pressure," as she described it, came from many directions to finish what she had started and not to change the jury in the midst of the trial.[98] Her colleague Mike Monroney said that her removal would be "catastrophic," but McCarthy was, of course, jubilant about the changes and bragged that he had "scared" Smith and Hendrickson off Elections.[99] Infuriated at the charge, Hendrickson changed his mind and stayed on the subcommittee. Smith handled the criticism by proposing the Benton resolution be handled in a different manner and successfully supported Senator Monroney's initiative to have the resolution discharged from the Elections Subcommittee by the Senate. The immediate result was that McCarthy remained unchastised, Smith was promoted, and the battle continued.

What Smith considered McCarthy's "most serious attack" on her came in early 1952 with the publication of *U.S.A. Confidential* by Jack Lait and Lee Mortimer.[100] Lait, editor of the *New York Daily Mirror,* and Mortimer, a gossip columnist for the paper, were supporters of McCarthy, and Mortimer, who actually wrote the book, conferred with the Wisconsin senator during his research. Smith characterized the book as "vintage McCarthyism" in its use of falsehoods, distortions, and half-truths to accuse her of being pro-Communist, a fellow traveler, and a "stunted visionary who made boneheaded speeches."[101] As infuriating to Smith, the book quoted an anonymous Senate doorman saying, "There's too many women in the Senate!" Smith, the authors concluded, was "a lesson why women should not be in politics": she "lies awake nights scheming how to 'get even,' " "reacted to all situations as a woman scorned, and not as a representative of the people," and was "under the influence of a coterie of left-wing writers."[102] Book advertisements declared, "Every word is true. Every statement has been checked and verified."[103]

Fed up, Smith filed a libel suit against Lait, Mortimer, and Crown Publishers on 7 May 1952. She employed New York attorney Richard H. Wels, whom she and Lewis had known as a former special counsel for the House Naval Affairs Committee. Lewis prepared the analysis of the book's charges and, as he wrote, "their falsity and malicious nature," and he did so with the thoroughness and detail for which he was becoming known.[104] He began with the general attack on the Declaration of Conscience as "un-American" and "designed to shield pro-Communists."[105] He refuted the charge with references to national editorial praise of the declaration for upholding American values and, in particular, on the award Smith had received for the speech from the conservative-to-reactionary Freedoms Foundation, many of whose board members were specified as McCarthy supporters.

Lewis spent considerably more effort and space in refuting the accusations that Smith was a fellow traveler and "pal" of Esther Brunauer, a State Department employee whom McCarthy had accused of Communist affiliation and who had been suspended on security charges.[106] *U.S.A. Confidential* alleged that Smith and Brunauer had traveled together to the UNESCO conference in Italy, shared a hotel room, and discussed Brunauer's Communist sympathies. Lewis documented that Smith had traveled alone to Italy, arrived weeks later than Brunauer, roomed alone, never met Brunauer until the conference and then only twice briefly, had no knowledge of her actions, and had no reason to accuse or to defend her. Lewis hit his stride in refuting the charge that Smith was under the influence of left-wing writers like "Doris Fleeson, Marquis Childs, Alan Barth, Drew Pearson, Cabell Phillips, Robert Allen, Elmer Davis, Joseph Alsop, and Stewart Alsop."[107] He secured from each journalist, except Drew Pearson who did not respond, a statement of having little to no contact with Smith, certainly no influence on her, and a personal denial of being left wing. To rebut the charge that she was a "left-wing apologist," Smith wrote to senators John W. Bricker, William E. Jenner, Styles Bridges, and Pat McCarran, all acknowledged by Lait and Mortimer as "good Americans" who defended democracy. Each predictably refused to accuse her of anything in writing and instead wrote highly complimentary responses while castigating the "scurrilous" accusations against her.[108] Lewis also contacted all the Senate doormen and secured from each a denial of having been the one to criticize Smith, as *U.S.A. Confidential* maintained.

Lewis's analysis was 17 pages long, while *U.S.A. Confidential* in its 404 pages mentioned Smith on 3 pages. These references totaled two paragraphs, a phrase, and her name in a list of six other senators. Literally hundreds of other people were casually libeled along with her in what the authors boasted was "a shotgun book."[109] Lait and Mortimer characterized Eleanor Roosevelt as the "chief tub-thumper for socialism,"[110] Justice Felix Frankfurter as the "evil genius of the socialist revolution,"[111] senators William Benton as "a fanatic for queer radical ideas,"[112] John Pastore as "chosen by the Mafia,"[113] and Wayne Morse as a "socialist schemer."[114] The "stunted visionaries" included senators Herbert Lehman, Irving Ives, Leverett Saltonstall, Paul Douglas, and Charles Tobey.[115] Of the signers of the Declaration of Conscience, the authors forgot to slur George Aiken, Robert Hendrickson, and Edward Thye, but, then, the book was not limited to the U.S. Senate. Its hit list included the Mafia, unions, Negroes, homosexuals, and assorted states and cities. Of all those whom *U.S.A. Confidential* castigated, only Smith sued. In Smith's opinion, her suit was justified because the book "held her up as an incompetent, irresponsible and faithless public servant" and as an "object of hatred, contempt, scorn, derision, and aversion among her neighbors, associates, and constituents."[116]

For four and a half years Smith's suit languished in the courts while the authors and Crown Publishers employed various delaying tactics. First the defendants stalled for six weeks in documenting sources for their statements against Smith, which they never produced. Then they secured from federal judge Thomas F. Murphy a decision that they would not have to file an answer to the complaint until they completed Smith's deposition. They delayed nearly two years in deposing Smith. During this period Smith's attorney presented Lait and Mortimer with written interrogatories that the judge directed be answered. Smith, as plaintiff, wanted to know on which nights they believed she lay awake scheming how to get even and elicited the response from Mortimer that he did not know "because he had never slept with her."[117] Other delays included the defendants' attorney suffering with a virus, traveling out of the country, being fired, having a petition for disbarment filed against him by former clients, and being replaced by his client, Mortimer, who chose to represent himself.

During this lawsuit-as-carnival McCarthy remarked on the Senate floor that "Jack Lait wrote a book in which he pointed out that one of the Senators traveled to Italy with Mrs. Brunauer, and the Senator, who has defended these innocent people constantly, has sued Lait for $2,000,000 because she thought her character was injured to that extent by the story that she had known the Brunauers."[118] When Smith came up for reelection in 1954, she was told by the people involved in the lawsuit that she best drop the charges "to save herself embarrassment" in the campaign.[119] Two weeks later when she had not, a candidate whom McCarthy had recruited entered the primary against her. By the time the case was settled, Jack Lait had died of cancer, and Mortimer accused Smith of "an evil conspiracy" that had caused not only his collaborator's death but also that of Mortimer's wife, mother, and father.[120] So determined was Smith that she secured court approval to substitute Lait's widow as the defendant because Mrs. Lait was the executrix of her husband's estate. Then Mortimer left the country on a world trip and delayed settlement still again.

The denouement came on 17 October 1956, when the trial finally began and ended. Stating that there was no need for the case to be tried, Mortimer admitted that his statements against Smith had been false. He, in Smith's words, "folded completely," agreed to pay $15,000 in damages, and published an apology and retraction in the New York and Maine newspapers.[121]

Concurrent with Smith's lawsuit, McCarthy ran for a second term in 1952.

His opponents urged Smith to campaign against him, but she responded that the people of Wisconsin did not need an outsider to tell them how to vote and that they already knew how she felt about him. To her dismay, Dwight Eisenhower did campaign for McCarthy, as did the party's vice presidential nominee, Richard Nixon, which is to say that Smith was embroiled with McCarthy at the time she had been considered for the vice presidency. The 1952 Republican victory was the second Smith had experienced since entering Congress in 1940, but McCarthy was part of the party's majority. When he entered the Senate chamber on 3 January as part of the Republicans' forty-eight to forty-seven majority over the Democrats, the gallery was quiet. Always the showman, McCarthy entered as though the conquering hero, grinning maliciously, slapping Carl Hayden on the back, and winning some applause at last. Then Smith entered jubilantly with former Maine governor Frederick G. Payne, who had defeated her old adversary, Owen Brewster, by some three thousand votes, and was greeted with thunderous applause.

McCarthy's seniority made him chairman of the Government Operations Committee, and the Eighty-third Congress was barely underway when he bragged to the press that he was getting Smith "kicked off" of his committee.[122] Since he had succeeded earlier in removing her from the full committee's Investigations Subcommittee, Smith took his threat seriously and went directly to the chairman of the Republican Committee on Committees, Senator Hugh Butler of Nebraska. During her four years in the Senate, Smith had not received a major committee assignment and believed Butler had discriminated against her in favor of senators junior to her. Butler assured her that this time he would consult with her before he made his assignments, but Lewis later heard a press rumor that Smith had been assigned to Appropriations and Armed Services but taken off Government Operations. Angry, Smith went immediately before the full Committee on Committees in an old red plaid dress in which she had been cleaning out files. She castigated Butler for not keeping his word, and although pleased with her assignment to two major committees, argued that Government Operations was a committee a senator could keep as a third one. She had not agreed to leave Government Operations and wanted to keep her seat. Francis Case of South Dakota called Smith "selfish," and Butler said that he did not think she would want to be on a committee where she was "not wanted by the Chairman." Smith responded that she would not let McCarthy's "dislike" impair her rights as a senator and that she would take this fight to the Republican Conference and to the floor of the Senate if necessary. A few hours later the committee announced assignments; Smith was still on Government Operations. When McCarthy learned of Smith's victory, he snarled, "There's too damn many women in the Senate," a comment Smith considered "strangely similar to the alleged doorkeeper's" in *U.S.A. Confidential.*[123]

McCarthy's final effort to, in Smith's word, "destroy" her came during her 1954 reelection campaign.[124] Directly after she halted his attempt to issue reports for the Investigations Subcommittee, McCarthy called Owen Brewster in Maine to see if he knew anyone who would run against Smith. The speculation had been that Brewster would challenge Smith, but Brewster told McCarthy that he did not know of any potential candidate. When Smith learned of McCarthy's inquiry, she told Brewster that "there isn't anyone I'd rather run against than you."[125] Undaunted, McCarthy assured Brewster that he could get "plenty of money" for anyone who would run. At the same time, Lee Mortimer, writing Walter Winchell's 25 August 1953 column while Winchell was on vacation, said that McCarthy would take "to the hustings in the states of his opponents, and especially in Maine where La Smith is up for re-election in 1954. (Remember what happened to Tydings?)"[126] McCarthy "desperately," Lewis said, chose Robert L. Jones, who had managed Brewster's unsuccessful 1952 reelection campaign, to be his champion against Smith.[127] After Jones had lost his job on Brewster's staff, Congressman Charles P. Nelson of Maine had told Senator Charles E. Potter of Michigan that "Jones, his wife and four children were on the verge of starvation" and persuaded him to employ Jones as a research assistant.[128] Potter was on the Investigations Subcommittee and possibly McCarthy knew Jones through that connection. By late August 1953 McCarthy had added Jones to his entourage as Potter's representative on investigation hearings in New York and New Jersey. Lewis observed that "the build-up was on for Jones," because McCarthy encouraged Jones to ask questions at the hearings and make statements to the press "as though he was a Senator."[129]

The McCarthy-Smith feud had profoundly disturbed conservatives in Maine, and there were press reports that the Republican party had been "rocked" by their confrontations.[130] Albert Abrahamson, a longtime Smith adviser, reported that there had been "a great deal of criticism of her" because of "her failure to come around and see people."[131] Also a rumor was circulating that her old supporter, and arguably the most influential man in Maine, Guy Gannett, would support her opponent if "a likely one appeared."[132] In November McCarthy "invaded" Maine, as Lewis saw it, and he brought Jones and what eventually turned out to be Jones's campaign staff with him.[133] The state Veterans of Foreign Wars, which Smith had been courting for years, invited McCarthy. Maine's junior senator, Fred Payne, who had promised in running against Brewster to cooperate with Smith, not fight her, welcomed McCarthy to the state by sending him flowers. No prominent Republicans appeared with McCarthy, but the press reported a charged atmosphere and a fear that the old McCarthy-Smith "fireworks" would start again.[134] Instead, the wily Wisconsin senator praised Jones as a "fighter of Communism" and the "kind of young man the people of Maine should send to Washington." McCarthy made the mistake at his Portland news conference of asking reporters if there was anyone politically stronger than Smith in Maine. He was told, "Yes, Almighty God."[135]

Undeterred, McCarthy visited Hugh Roy Cullen, the Texas oil man, and secured his financial backing for Jones. That meant "unlimited campaign funds" for Jones, Drew Pearson reported.[136] Personally, McCarthy introduced Jones to Gannett as Maine's next senator and continued to promote Jones as the Army-McCarthy hearings got underway by referring to him as "Senator Jones."[137] Privately, McCarthy bragged to Brewster that Jones's candidacy would "(1) ruin Smith financially, (2) ruin her perfect voting attendance record, and (3) cause her worry and harassment," if not defeat.[138] All of this Lewis referred to as "Jones' conspiracy to run against Senator Smith" in the report he prepared for her.[139]

Back in Washington for the new term, a press poll declared Smith the most popular of senators and McCarthy the most controversial. Even better as a springboard for the election year, the Chi Omega Sorority Achievement Award Committee, chaired by Eleanor Roosevelt with Mamie Eisenhower as honorary chair, selected Smith as their 1954 recipient. Carrie Chapman Catt, Madame Chiang Kai-shek, Anna Rosenberg, and Frances Perkins were previous winners, which made the award prestigious enough to be presented to Smith at the White House by President Eisenhower. Her longtime friend Frances Bolton, before an audience of members of Congress, the Supreme Court, and cabinet, praised Smith for overcoming "the animosity of jealous and angry men and women. And how they fought you, not cleanly, not fairly . . . , but you stood smiling against the vilification." Bolton believed that if Smith had done nothing more "than give the country your simple Declaration of Conscience, you would have made a . . . contribution toward a renewal of national honor."[140]

Two days later on 7 January 1954, Smith listened to Eisenhower's State of the Union address and noted that his loudest applause came with his condemnation of American Communists. Ike wanted convicted Communists stripped of their U.S. citizenship, and while many debated the constitutionality of such legislation, Smith immediately introduced a bill to carry out the president's wishes. Her emphasis was on conviction for advocating overthrow of the government, because the Smith Act (no relation to Margaret Chase Smith) already took away citizenship for the attempted overthrow of the government, and the McCarran-Walter Immigration and Naturalization Act withdrew citizenship from anyone convicted of treason. Earlier, Smith had tried to bolster her preelection anti-Communist stance by introducing legislation to outlaw the Communist party, but the Judiciary Committee had referred the bill to the Department of Justice for review. Despite the committee's persistent efforts to secure a report from the department, 1953 had passed without a ruling or political dividends for Smith. Now she went on television to call for letters to the attorney general in support of her proposals. McCarthy cavalierly dismissed Smith's efforts by saying that before the elections, he expected a flood of bills from those who were "soft on communism."[141]

According to a *Congressional Quarterly* survey, fourteen bills to outlaw the Communist party had been introduced from 1941 through 1952, and in 1953 and 1954 nineteen more were forthcoming, fifteen in 1954 alone. In the Senate, in addition to Smith, Charles Potter of Michigan, Mike Mansfield of Montana, and Homer Ferguson of Michigan authored similar bills. In the House Martin Dies of Texas was the primary proponent of the legislation. Despite the Eisenhower administration's being as much McCarthy's captive as the Senate was, the president, advised by Attorney General Herbert Brownell, Jr., opposed efforts to outlaw the Communist party. The rationale partly was that such a law would drive the party underground and make surveillance more difficult. Given the near-hysteria of American anticommunism, there was limited concern for the constitutional rights of the individual but significant interest in the Department of Justice to prevent any new legislation from conflicting with or invalidating existing laws. In addition to the Smith Act and the Hatch Act, cold warriors had passed laws requiring foreign agents and Communist action or Communist front groups to register with the attorney general. Brownell acknowledged that if it was illegal to be a Communist in the United States, registration would involve self-incrimination. Still, superpatriotic groups like the American Legion, Veterans of Foreign Wars, and Daughters of the American Revolution pressed for more legislation, and politicians desiring votes introduced more bills.

Smith's supporters had difficulty with her accepting the political reality that in 1954 anticommunism was good politics, possibly the best politics when one had Joseph McCarthy as an enemy. Columnist Roscoe Drummond insisted that Smith was "demonstrably not a witch-hunting, hang-the-Communist-even-if-you-hang-free-speech advocate."[142] She did not see a subversive at every Washington desk; she just thought the Communist party should be branded for what it was, he weakly concluded. Expediency aside, in promoting anti-Communist legislation, Smith accepted McCarthy's premise that the government was threatened by subversives and was now his competitor in safeguarding the nation. To express her concern, she even voted for the Senate's $214,000 appropriation for McCarthy's investigative committee along with the majority.

Smith announced for reelection in January, and Jones followed in February. He referred to Smith as "silent, puzzled, uninformed, and weak-willed" and promised a "bitter political showdown in Maine between the forces of Americanism and international liberalism." He expected opposition from "devious left-wing elements" and made no apologies for being McCarthy's "protege."[143] Indeed, Jones expected McCarthy to tour the state in March. The thirty-four-year-old Jones put on a good show for the press and came off to their surprise as personable and dynamic. He introduced his attractive wife, Anita, their four children, ages three to thirteen, and his parents who lived in Biddeford. Reminiscent of Smith's use of *Mr. Smith Goes to Washington,* Jones used the popular song, "The Whole Town's Talking about the

Jones Boy." Given the disparity in their ages, Smith must have appreciated the last lyric, "and he's only nine days old."[144]

May Craig reported that all of Washington was watching Maine and fearful for Smith as the state became the testing ground for McCarthy's influence. McCarthy would immeasurably strengthen his power base if he could defeat his long-time nemesis, because Smith was the first Republican whom he had gone after. Writing that McCarthy's greater goal in the election was to dominate the Republican party, Walter Lippmann maintained that McCarthy "respected nobody, no office, and no institution in the land."[145] Craig believed McCarthy would bring his traveling "Communist hunt" to Maine and hold hearings in which Jones would participate to boost his candidacy.[146] The *Washington Post* added that the Smith-Jones primary fight would be "the dirtiest in the nation."[147]

Smiling confidently, Jones held his first press conference in Portland and calmly answered rapid-fire questions from reporters for forty-five minutes. Not missing a beat, Jones said that he planned a "bare knuckles" campaign, endorsed McCarthy "100 percent," and equated Americanism with McCarthyism. "I think Joe McCarthy is a great American, a great patriot, and is doing a fine job," Jones said, and, when asked if he also endorsed McCarthy's methods, added, "methods are secondary." As to his allegation that Smith was "silent, puzzled, and uninformed," "that's obvious," Jones said, "to anyone who has seen her on the floor of the Senate."[148] Enhancing his boyish appeal, Jones launched a "poor man's campaign, from a trailer." With his family and small staff, he began traveling across the state. To poor potato farmers and fishermen, Jones forthrightly acknowledged his French-Canadian ancestry, still considered a source of stigma by many Mainers but positive for his audience. "Make Maine potatoes the main dish at the main meal," Jones said, to the delight of farmers.[149]

The only political role Smith had known was underdog, but as potentially threatening as a McCarthy-sponsored opponent was, she had reason for optimism from the beginning. Maine's politicos did not give Jones "a ghost of a chance," because he was a political unknown sponsored by outside money, the press reported.[150] The entire Maine congressional delegation, including a repentant Payne who now endorsed Smith "100 percent," declared their opposition to both out-of-state funds and personalities being injected into the campaign.[151] Governor Burton Cross told the press that he had "very high regard and respect" for Smith, and the Gannett chain, as well as the Bangor, Bath, and Rumford papers, all endorsed her.[152] Surprisingly, both Brewster and his wife signed Smith's renomination papers, and Senate colleagues braved McCarthy to endorse her. Homer Ferguson, Republican of Michigan, described Smith as "able and conscientious"; John Bricker, Republican of Ohio whose Bricker Amendment was under debate, said that she was "diligent and attentive to her duties"; Clyde Hoey, North Carolina Democrat, called Smith "one of the most valuable members of the Senate" because she had "sense, judgment, wisdom and discretion"; and Harry Byrd, a Virginia Democrat, commended her "facility for digging out the facts."[153] Better, in front of several senators and a reporter, Eisenhower called Smith his "favorite Senator" and added, "I mean what I say, not favorite woman Senator, but my favorite Senator."[154] At the same time as the troops circled the wagons in Smith's defense, Senator Potter fired Jones and declared that he was Smith's "friend."[155] Jones insisted that he had resigned, but the press learned that Jones had, without authorization, stated that Potter supported McCarthy's attack on the army, and that was why Potter fired him.

Primary among Smith's advantages in the 1954 campaign was Joseph McCarthy's disastrous decision to investigate the U.S. Army. The investigation proved both a diversion from Maine for McCarthy and, unlike the Department of State and the U.S. Congress, too sacrosanct an institution for him to attack. Or perhaps it was that after four years, the nation had witnessed his unseemly bullying, insulting, and humiliating tactics for too long, and without a single dangerous spy ring or despicable act of subversion uncovered. Even the theater of popping flashbulbs, scribbling reporters, and enthralled audiences in the ornate Senate-caucus-room-become-stage-set with America's aggressive protector relentlessly shouting, "Are you now or have you ever been a member of the Communist party?" had palled. The show had run too long, the critical reviews had multiplied, and the army had weapons of its own, foremost among them Boston attorney Joseph Welch, who represented the army and proved himself McCarthy's match. Fortunately for Smith, the Army-McCarthy hearings took place during the last two months, April and June, of her primary campaign against Jones. For the first time on television Americans had a first-row seat from which to watch McCarthy crudely snarl, accuse, and threaten. His shrill "point of order, Mr. Chairman, point of order," soon repelled viewers because it came to signal still another intemperate outburst and a transparent effort to keep the cameras on him. "McCarthy is not fighting the army," Robert Jones loyally proclaimed in Maine. "He is fighting Communists."[156] But as criticisms of McCarthy piled up, Jones said that the hearings were a "plot to destroy Senator McCarthy, to split the Republican party in order to lay the foundation for a socialistic administration in 1956."[157] Fearful of being caught in a backlash, Jones called on the Republican leadership to "gag" McCarthy's critics.[158] When that failed, Jones discounted the hearings as "absurd" and "a three-ring circus,"[159] and he said he was sure McCarthy did not mean it when he said General Ralph Zwicker was a "disgrace to his uniform."[160]

Smith's response proved less predictable. When Senator Stuart Symington, Democrat from Missouri, called her about the hearings, Smith assured him that she would vote with the Democrats on the committee against McCarthy's assault on the army. But since she had positioned herself under McCarthy's anti-Communist mantle, she competitively cross-examined Secretary of the Army Robert Stevens when he came before the Armed Services

Committee. The hearings were on the draft law for physicians, but Smith asked Stevens if the army was "coddling Communists," and when he replied that he was sure no one was, she persisted. "What effort was being made to find out if the army was coddling Communists," she asked, only to have Wilson again casually respond that "he hadn't run across any Communists but if they were there, they would be out as soon as the proof was in." "But do you have any plan to determine whether there is anyone coddling Communists in the Defense Department?" Smith pressed. "I do not pay much attention to it because I know it is not so," Wilson ineffectually replied. As relentless as McCarthy, if quieter, Smith pushed, "But do you have any plan; do you do anything about it?" "I do not need to because it is not true," was the best Stevens could do. McCarthy-like, Smith asked for names of "coddlers" but could not penetrate Stevens's insouciance.[161]

In Maine Smith campaigned as she always had. "Don't trade a record for a promise" was again her campaign slogan, and her practice, as before, was to come home only on weekends to campaign because Congress was in session. Not only was she "on the job," but this time the voting margin between the parties was also so close that "I don't dare be absent."[162] For the first time Smith claimed a perfect attendance record for 1953 and 1954 in the Senate, the only member who could do so, and more campaign evidence of her responsible, hard-working ethic. She also continued to be frugal in her spending. She refused to accept campaign contributions and relied on a volunteer campaign staff. With only twenty-two days left in the campaign, she had spent $810.25 to Jones's $2,085.28.

Desperate at the end of the primary battle, Jones announced that he was going "to take off the wraps" and "really go at Mrs. Smith."[163] He increased the pace of his already frenetic campaign, began making two or three speeches a day, concentrated on television coverage, and, according to one reporter, rushed around "like a frustrated toreador."[164] His rhetoric escalated also. Using the *Congressional Record* for evidence, Jones said Smith's attendance record meant only that she voted, not that she spoke out on issues or debated on the floor. She was a "do nothing, say nothing" senator who had done nothing for Maine, "absolutely nothing."[165] Jones also claimed that a man from a "liberal leftist group" had offered him $25,000 to drop out of the campaign. "Who's getting outside help," he asked, "Mrs. Smith or me?"[166] In his last mailing Jones described himself as "a personal disciple of Senator McCarthy's" who had "set out to drive Senator Smith from public life" because of her "hostility" to McCarthy.[167]

Toward the end, McCarthy cooperated by attacking a young lawyer in Joseph Welch's firm, and the nation watched on television as Welch rang the death knell on McCarthy. "Until this moment, senator, I think I never really gauged your cruelty or your recklessness," Welch sadly responded. When McCarthy angrily tried to cut off his response, memorably Welch blasted, "Have you no sense of decency, sir, at long last? Have you no sense of decency?" and with America behind him walked out on McCarthy.[168]

On election night, photographers found Smith in the kitchen of her Skowhegan home. The results exceeded Smith's expectations. In nineteen precincts Jones did not receive a single vote, and in the state Smith defeated him five to one. Her triumphant total was 96,457 to Jones's 19,336, and, with her total expenditures of $3,814.85, that came to about twenty-five cents a vote. "As Maine Goes the Nation Would Do Well to Follow," was one of the headlines Smith read the next morning, although she might have preferred another paper's choice: "As Maine Goes So Goes the Nation's Conscience." A third crowed "A Mighty Smith Is She,"[169] but most also mentioned McCarthy: "McCarthyite Snowed under in Maine Vote," "Senator Smith Beats Friend of McCarthy," "Victory Seen as Blow at McCarthy," "McCarthy Challenger Cut down in Maine Primary."[170] After Jones acknowledged his defeat in a concession telegram to Smith, he insisted that the defeat was his, not McCarthy's. "After all, I was the candidate," he wrote.[171]

Smith's victory was a body blow to McCarthy, because his political power had been his ability to defeat his critics. Now Eisenhower dared say that he was "highly pleased" about Smith's triumph, and her colleagues filled her office with congratulatory flowers, telegrams, and messages.[172] "The fact that a mere woman could give McCarthy a five-to-one shellacking in a conservative state like Maine," Bill Lewis said, "had a tremendous psychological effect on the Senate."[173]

Senator Charles Potter had difficulty understanding Smith's triumph. "Perhaps it was her cool, calm fearlessness," he speculated, "her refusal to panic, her ability to wipe off the mud and the poison." She handled McCarthy as if he was a "lawless adult delinquent," Potter continued, and "slapped him down with dignity."[174] At the end of June, she returned to Washington for the kill. Senator Ralph Flanders, Vermont Republican, introduced a censure resolution against McCarthy in July, and Smith immediately announced that she would vote for it. Majority leader William Knowland postponed the inevitable until the elections were over, but Smith had one triumphant moment of her own with McCarthy. One day before she returned to Maine and her almost forgotten Democratic opponent, she rode several times with McCarthy on the little subway train that connected the Senate Office Building with the Capitol to answer quorum and roll calls. On the last ride McCarthy commented nervously, "Margaret, we seem to be following each other and riding together." "Yes, Joe," she replied. "If you don't watch out, people will say that we are fellow travelers."[175]

Paul Adrian Fullam, professor of history and government from Colby College in Waterville, received the Democratic nomination for the Senate without a primary opponent. Being unchallenged was not unusual because before 1954 Maine had largely been a one-party state. In this general election, however, the resurgence of the Democratic party began. The revitalization of the Democrats was due largely to the personal appeal of a mostly unknown challenger to Governor Burton M. Cross, Edmund S. Muskie. When Fullam first arrived in Maine, he had been told by a Colby colleague, William J. Wilkinson, that "he would get nowhere in the State of Maine being a Democrat, so he had better be a Republican."[176] Over the years Fullam had, like many other Democrats, registered as a Republican in order "to make his vote count" in the only real election the state had, the primary.[177] But in 1954 with Muskie heading the ticket, the thirty-nine-year-old Fullam agreed to run against Smith in the interest of creating a two-party system. Muskie considered Fullam "a very attractive candidate" who could not win against Smith, "a formidable opponent," but who could "cut into her majority."[178]

Smith knew Fullam because she had lectured to his classes at Colby, but she did not pay him much attention until he began to attack her politically. Smith had always been thin-skinned, but now at the height of her popularity, she began to personalize criticisms as well as to continue advertising them as smears. Low-key but engaging and articulate, Fullam used humor against Smith and called the last-minute Republican campaign a "snow job"; he gave Republicans an "A for rhetoric but flunked the whole lot for content."[179] In another speech Fullam said, "They say vote for Ike and a Republican Congress and save General Motors, not save the world." "Confusion reigns in Washington, and I shudder to think what may happen," he told one audience.[180] Then Fullam challenged Smith's anti-Communist stand by calling for "aggressive containment"[181] of the Soviet Union because "1955 might be the year of a Soviet attack."[182] Republican mismanagement had left the United States unprepared. Smith herself, Fullam charged, voted for a $5 billion cut in the air force budget. "If we deal with the Soviets on the basis of what we can afford," he said, "we shall be selling our birthright for a message of pottage."[183] On 1 September in Rumford Fullam spoke on Smith's voting record, which he characterized "as a shame" and asked her a series of "are you proud of" questions on her votes.[184] Lewis, hearing about the speech but not having a copy, exaggerated it to Smith as Fullam's "pointing a finger of shame at her." Smith accepted Lewis's exaggeration and began referring to Fullam's attempt "to shame" her.[185]

Muskie observed that Smith surprised Democrats in Maine by interpreting Fullam's campaigning as "a personal attack on her" instead of the rather ordinary politicking it was.[186] As part of common political practice, the national Democratic leadership, enthusiastic about the rebirth of the party in Maine and determined to regain control of Congress, became involved in the election. In particular, John F. Kennedy, Democrat from Massachusetts elected to the Senate in 1952, came to Maine to campaign for Fullam. Smith saw this as a "personal affront" because Kennedy "had pretended to be a friend of hers.''[187] Retaliating, Smith linked Kennedy with McCarthy as the only two senators who had ever come to Maine to work against her.

As metaphor for the Democrats' resurgence, hurricane Edna swept through the state two days before the 12 September election. A freak storm that split into two eyes, Edna simultaneously devastated the coast and tore up the interior of the state. The storm washed out presumably impregnable bridges, ripped up ancient trees, and destroyed homes, businesses, and crops. Overwhelmed by the damage caused by the wind's fury and the torrents of rain, Governor Cross lost still more ground to Muskie, who also saw an advantage to a low voter turnout. A last-minute bit of sloganeering advised votes for "M and M, Margaret and Muskie," and neither of the candidates argued against a voter splitting the ticket.[188]

As unexpected and furious as Edna, Smith went on television the night before the election to blast Fullam. As with Robert Jones, she had not mentioned Fullam in her earlier campaigning, but now she maintained she wanted to "straighten the record," not "get votes."[189] She waited until election eve when "she felt the minimum number of votes would be affected," she told incredulous Democrats who realized Fullam would have no time to respond. In Portland at the WCSH-TV studio at 11:05 P.M. Smith "corrected" Fullam's "serious misrepresentations," "accusations," and "lies."[190] She portrayed herself as "personally attacked," "ridiculed," "accused," and "derided" by an opponent who had called her "unfit," guilty of "monstrous injustice," and "lacking in conscience," of all things. Now, Smith said, reading from an enumerated fifty-five-point typescript prepared by Lewis, she planned to answer each "finger of shame" pointed at her. With point number four, she promised, "At the end of this address I shall give you the biggest political surprise of this campaign. So keep tuned in." Smith proceeded, Fullam pointed out on the Friday following the election when the station gave him time to reply, to answer charges that he had not made and to exaggerate the ridiculous points he had used in the campaign. One charge Smith did not make was that she had been "smeared"; the word, for once, was absent. In point fifty-five she asked for the votes of Democrats and independents as well as Republicans, but the highlight of her best political performance ever was when she delivered the coup de grace. Dramatically, she held up her primary nomination papers and showed the audience signature number thirty-two, "Paul Fullam, Sidney, Maine."[191]

"The Sunday night you were on TV," Elsie M. Wyndham of Lisbon Falls wrote Smith, "I was alone in my living room, no, you were with me, honestly I felt you were right in the room with me, and when you held up the nomination paper I just clapped my hands I was so overjoyed."[192]

Fullam and his supporters were not. Accusing Smith of "McCarthyism," Fullam told the press the next day but too late for publication until after the election, "As Welch said to McCarthy, as sure as there is a God in Heaven, your evil ways will not prevail."[193]

"M and M" won, but Smith's 58 percent of the vote was, Walter Lippmann said, a "sensational decline" from the 71.4 percent she had received in 1948. Fullam, a political unknown who had never before been a candidate, polled 937 votes to Smith's 1,157 in Skowhegan, and for the first time Smith had a candidate who underspent her $2,850.37 to her $5,000 from the GOP Senatorial Campaign Committee.

Smith took the victory and ran, literally, around the world on a tour she had planned for Edward R. Murrow's "See It Now" program on CBS-TV. Murrow and his producer, Fred Friendly, had sent a crew to Maine during Smith's primary race against Robert Jones. The result had been a devastating composite of campaign clips that revealed Jones, Lewis said, as a "junior grade Joe McCarthy," who "aped Joe in mannerisms, hesitant and repeated phrases, tonal inflections, scowls, smiles."[194] Given their common animosity toward McCarthyism, Smith and Murrow developed a mutually beneficial relationship. In the interest of both his program and her political future, Murrow asked Smith to travel with CBS cameraman Charles Mack and soundman Bobby Huttenlock to interview a series of world leaders. Smith made it clear that the trip was "not official and not at government expense"; in fact, she would receive no fee. As for the censure vote on McCarthy, she "certainly would not miss that session," she told the press. No other senator had ever made such a trip, and Smith wanted to "talk with farmers in Italy and France and Southeast Asia who have been attracted to Communism and figure out why. I even want to argue with a Communist." Accompanied by Lewis, on 7 October Smith flew from New York's Idlewild Airport on Pan American for London.[195]

Smith's tour of European capitals and brief audiences with world leaders became the prototype of such junkets for later presidential candidates. Unique at the time, the trip gave Smith stature in international affairs as she met with a dazzling array of European politicians: Winston Churchill, Anthony Eden, Aneurin Bevan, Pierre Mendès-France, Charles de Gaulle, Edgar Fauré, Georges Bidault, Konrad Adenauer, and V. M. Molotov. She delighted the press with a story about brandy-devotee Churchill's drinking a glass of water and commenting, "I do that just to show you that I can."[196] Meeting with Mendès-France, Smith looked down to see that she was wearing one black and one blue shoe. When asked by a reporter what she did, she replied, "I just put my best foot forward."[197] Smith insisted that she not meet only officials but also "the little people . . . the common everyday people." In London she spent an afternoon with a middle-class London family, and in Germany she "studied people on the farms from the train" and went into the stores of East Berlin.[198] Veteran columnist Irene Corbally Kuhn criticized Smith's trip as "foolish" and said that the senator "simpers like a schoolgirl for the TV cameras." Smith "gushed" over Churchill, Kuhn wrote, "like a bobby-soxer keening for crying crooner Johnny Ray," and the press "shuddered" and felt "sorry for her."[199]

In East Berlin, although traveling with State Department official Elmer Cox, policemen arrested the two CBS newsmen, Lewis, and Cox. Angered by the television camera, the policemen started toward Smith, but CBS reporter Richard C. Hottelet said that he "brushed aside a few Communist busybodies who were wearing Communist badges and bundled Mrs. Smith into the auto." A policeman tried to stop the car, but Hottelet took off down the busy Alexanderplatz while out the rear window Smith watched four plainclothesmen take Lewis and the others to police headquarters. There they were detained for an hour until Cox could establish their identities. He had Lewis and the others show their tickets to Moscow, and "that impressed them; they said we could go."[200] Back home, McCarthy diehards, hearing of the incident, referred to Smith as "Moscow Maggie" and wrote about the "kidnapping of her administrative aide."[201] "But tell us, Marg," the *New Hampshire Sunday News* asked editorially, "after a good look at [Soviet Premier] Malenkov's methods, are you still going to vote to censure Senator McCarthy?"[202]

In 1954 visas to the Soviet Union were rare, but in the previous eighteen months or so, a few American officials, journalists, and students had been allowed to visit. Still, Smith was the first U.S. senator to be welcomed in Moscow since the 1930s. Her party traveled there by train from East Berlin through Prague, which, she said, was not the gay city she had expected but "gray, ashen . . . like a city whose soul had been killed, whose heart had been torn out" with people like "zombies."[203] Ambassador Charles Bohlen met Smith's party and made arrangements for her to have her hair cut and to visit a Russian fashion show, if not to visit with Malenkov. Smith did visit with Foreign Minister V. M. Molotov for a surprising hour and told the press that the filmed interview would be titled, "I Talked to a Communist." She enjoyed walking the streets of Moscow, riding the subway, eating in the restaurants, and visiting a collective farm, hospital, and elementary school. Instead of the benefits of direct communication being the result of the Soviet visit, an exacerbation of tensions was. "I would not be surprised," Smith unwisely told the press as soon as she left Moscow, "if relations [between the United States and the Soviet Union] would be broken off at any time by either side." Her intemperate remark came as a result of her concern for the wives of American envoys who had been involved in a picture-taking incident in a Russian factory. They had been labeled "undesirable" by Soviet officials and asked to leave the country.[204] Neither Washington nor Moscow had considered a rupture in relations because of the incident, and the Soviet press accused Smith of "hooliganism," calling her an "Amazon warmonger hiding behind a rose."[205] For Smith these were the best of all possible headlines to herald her return to the United States for the censure vote on Joseph McCarthy.

Smith did not assume a leadership role in marshaling votes against McCarthy. Instead, her New England colleague, seventy-four-year-old Ralph E.

Flanders, led the final assault by introducing Senate Resolution 301: "Resolved, that the conduct of the Senator from Wisconsin, Mr. McCarthy, is unbecoming a member of the United States Senate, is contrary to senatorial traditions, and tends to bring the Senate into disrepute, and such conduct is hereby condemned." A devout Mormon from Utah, Arthur Watkins, chaired the select committee of three Republicans and three Democrats to which the leadership referred the resolution with the requirement that the committee report before the Eighty-third Congress adjourned. McCarthy did not consider the committee a threat and referred to it as "the unwitting handmaiden of the Communist conspiracy."[206] As intemperate as ever, he pressed Smith for approval of Robert Jones on the Government Operations Committee staff and of Owen Brewster as Roy Cohn's replacement as the committee's chief counsel. When Senator Barry Goldwater of Arizona attempted to secure an apology from McCarthy to those senators whom he had insulted as a way to avoid censure, McCarthy threw his pen across the room and swore at Goldwater. The Senate met as a committee of the whole on 2 December 1954 to hear Watkins report that his committee unanimously recommended censure and to ask, irrespective of Smith's role in McCarthy's downfall, "Do we have the manhood in the Senate to stand up to a challenge of that kind?"[207] Perversely, Smith's only comment during the debate was that it was "strange that we can verbally attack anyone else without restraint and with full protection and yet hold ourselves above the same type of criticism here on the Senate floor."[208] For the sixth time in its 163-year history the Senate, hushed and tense, voted sixty-seven to twenty-two that McCarthy's conduct was "contrary to senatorial traditions and is hereby condemned."[209]

Censure did not hold McCarthy responsible for assaulting the Bill of Rights, remove him from the Senate, take away his vote, or withdraw him from his committees, but Robert Byrd, West Virginia Democrat, called it "an awesome punishment" from which McCarthy "suffered mightily."[210] His colleagues shunned him, the press ignored him, and President Eisenhower hosted a reception at the White House to which every member of the Senate except McCarthy was invited. Twice during his purgatory McCarthy contacted Smith. Once he called to commend a vote of hers, only to have Smith blast him in writing that she was surprised because earlier he had referred to her statements as "boneheaded" and to her as "a lesson why women should not be in politics," "a woman scorned," and a "left-wing apologist."[211] Recognizing those statements as the ones in *U.S.A. Confidential,* McCarthy called Smith again to say, "I just want you to know, Margaret, that there is not a word of truth in what [Mortimer] said."[212] A longtime alcoholic, McCarthy began to drink more, and two and a half years after censure in May 1957 at age forty-eight, he died in office.

Even in death McCarthy continued to plague Smith. The staff of the Government Operations Committee prepared a resolution of condolence to

McCarthy's wife and daughter that Smith considered laudatory of his goals and methods. The resolution praised his work as chairman of the Investigations Subcommittee and stated that McCarthy had "conducted a most aggressive and courageous fight against communism, striving constantly to awaken the American people to the threat of the international Communist conspiracy to our government." Smith wrote committee chairman John McClellan that she would vote for a resolution that expressed sympathy only; she could not "conscientiously subscribe" to praising McCarthy. She realized that it would have been "politically expedient" to sign the resolution quietly because her failure to do so would be "distorted and exploited," but she was "willing to pay that price in order to live with my conscience." Alone at the end in her opposition as she had been in the beginning, Smith was the only member of the committee to refuse to sign the resolution.[213]

The press picked up the story, and the reaction Smith expected was forthcoming. She was also excoriated in an avalanche of mail that condemned her as "nasty," "narrow-minded," "unpatriotic," "disgraceful," and "contemptible" and referred to "the joy in the Kremlin tonight" and to "her strange conscience."[214] Lewis saw it differently. With the exception of her expulsion from the Investigations Subcommittee, he believed Smith had "baffled, outwitted, outmaneuvered, and defeated" McCarthy at every turn. "And McCarthy, in attempting to kill Margaret Chase Smith," Lewis wrote, "had dug his own political grave."[215]

Margaret Madeline poses with her parents, Carrie and George Chase. (Photo courtesy of the Margaret Chase Smith Library.)

Miss Margaret Chase at age six in 1903. (Photo courtesy of the Margaret Chase Smith Library.) (Photographer: Scott Davis)

Margaret Chase, second from right, on the 1916 championship Skowhegan High School basketball team. (Photo courtesy of the Margaret Chase Smith Library.)

There was more to Margaret Chase Smith's political career than roses, recipes, and roll calls. She was the most influential woman in the history of American politics with her thirty-two-year career in Congress. (Photo courtesy of the Margaret Chase Smith Library.)

Congressman Clyde H. Smith, circa 1938–1939. (Photo courtesy of the Margaret Chase Smith Library.)

Major General William Chesley Lewis, Jr. (Photo courtesy of the Margaret Chase Smith Library.)

During a 1951 visit, the Atlanta Telephone Women honored Senator Smith at a breakfast and asked her to pose before a Southern Bell Telephone switchboard. Smith had worked part-time as an operator while she was in high school and full-time for several years after her graduation. (Photo courtesy of the Margaret Chase Smith Library.)

Smith is with President Dwight David Eisenhower whom she secured as a visitor to Maine and to her small frame house overlooking
the Kennebec River. Smith has on the hat and white gloves she
commonly wore to the Senate. (Photo courtesy of the Margaret
Chase Smith Library.)

Smith and Richard M. Nixon were adversaries from 1951 when Joseph McCarthy replaced her on his investigations subcommittee with the newly elected Nixon. In 1952 and 1956 Smith's hopes for a vice presidential nomination were dashed when Nixon received Eisenhower's blessings instead. Nevertheless, Smith campaigned for Nixon during his 1960 presidential campaign. August 1960. (Photo courtesy of the Margaret Chase Smith Library.)

Smith is pictured at the White House on 16 July 1963 with President John F. Kennedy (to the right of Smith) and Senator Edmund Muskie (far left). (Photo courtesy of the Margaret Chase Smith Library.)

Smith and Lyndon B. Johnson served in the House of Representatives together and developed a long-lived friendship from their years on the Naval Affairs Committee. They both entered the Senate in 1949, and Smith considered Johnson the best majority leader under whom she served. (Photo courtesy of the Margaret Chase Smith Library.)

Chapter Six

THE FIRST FEMALE COLD
WARRIOR

*On the morning of 24 September 1963 Margaret Chase Smith took the seat
on the front row of the Senate that she had held since 1949. Dressed as
usual in a plain suit and heels but minus the hat and white gloves she had
worn since the 1940s, she appeared more solemn than usual. In startling
defiance of tradition, the Senate had voted for a group photograph of themselves sitting at their desks. Smith sat erect, chin lifted, unsmiling; her mind
was on the vote to be taken when the photographer finished.*

*She quietly rose to make the last speech before the Senate voted on the
Limited Test Ban Treaty, which outlawed nuclear testing in the atmosphere,
water, and outer space. In case anyone had forgotten her patent on politics
of conscience, she compared the emotional charges of her colleagues on both
sides of the treaty with what she had experienced in the 1950s. "I know—
because I was a target," she said, of the tactics of "guilt by association"
and "trial by accusation." She asked, "Have we lost all sense of reasona-
bleness? Cannot members of the U.S. Senate have honest differences of opinion without being charged with mental deficiency or treason?"[1]*

*When the clerk called Smith's name, she voted no with more moral cer-
tainty than she had when she read the Declaration of Conscience.*

During the post-McCarthy years, Smith blossomed like the rose she favored. She progressed from the "smeared woman" to the "woman of conscience" and basked in her moral certainty. As secure as a politician ever is,
with another six-year term before her, Smith chose to exercise her authority
in the theater McCarthy had vacated. In her long-nurtured role as military
expert she decided to confront the evil of world communism and became
the nation's first female cold warrior. Ironically what that meant was con-

tinued confrontation with the American military establishment she had long championed.

Smith's earliest experience in this context had come in the aftermath of the stalemated Korean War. Led to expect first victory and then unification of North and South Korea during the war, Americans instead saw their forces humiliated by the Chinese and the government humbled in stymied peace negotiations.

"If the current negotiations don't produce peace but do break down and war is resumed," Smith wrote, "then drop the atomic bomb on these barbarians who obviously in their past atrocities have proved that they have no concept of a desire for decency." Excessive in her zeal even by Cold War standards, Smith believed that "maybe the atomic bomb will bring the Red barbarians to their senses as it did the Japanese." "I know that some will protest that the atomic bomb is an immoral weapon. I agree that it is. But so are all other man-killing weapons of war," she continued. "War itself is immoral because it is nothing less than organized murder. Yet when we are attacked we do not refuse to fight simply because we know that war is immoral."[2]

A confused public looking for someone to blame voted the Democrats out in 1952 and gave Smith her second, and last, experience with a Republican majority in the Senate. She did not have the seniority for a committee chairmanship, but Leverett Saltonstall of Massachusetts, chairman of Armed Services, appointed her chair of the Preparedness Subcommittee investigating a rumored ammunition shortage during the Korean War. Scenting another possible scapegoat, Smith accepted the assignment with righteous eagerness.

President-elect Dwight David Eisenhower initiated the concern about an ammunition shortage when he returned from fulfilling his campaign promise to go to Korea. "In the strictly military sphere," he reported, "certain problems of supply have reached rather serious proportions and require early correction."[3] Then General James Van Fleet compounded the public's concern when he came back from a twenty-two-month tour in Korea as commander of the Eighth Army and told the Committee on Armed Services that a "serious and sometimes critical" shortages of supplies existed. "We could have won in the Spring of 1951," Van Fleet said, "and should have." "I cannot understand this situation," Robert Byrd of West Virginia responded. "We have appropriated $160 billion to the military for the last three fiscal years, spent $103 billion, and have not got enough ammunition to fight a war in Korea. This is a national scandal."[4] Although the secretary of defense, the secretary of the army, and the army chief of staff all testified to the contrary, and Eisenhower publicly supported them, the politics of the situation demanded a public investigation. Smith received this "political hot potato," as her subcommittee staffer, Fred Rhodes, called it and went to work.[5] Armed Services accepted that the shortages were real and authorized

Smith's committee to determine "the officials and conditions responsible" for it.[6]

With Byrd, John Sherman Cooper of Kentucky, Robert Hendrickson of New Jersey, and Estes Kefauver of Tennessee as members, the subcommittee first dealt with the most important controversy: whether their hearings should be televised. The hearings involving Truman firing General Douglas MacArthur and some of the Joseph McCarthy investigations had been televised, but many senators objected to the intrusion of the camera and the potential result of sensationalism. Smith did not object and in fact led and then pushed the subcommittee to agree on televised hearings.

Aware of the "intense" public interest, Smith, according to Rhodes, carefully orchestrated the hearings.[7] Like Byrd who said that the charges of an ammunition shortage shocked him more than anything else in Washington in years, Smith wanted answers and wanted the political credit for obtaining them. As the first woman to conduct a major senatorial investigation, Smith also wanted to avoid the pitfalls associated with gender. Her intention was to be prepared, thorough, tough, and, above all, fair. Accordingly, she announced that her objectives were "to obtain the facts and the truth, to determine responsibility, and to put in place safeguards to prevent future shortages."[8]

The hearings began in April 1953 in the Armed Services Committee room, ornately decorated with three huge crystal chandeliers, a fireplace with a massive marble mantle, an enormous gilt-leaf mirror, and a twenty-foot-long conference table. Smith entered on the stroke of 10:00 A.M. to find the room crowded to the doors with extra chairs, six tall television cameras, and their blinding lights. Quietly she eased her way through the crowd to her place in the center of the far side of the table. Across from Smith stood the first witness, Van Fleet, at near military attention and in uniform. Smith pleasantly greeted him and shook his hand, and the other committee members, as they arrived, followed her example, with Kefauver, who arrived late, the last. Then Smith quietly tapped her pencil against a glass and began the meeting by reading an eight-page statement on the purpose of the investigation. With no histrionics or extemporaneous comments, Smith began questioning Van Fleet, as she had always done in hearings, by following the script Bill Lewis had prepared for her.

Van Fleet repeated his accusation that the ammunition shortage caused the United States to lose the Korean War, because the shortage "substantially restricted the action of our troops and endangered our defensive lines."[9] He related a June 1951 amphibious landing behind enemy lines, which he was convinced "could have destroyed Communist forces" but he was unable to carry out.[10] "Should the enemy start something which is unpredictable," he concluded, "then do we have enough to meet this offensive, and I say 'No.' "[11] Other military commanders supported Van Fleet while members of the administration blamed "the system,"[12] "waste,"[13] and Congress. Witnesses lined up to testify that confusion over the purpose of the war (to win? to fight communism? to police the area? to manifest American power?) led to a failure of industry to respond.

The press reported that Smith was "fair and has plenty of courage"; "she is one person whom the high brass has not been able to soften up."[14] Smith started each day's session on time with a summary of the previous day's testimony, the first chair in press memory to do so. She kept a "tight rein," one reporter wrote, on the hearings, and when witnesses responded that they did not have her requested information, she said, "You'll look it up for us, won't you, General."[15] The next day she went back to her original request and incurred, several reporters wrote, the Pentagon's "displeasure" for her persistence.[16] Determined to fix responsibility, Smith tried to follow Van Fleet's daily reports of shortages to his superiors, but no one would admit to receiving them. She then tried to untangle the web of ordnance supply and learned that one order for ammunition passed through forty-two separate agencies and had to be cleared by more than two hundred people before it was contracted to a defense industry. Frustrated, Smith had the subcommittee adopt a resolution requiring the army to provide the names and positions of everyone from beginning to end who handled an ammunition requisition. One senator suggested instead that they should resolve that the Joint Chiefs of Staff be fired.

Smith sent the interim report of the committee to perennial presidential adviser Bernard Baruch, who responded with "admiration" for her work and suggestions. Baruch's recommendations and the committee's acceptance of them led eventually to the United States' going on permanent military footing during the Cold War and a proliferation of congressional staffers to be certain the military never again placed the United States in a vulnerable position.[17] The basic mistake of President Truman, his National Security Council, several members of his cabinet, and the Joint Chiefs of Staff, the committee report concluded, was "miscalculating the aggressive designs of International Communism. A repetition of this type of miscalculation and inability to plan for the defense and security of the United States could result in catastrophe for this nation."[18]

Later Smith said that "what we found in that shocking story" about an ammunition shortage "made a very deep and lasting impression on me. I do not want to see that tragic condition repeated."[19] She immediately had another opportunity to buttress American defenses when the Eisenhower administration decided to reduce the air force to 114 wings by cutting the service's appropriations by $5 billion. The Committee on Appropriations conducted hearings on the proposal, with Smith as a member concerned that "history will not repeat itself as on the tragic experience 3 and 4 years ago when the then President cut our Air Force down shortly before he ordered our intervention into the Korean War."[20]

Eisenhower's new secretary of defense, Charles E. Wilson, who had been told by his predecessor, Robert A. Lovett, that he would have to spend six months of every year dealing with Congress, defended the cuts to Smith. Unprepared and uninformed, Wilson smoked cigar after cigar during the hearings and exasperated Smith with his delaying tactic of small talk about the weather. "I'm sure you didn't come here to talk about the weather," she snapped and turned to her inevitable list of questions.[21] "Is the new budget based on economy or security," she asked, and received a muddled reply. "How can you cut more than $5 billion from the Air Force appropriations, cut back the Air Force's strength to 114 wings and still say that the Air Force will be more powerful?" Smith continued and elicited a more imprecise response. Altogether Smith had a list of thirty-two questions: "How has Soviet strength changed . . . so that we can reduce our forces?" Is there now "less danger of aggression?" "Hasn't the main deterrent been our long-range Air Force, with its atomic capability?" "If the Communists . . . break out of containment elsewhere, as in Indo China, do we plan to send . . . American troops to contain them?"[22]

One reporter present commented that "the nation's tragedy" was that Mr. Wilson was not only unable to answer but also that he acted as if many of "the questions were new to him."[23] The political cartoonist Herblock published a cartoon of Wilson saying that less is more, and Smith asking that he explain that to her.[24] Committee member and former air force secretary Stuart Symington of Missouri counted eleven times that Smith asked about the position of the Joint Chiefs on the cuts and never received a direct answer. The publicity on these hearings strengthened Smith's earned reputation for being a tough examiner. "She's unbelievably meticulous," one senator said. "She comes in with a good case or she doesn't come in at all. She's a very gracious woman, and she doesn't like to pick a fight, but the questions she asks can be very sharp. God help the man who gives her a smart answer. Give her a horsy answer and she'll fly all over you."[25]

Although Smith learned that the Joint Chiefs had been "told, not asked" about the cuts and told only "a few hours" before their public announcement, she was the only committee member to cause a "row," the press said.[26] The reason was that air force chief of staff General Nathan F. Twining, chairman of the Joint Chiefs Admiral Arthur W. Radford, army chief General Matthew B. Ridgway, and naval chief Admiral Robert Carney all refused to protest the cuts. Only retiring air force chief General Hoyt S. Vandenburg opposed the cuts, and even he did not, in Smith's opinion, "feel strongly and deeply enough on it to take issue with the President." Smith concluded that if "military discipline" silenced witnesses, surely they did "not feel deep down in their hearts that tragic consequences will be caused by this cut."[27] Reluctantly she voted with the majority to cut a military budget that had grown from a pre–Korean War $15 billion to $50 billion in 1952 back to $40 billion in 1953.

In 1957 when the air force decided to give a star to a star, Senator Smith again confronted the military establishment. The issue this time was the promotion of James Maitland Stewart, better known as the actor Jimmy Stewart, to brigadier general in the Air Force Reserve. A longtime advocate of the reserve forces, Smith received information on Stewart and the ten others on the same promotion list from reserve officers who claimed that deserving men were being overlooked in favor of celebrities. In her own office Smith had, in her opinion, proof of the complaint, because Bill Lewis was a colonel in the Air Force Reserves and eligible for promotion.

At one of their usual "end-of-the-day conferences," as Smith called them, she told Lewis that she wanted to check out the eligibility of those on the promotion list. Smith cautioned, "You know, Bill, if I do investigate, you must realize you will be accused of getting me to do it. You will take a lot of abuse." "So will you," he responded, "but I can't ask you to refuse to investigate." "Then it's settled," Smith concluded.[28]

Smith came to the Armed Services Committee meeting girded for battle and armed by Lewis with a large notebook of research materials and a long list of questions. She found not only a committee expecting routine confirmation but also the legendary Lieutenant General Emmett "Rosie" O'Donnell, air force chief of personnel, waiting to testify. A hero to many as a decorated officer in both World War II and Korea and to others as a West Point athlete and coach, O'Donnell confidently presented his nominees as deserving men. In contradiction, Smith asked why Stewart was being promoted over nineteen hundred other eligible colonels when he had had only nine days of training in eleven years and could not fly any of the current air force planes. O'Donnell used Stewart's World War II record of flying twenty bombing missions over Germany and being decorated for bravery as his justification. Unspoken but in everyone's mind were the roles Stewart had played in *The Spirit of St. Louis* as Charles A. Lindbergh and in *Strategic Air Command* on the Eisenhower administration's new preparedness program. Smith continued questioning O'Donnell on the other nominees, with the predictable result that her homework was clearly better than his. Soon his angry, flushed face revealed the reason for his nickname as he continued to bluster and to make mistakes in fact, each of which Smith noted. In the marathon three-hour session, Smith clearly had not only the facts but also the upper hand. She was herself a reserve lieutenant colonel who had put in her required fifteen-day training period every year since 1947. In addition, she had written the 1954 Reserve Officers Personnel Act, which established promotion criteria. Secure in the correctness of her own position, Smith resented O'Donnell's "openly derogatory" attitude toward her and his implications that she was "making misrepresentations" or "did not know what I was talking about."[29]

The committee honored Smith's objections and rejected Stewart's promotion for the time being. What kept the issue alive and allowed it to fester into what many called "one of the bitterest feuds Washington has witnessed" was Smith's actions the next day.[30] She entered into the *Congressional Record* what she saw as the facts but what others, certainly O'Donnell, saw as a bitter attack on him. First, Smith chastised O'Donnell for defending Stewart's unqualified promotion to what would have been the third leadership position in the Strategic Air Command in the next war. "Does that make sense?" she asked. Then she said O'Donnell had engaged in "extensive false testimony" and "betrayed a shocking lack of knowledge" before the Committee on Armed Services. To protect himself, O'Donnell had next engaged in "wholesale rewriting" of the committee transcript, which had been given to him as a common courtesy to correct grammatical errors. He changed his answers on sixty-two pages of the eighty-three-page transcript.[31] Smith had considered making a few changes in the transcript to improve her grammar, but Lewis advised her not to make any changes. "You give them something to put their hat on, Senator, and they'll end up putting a whole wardrobe on," he said.[32]

Jimmy Stewart, true to his nice guy image, did not remonstrate with Smith over the beating he took in Congress and in the press. Instead he quietly said that he had been "honored to receive the nomination by President Eisenhower and the Air Force" and affirmed that he would do his best to fulfill his duty requirements.[33] O'Donnell was a different matter. He announced that he was "shocked at the harsh language of her assertion" and was "at a loss to understand her action." He had answered the "full gamut" of questions "to the best of my ability and knowledge at the time," and when he had received the transcript "with instruction to correct it, I did just that."[34]

After that, the situation became byzantine, with Smith rebutting O'Donnell's statement paragraph by paragraph and rumors and accusations beginning to fly about town. Senator Styles Bridges of New Hampshire, a friend of Smith and defender of the Eisenhower administration, tried to end the conflict before it got out of hand, but Smith would have none of it. Angered by her adamancy, Bridges said that "she's the hardest woman in the world to deal with. I give up."[35] Smith alleged, without naming Bridges, that a senator had privately told her, "Miss Margaret, I am authorized by the Air Force to warn you that if you don't remove your objections, your name will be blackened from coast to coast along with that of Bill Lewis." When Smith refused, the senator added as carrot to stick, "Miss Margaret, if you will relent and let these nominations be approved, I promise you I will do everything I can to get Bill Lewis made a General." "Senator, you don't know either Bill Lewis or me very well," Smith replied. "I have no intention of withdrawing my opposition."[36]

Drew Pearson broke the story in the press under the headline, "Woman Senator Defeats Brass," and referred to the "backstage battle" as "rough." "Air Force propagandists," Pearson wrote, were putting out stories that Bill Lewis was "holding up other promotions because he was not promoted himself." Other rumors were that Smith was "irked" because she wanted to be commander of the WAFs and wanted her reserve commission, which expired on her sixtieth birthday, 14 December, extended so no one would know her age. In his notoriously sexist manner, Pearson affirmed Smith by ending his column, "Moral: It doesn't pay to argue with a lady."[37]

Smith identified the air force propagandist as Stephen F. Leo, former director of public relations for the air force, whom she asserted was coordinating "the publicity campaign to discredit her."[38] "Smear stories were planted by Air Force representatives," she wrote, "against me with various segments of the press."[39]

The feud reached the comic strips when the cartoonist for the Steve Canyon strip had Canyon's promotion blocked, and when a character asked why, the reply was, "Probably can't get by Senator Margaret Chase Smith."[40] Amused, Smith said that she had never understood why Canyon had not been promoted earlier "unless it was because of the restrictions placed in the regulations by the Regulars against the Reservists on extended active duty."[41]

Not noted for humor, Smith engaged in a public exchange over Stewart's promotion with an air force officer who said Stewart's role in *Strategic Air Command* alone justified his promotion. "You do not seriously believe Jimmy Stewart rates a Brigadier Generalship for playing in a movie. . . . That surely cannot be considered Reserve duty and participation!" When her opponent said, "Yes, he did," Smith countered with, "Then why don't you make June Allyson a Brigadier General for playing the female leader in *Strategic Air Command*."[42]

In 1959 Eisenhower nominated O'Donnell for commander in chief, Pacific Air Forces, and Jimmy Stewart again for brigadier general. Before the Armed Services Committee met on the nominations, Smith wrote to chairman Richard Russell on 19 May that she could not vote for O'Donnell's promotion because of his "serious misrepresentations and untruthful statements" in 1957. These actions, she believed, indicated "an attitude of defiance and arrogance toward the Committee" that she thought continued on O'Donnell's part. Smith also faulted O'Donnell's management of personnel, which she had been told by "many well-informed persons" was the "greatest weakness of the United States Air Force." Then on the last page of her five-page, single-spaced letter, Smith got to the point. She charged O'Donnell with "personal attacks and smears" against her, of making "malicious statements against me," and of causing "false statements in the newspapers, magazines, radio and television against my integrity and character." Because of her experience, she was disqualifying herself from voting on O'Donnell and did not want what had happened to her "to in any way influence" committee members.[43] By a vote of twelve to one, Armed Services promoted O'Donnell, with Harry Byrd casting the lone negative vote.

On the same day as the O'Donnell vote, Smith confounded her party and the president once more. Lewis L. Strauss, Eisenhower's controversial nominee for secretary of commerce, was up for confirmation, and, true to her past practice, Smith had not announced how she would vote. She studied the transcript of Strauss's testimony and questioned Senator Clinton Anderson of New Mexico who opposed the nomination because of Strauss's actions while he was chairman of the Atomic Energy Commission. Strauss had used, in the opinion of his critics, McCarthy-like tactics to remove the security clearance of scientist Robert Oppenheimer. "I had no idea how I was going to vote on Mr. Strauss," Smith said, "until in the third day of hearings he defeated himself." He gave "half facts, misrepresentations, and challenged the integrity of official transcripts."[44]

On the day of the vote Smith said she "changed into a bright red dress" because "sometimes when I'm feeling a little low I put on a red dress, and went over to the Senate."[45] Before a packed gallery and on an issue the White House saw as a party test vote, Smith voted against Strauss. A loud "Oh" from the gallery drowned out the angry "No" from the Republican senators but did not cover Goldwater's "God damn it" as he slammed his fist onto his desk. "She won't get one cent of money from my committee for reelection."[46]

By a vote of forty-nine to forty-six, Strauss became the eighth cabinet nominee in history to be rejected and the first since 1925, when the Senate turned down Calvin Coolidge's nomination of Charles B. Warren for attorney general. "I don't care how she votes," a party leader told the press anonymously, "but the decent thing would have been for her to tell us ahead of time, so we would have had time to protect ourselves."[47] According to *Life* magazine, Smith "had been infuriated when her party colleagues refused to back her fight" against O'Donnell, and she refused "in turn to view the Strauss nomination as a party matter."[48] Smith saw it differently; she had done the right thing. "I like integrity and I like others to be honest," she said. "I could not vote for that man."[49]

Not long afterward, the air force again nominated Jimmy Stewart for promotion. With another loose-leaf notebook filled with documents and "undoubtedly prepared by Mr. Lewis," May Craig said, Smith again fought his promotion.[50] The senator complained to the committee that although Stewart "lived in California and there were SAC bases in California," the air force had hastily sent him to Maine before the hearing for the training she had faulted him for not receiving earlier. "It was clear and obvious," she maintained, "that this was done deliberately to embarrass me in my home state."[51] In his laid-back, aw-shucks manner, Stewart joined in the criticism of Smith with references that she "squared her jaw" at him, and he said, "I'm not sure that the Senator fully understood that nobody was expecting me to climb into a modern jet bomber and fly it."[52] A friend reassured Stewart by saying maybe Smith never saw any of his movies, but Stewart replied that maybe the problem was that she had.

Smith pointed out that the air force now had Stewart assigned as the chief of staff for the Fifteenth Air Force and managed to hold up his promotion for four months. Finally the air force changed Stewart's mobilization assignment to the information office, albeit seventeen months after Smith had first suggested it in 1957. Stewart maintained that he had been slated for information duty before Smith's criticisms, but she let that pass. He also completed the bare minimum training required for promotion right before the committee voted, and Smith contented herself with the observation that Stewart still had the "poorest and smallest" reserve training of any of the twenty-nine officers on the new promotion list.[53] Nonetheless, to end the impasse, she allowed the star to receive a star. Appropriately, Stewart was on location filming a war movie and costumed in an officer's shirt when the film's technical adviser, a retired army brigadier general, pinned the stars on his collar.

On the same promotion list, Senator Barry Goldwater of Arizona involved himself in the affair by sending Styles Bridges a list of questions Smith had asked of a Pentagon officer for answers in reference to Goldwater's activities as a reserve officer. This "indicates the extent to which her Administrative Assistant is going," Goldwater wrote, "to effectively block promotions in the Reserve." Goldwater concluded by asking Bridges to request a "background sketch" of Lewis from the air force.[54] Goldwater called Smith to say, "If my name being on those orders causes you discomfort, I'll be glad to withdraw my name," but said she replied, "Oh, no, no, no, it's not you; it's Stewart's background." About Lewis, Goldwater learned that he had gone "to all the schools he could find and took correspondence courses in the schools he couldn't get to. So he was qualified."[55] Smith never challenged Goldwater directly, and he was promoted along with Stewart.[56]

By the end of the 1950s, Smith concluded that winning the arms race with the Soviet Union was as good for Maine as for the United States, which was to say it was good politics. "Maine is just one big air base," she said about the importance of Loring Air Force Base in her home state and could have added to the militarization of Maine the intercontinental missile bases in Arrostook County, the atomic submarine construction at Kittery Naval Shipyard, and the building of two guided missile destroyers at Bath Iron Works.[57] Before the end of the decade there was an important radar installation at Topsham, a missile base at Presque Isle, and a tanker unit at the Brunswick Naval Air Station. By 1959 only the paper-pulp industry surpassed the federal government's payroll in Maine, and the state, Smith proudly concluded, was "one of the most important advance fortresses within the continental limits of the United States."[58]

Smith also succeeded in passing legislation that raised the wages paid at the Portsmouth Naval Base next to Kittery, Maine, to equal those paid by the government at the Boston Naval Yard. For ten years the navy had resisted efforts to, in Smith's words, "correct this injustice," because of cost-of-living differences in the two areas.[59] Now the navy persuaded the president to veto

Smith's bill. Advised to drop the issue by Republican leaders because the Congress had not overridden one of Eisenhower's vetoes, Smith refused and forced the vote. Republican minority leader William Knowland defended the president and said that Eisenhower planned to announce later in the day a wage increase for Kittery workers, so there was no need for override. Smith criticized the president's waiting "until the very last minute with a desperate eleventh hour promise." He was too late—"ten years too late"—Smith argued, but, in tandem with Knowland, Karl Mundt moved to recommit the issue to committee. "Senator Smith jumped to her feet and moved" to table Mundt's motion, Bill Lewis said, and "almost instantly the Senate roared its approval. . . . Later Mundt told Senator Smith that she had acted so fast and devastatingly that he never knew what hit him." The vote was sixty-nine to twenty to override "the President's cherished, spotless record," and, according to an observer, the vote was really 69 for Smith to 20 for Eisenhower." Majority leader Lyndon Johnson agreed and called the vote "the greatest personal victory he had ever seen in the Senate."[60] Although a majority in the House voted to override, the issue failed for lack of a two-thirds margin. The president had the Department of Navy order the announced raise anyway.

The result of Smith's militarization of Maine was, she realized, to make the state "a prime target for Russian attacks,"[61] but she believed that the state and the nation would "survive any onslaught of a godless country that makes its advancements through enslavement of its people."[62]

While Smith persistently confronted the president, she championed his controversial secretary of state, John Foster Dulles. Known as a liberal Republican on domestic issues, on foreign policy Smith was a conservative and supported the party's platform criticisms of the Democrats' containment policy as "futile" and "immoral."[63] She agreed with Dulles's call for massive retaliation with nuclear weapons to halt Communist aggression, a policy the press dubbed "brinkmanship."

When Eisenhower moved away from Dulles and tried to ease Cold War tensions through summit meetings with Stalin's successor, Nikita Khrushchev, Smith was wary. In one of the series of radio broadcasts she did in Maine for May Craig, Smith rebutted the criticism of Dulles as a "snow man with a frozen foreign policy unyielding and unwilling to negotiate and talk on peace." She said Dulles had "called the bluff" of the Soviets on summitry by "brilliantly" asking for a specific agenda on disarmament, arms inspection, and German unification. When Khrushchev refused, Smith believed, he revealed his interest in a summit as "the actual fraud that it was."[64] Eisenhower went ahead and met with the Soviets and convinced many Americans that the talks could contribute to peace. But Smith remained on guard because "Russia has a long record of duplicity, doubletalk, and doublecross on agreements."[65] "Someone must have been feeding raw meat to our lady Senator from Maine," one reporter concluded, "the way she has been rampaging about lately at Washington in her votes against the Administration."[66]

On possibly the gravest of Eisenhower's foreign crises, the 1954 shelling by the People's Republic of China of the Nationalist-held islands of Quemoy and Matsu, the president had Smith's support. "There is no choice," Smith said on the floor. "The circumstances do not permit us the liberty to differ with the President."[67] Believing the shelling was preliminary to a Chinese invasion of Formosa, Smith met, she said, "day and night" with the Armed Services Committee to do some "straight thinking" on what the United States should do if the invasion occurred.[68] The result was committee, and eventually congressional, support of a security treaty with Chiang Kai-shek and a resolution authorizing Eisenhower to defend Formosa and the offshore islands. To refuse support, Smith said, would give the "impression that we did not have the will to resist communist aggression."[69]

Smith also supported Eisenhower's extension of American power into the Middle East during the 1956 Suez crisis, and she backed Eisenhower when he went further and sent American marines into Lebanon in 1958 to prevent a civil war. Nor did she criticize his covert actions in using the Central Intelligence Agency to overthrow anti-American governments in Iran and Guatemala and to install pro-American, anti-Communist leaders. Cold War morality, not raw meat, motivated Smith, and when the administration's actions coincided with her beliefs, her support was there.

"My job is my life," she said in the mid-1950s, and her life, as well as Lewis's, continued to be one of unremitting work.[70] The two had been living together since 1951 when Lewis had built a modern, six-room, two-story house in Silver Spring, Maryland, for himself and his parents. Smith, noting that the lower floor was planned as a recreation area, kept asking Lewis how he intended to use all that space. Lewis finally asked if she was "hinting" about it, and when she said yes, he asked, "Would you like to come out here to live," and she replied that "she sure would."[71] The senator did not say when this conversation took place, but as early as July 1949 Lewis wrote to his parents that he and Margaret were shopping for carpet and drapes. "Margaret's bedroom," Lewis told his parents, "will have the blue colors that Mother picked. The bathroom will be a light blue."[72] Smith rented the lower level as a small apartment and furnished it in near-monastic simplicity with a single bed and little else. Although Smith failed to inform her constituents of her living arrangements, she commented in her radio addresses on Silver Spring as a near-rural area, reminiscent of Maine. Once she told her listeners that Lewis had picked eighteen quarts of wild strawberries behind his house, which Smith cleaned and froze, a surprising treasure in the "hurly-burly Washington area."[73] A typical morning for the two of them was to arise at 7:00 A.M., arrive at the office before 8:00 A.M., and have a cafeteria breakfast of grapefruit, toast, and coffee at their desks while reading the newspapers.

Seniority had provided a large, six-room office for Smith in the new Senate

Office Building, and although she told her constituents that she preferred her old office, she added that hers, number 2309, was one of the "choice suites."[74] The only reason she had moved, she insisted, was to please her staff by placing them closer to the cafeteria, mimeographing, duplicating, and especially the mail offices. Her "political enemies," she said, "constantly criticize me" for concentrating on mail, but "I welcome such criticism" because it meant she was "doing her best."[75] Smith's office became a model of administrative efficiency in handling constituent problems dealing with Social Security, the military, civil service, and pensions. Her office files contain thousands of letters documenting not just the problems but also the solutions her staff, under Lewis's direction, found for grateful voters.

Blanche Bernier Hudon on a $7,099 salary continued as Smith's receptionist, but Joseph Bernier, husband of Smith's sister Laura, and Blanche's brother, was a new staff member on a $15,731 salary. Lewis earned $16,300, but as Frances Bolton pointed out, he was independently wealthy and did not have to work; "he can afford to argue with Smith."[76] The new office building also had a beauty shop in its basement along with the traditional barber shop, and Smith went down once a week at 5:00 P.M. for a fifteen-minute shampoo and pin-curl set. She covered her head with a scarf and went back to her office to work while her thinning gray hair dried. There was no subway from the new office building to the Capitol, just an old navy station wagon to shuttle senators back and forth. Smith and Lewis preferred walking, outside in good weather and in the connecting tunnel if it was inclement. The best evidence of Smith's improved position was an office in the Capitol with a fireplace and, most significant, a little bathroom. A Capitol hideaway was what every senator coveted, and seniority, not gender, provided Smith's.[77] There was consideration of a swimming pool for Smith to supplement the one her male colleagues still used in the nude. She demurred to the belated gallantry, righteously adding that she was proud of not costing the taxpayers money. Along with the powerful Armed Services where she was the third-ranking member and on Appropriations where she ranked fifth, Smith continued on Government Operations where being second in seniority made her chair of the Reorganization Subcommittee.

For all of Smith's righteous opposition to the Eisenhower administration, she never broke with the president or he with her. Politically, both were too astute. Smith's coup with Ike came in 1955 when he accepted her invitation for a fishing vacation in Maine and a lobster bake in her backyard. Maine, in its love-hate relationship with tourists, had billed itself "Vacationland," and Smith's triumph in luring the popular president there was triumph for the whole state. The trip also became something of a problem for the whole state. Ike's favorite fishing involved wading upstream for trout, while Maine's best fishing was from a boat in one of the state's hundreds of lakes. The president did not care for boat fishing, because "when I go out in a boat, every other boat on the lake goes out too," he said. "This annoys the president, the fish, and the Secret Service," an aide pointed out.[78] As it happened, it delighted the state's black flies, an infamous and unadvertised characteristic of "Vacationland," which were also impervious to all the Secret Service's insect repellents. A much-bitten Ike arrived at Skowhegan and rested briefly at Smith's house in Lewis's rooms, from then on referred to as the "Eisenhower Suite," before appearing in her backyard for a picnic. An elaborate stone platform surrounded by a rock wall had been built for the lobster bake, but a barbecue grill was also available for those who preferred steak. The president insisted on cooking his own steak and after dinner visited with Smith's guests on the beautiful green lawn that sloped down to the Kennebec.

In addition to having the president as a guest, Smith offset the negative publicity she had received in her battles with the administration by introducing her rose bill in 1955. In cooperation with her old friend in the House, Frances Bolton, Smith asked that the rose, symbol of peace, courage, loyalty, love, and, she could have added, herself, be declared the national flower. While reporters made references to "sniffing out the story," "the Senate smelling mighty like a rose," and a "Second War of the Roses," Bolton sent a rose to each of the 435 House members. There was an immediate controversy with a deluge of letters, telephone calls, telegrams, and postcards as the effort to designate a national flower became a national issue. Proponents and opponents argued respectively that the United States was the only major nation without a national flower, the rose was England's designated flower, 30 million Americans grew roses, and the rose was not native to the United States. Champions of goldenrod, laurel, columbine, and arbutus introduced bills of their own, with the predictable result that none was selected.

Eisenhower again motivated speculation about the vice presidency when he announced that he would run in 1956; he praised Vice President Richard Nixon but did not say that he wanted Nixon on the ticket again. Instead Ike called for an open convention, an idea Smith immediately supported. "While there is merit in the tradition of permitting the presidential nominee to make a personal selection of his vice presidential running mate," she said, "to take that right from the delegates at the convention is not consistent with the principles and tradition of our republic. The convention should be just as open on the nomination of the Vice President as on the nomination of President."[79]

Republicans in Maine at their state convention immediately endorsed Smith for a "favorite daughter" nomination for the vice presidency at the national convention. The first state ever to agree to nominate a favorite daughter, Maine celebrated Smith in 1956 as never before. During the convention at the Falmouth Motel in Portland, Smith was mobbed by well-wishers wanting to see "Margaret." The press observed that almost everyone assumed they were on a first-name basis with her. In a dark blue taffeta dress with a wide portrait collar and flaring skirt, her ever-present pearls, and the expected red rose, Smith greeted visitors to her reception room surrounded by gifts of giant bouquets. She frankly told the press that she "wouldn't be human if she wasn't pleased with the idea of nomination," but added that she "was not seeking it."[80] Smith had not attended a national convention except for the brief appearance she had made following her primary victory in 1948. She received a last-minute invitation to speak in an unimportant role in August 1956 and, offended, refused. When the Republicans gathered in San Francisco's Cow Palace without her for their centennial convention, they heard their perennial candidate Harold Stassen say that polls showed Richard Nixon would take a million votes from the ticket. Some delegates wore "Dump Nixon" buttons, others had "Dump Everybody," but seasoned politicians murmured that Smith did not have a chance. As party leaders planned and plotted, connived and compromised, Owen Brewster emerged as her unlikely supporter.

Drew Pearson characterized Brewster as "Sir Lancelot in defense of the lady," and desiring to be queen-maker, Brewster secured serious, if temporary, consideration of Smith's nomination from party leaders.[81] In the end Nixon's forces overwhelmed all opposition from the floor as they had in 1952, and Ike issued a last-minute statement in favor of retaining him as vice president. The Maine delegation succumbed to the president's call for party harmony, and state chairman John Weston told Joseph Martin, convention chairman, that "since no serious contender had appeared to run against Nixon, Maine is happy to join in support of the renomination of our great Vice President." "Okay," replied the crusty Martin who considered Smith one of the "graduates of the famous Martin school of politics," but "give her a good plug."[82] Smith made no public comment about being bypassed for the second time and when asked later how long it would be before a woman received a nomination said, "Maybe by 1960."[83]

Smith limited her campaign efforts to Maine with the exception of speaking in favor of Eisenhower on the CBS television show, "Face the Nation." The program had never before had a woman as a guest, but at the president's suggestion, the women's division of the Republican National Committee asked Smith to debate Eleanor Roosevelt, championing the Democratic nominee, Adlai Stevenson, on the program. Hesitant because of her difficulty with public speaking and respectful of Roosevelt's "breadth and depth of knowledge of issues," Smith at first refused.[84] Reluctantly persuaded by Eisenhower to change her mind, she and Lewis carefully planned her appearance. Confident that Roosevelt would not have much time to prepare for the program because of her busy schedule and natural confidence, Smith and Lewis decided "to do detailed and meticulous homework." Surprisingly, their second consideration was appearance. "What would I wear? How would my hair be styled?" Smith said. "These weren't just my questions— they seemed to be of consummate interest to Bill too." What they wanted was a "favorable sharp contrast," and Smith said, "I felt that this would be as important, if not more important, than whatever we said in the debate."[85] In Smith's six-page account of the debate, she discussed at length the selection of her simple dark dress, softly waved hair, and "demeanor or conduct—air or style some might say," and not one word about issues.[86] Smith and Lewis assumed that Roosevelt's "towering height," "top-heavy appearance," and "decidedly partisan manner" would give Smith an edge as long as she answered the questions "as briefly as possible, slowly, deliberately, in a low, even-pitched tone."[87]

Much rehearsed, Smith presented, Lewis believed, a "nicely telegenic" appearance but said so little that the program director moaned, "Talk more, Senator Smith. Eleanor is monopolizing the discussion."[88] The Smith-Lewis ace in the hole, learned possibly from her election eve remarks against Paul Fullam in 1954, was a prepared closing statement, a "series of unanswerable arguments."[89] "What was surprising about it," Smith said, "was my abrupt change in delivery. It was not the soft, restrained, measured delivery in deferential tones—nor was it said with a smile. Instead it was a biting staccato." What she said, "as one who has publicly condemned irresponsible accusations of treason and pro-Communist," related to the "moral principle" and "moral leadership" of the Eisenhower administration. Smith asked Americans to "choose principle instead of politics" and vote for Eisenhower.[90] Furious at what she saw as Smith's righteous underhandedness, Roosevelt refused to shake hands with her, Smith said, "pulled away, turned her back, and said to her companions as she walked away, 'Did you hear what she said?' "[91]

Closer to home, Smith was also having difficulties with Democrats, specifically with the ongoing Democratic resurgence in Maine led by Edmund Muskie. Muskie topped his historic election as governor in 1954 by winning a second term in 1956 with 180,000 votes, more than any Republican candidate for the office had ever received. Then the state's junior senator, Frederick Payne, got caught up in the Bernard Goldfine scandal of the Eisenhower administration. Goldfine was the wealthy industrialist who dispersed vicuña coats and varied other monied favors to Republicans as well-placed as presidential adviser Sherman Adams in the White House. Payne was not only walking around in a vicuña coat, he was sleeping in a house Goldfine had bought him and staying in hotel rooms on various trips that Goldfine financed. Peculiarly, Smith had never met Goldfine, although he owned four textile mills in Maine and contributed heavily to the state party.

Muskie challenged Payne for the Senate, and Mainers in 1958 voted a near-straight Democratic ticket. In all of Maine history there had been only two Democratic senators, the last in 1911, and now Muskie became the third. The Democratic sweep included Clinton A. Clawson for governor, the state's first four-year executive, and two of the three representatives, James C. Oliver and Frank M. Coffin. "I feel a little lonesome politically," Smith lamented and referred to herself and reelected Congressman Clifford Mc-Intire as the "last remnants of the two-party system in Maine."[92]

Relations between Smith and Muskie were frosty from the beginning. Although she had always been a maverick Republican, Smith now became the champion of the party and inserted her seniority in the dike to hold back the Democratic flood. When the press reported that Smith had given Muskie a "tongue lashing" during an early trip he had made to Washington, she retorted that if Muskie had felt that way, "he was not man enough to say so to me to my face" but added that perhaps he enjoyed "the publicized martyr role of bitter, self-imposed silence." He would have to live with his conscience, Smith went on, "in spite of any political gain" and "any personal satisfaction" he may "have gained in hurting me."[93] As the senior senator, Smith made it clear that she was chairman of the state delegation and expected the Democratic majority to follow her lead.

In response, Muskie saw Smith as a loner in reaching political decisions and one who made little effort to achieve shared positions. He also faulted Lewis as "reluctant to see a congenial relationship" between the two senators and referred to Lewis's "hostility" toward him. Lewis, Muskie believed, was the one who did not want "a working relationship between our offices."[94] Muskie did not say that Lewis dominated Smith, as many others did, but neither did he consider that by now Smith was politician enough to enjoy Lewis as her lightning rod, attracting the bolts of criticism while she continued to smile and ingratiate. Muskie was all that Smith was not when he arrived in Washington in 1959: young, attractive, not only a graduate of Bates College but also a member of Phi Beta Kappa, an attorney, married with children, and a decorated World War II veteran. Most important, Muskie was a Democrat, and the party had regained control of the Congress. In the Senate the Democratic majority was almost two to one: sixty-five to thirty-five.

The one presumed advantage that Muskie did not have but Smith did was ten years of Senate seniority, which among all Republicans made her eleventh in seniority and in the whole Senate thirty-second. This status allowed Smith to retain her fifth ranking position on Appropriations and third ranking on Armed Services but to give up her second ranking position on Government Operations to become third in seniority on the new Aeronautics and Space Committee.

Initially, Smith had a better working relationship with the Democratic leadership, especially majority leader Lyndon Johnson, than did Muskie. In preparing for passage of a new civil rights bill, Johnson had asked for Muskie's support in voting against a northern liberal effort to change Senate rules to limit filibusters. Muskie refused, but Smith agreed. Smith and Johnson had served in the House together, came to the Senate the same year, and served on Armed Services together. The two liked each other, and Smith considered Johnson the best majority leader under whom she had served. Robert Taft and William Knowland were the only two Republican majority leaders briefly in power during her tenure, and her Democratic standard of comparison included Scott Lucas and Ernest McFarland. Unlike his predecessors, Johnson, in Smith's opinion, brought energy and enthusiasm to the position and became a master at persuading, coaxing, cajoling, and threatening his colleagues in order to reach consensus. With Smith, Johnson was in turn courtly, affectionate, and flirtatious, and she, without any loving relationship in her life, responded glowingly to his hugs, pats, and compliments. Big, lean Lyndon with his loose, gregarious, voluble manner and tiny, taciturn Margaret with her aloof-to-chilly reserve were an odd pair: Democrat and Republican, southerner and New Englander, conservative and liberal, Senate club member and Senate independent, majority leader and minority female. But politically the two understood each other and worked well together, and the civil rights controversies of the Eisenhower administration illustrated both their collegiality and the anomalies of their relationship.

With a negligible black constituency in Maine, Smith viewed civil rights as an issue of conscience more than of politics. She could have been silent on the subject or a "mental mute," as she said, because she was aware of the Senate dominance of Richard Russell, the undisputed leader of the "inner club," and his cohorts: Walter George, also of Georgia, Kenneth Mc-Kellan of Tennessee, and others who chaired the key committees. She had chosen instead to support the integration initiatives of Harry Truman, the first president to attempt to end racial discrimination in the United States, and she spoke out in favor of the 1954 Supreme Court decision in the case of *Brown v. Board of Education of Topeka*. She also supported Eisenhower in 1957 when he ordered a thousand paratroopers to Central High School in Little Rock, Arkansas, to protect nine black students who were integrating the facility, and she voted for his civil rights bill, the first since Reconstruction. Continuing to use the Cold War as her sine qua non, Smith argued that "in a struggle to the end with world Communism," the United States could no longer act "as if the only people who had the right to rule were white."[95]

When the Eisenhower administration introduced a second civil rights act in 1959 to ensure black rights in the South, Smith signed on as a sponsor and kept Mainers informed in a monthly series of radio broadcasts. She believed the addition of four senators from the new states of Alaska and Hawaii cost southern conservatives "the strong and tight hold" they had on the Senate and that Johnson would secure passage of a voting rights bill.[96] The southern block, led by Richard Russell, began the longest and most strenuous filibuster of Smith's career. Maintaining strict discipline to break the southerners, the majority leader kept the Senate in continuous around-the-clock session for over a week, which meant the maintenance of a quorum to answer the filibuster's frequent calls. Only a few senators willingly supported Johnson, Smith among them—as much to maintain her consecutive roll call record, which was then over seven hundred as to support the civil rights bill. Johnson ordered the sergeant-at-arms "to go out and haul in absent Senators—to even arrest them if necessary to get them to the Senate floor to answer the roll call."[97]

Because every few hours the quorum bell rang "as loud as a fire alarm," Smith said, male senators slept on army cots in the Capitol's old Supreme Court chamber a few feet away from the Senate.[98] "Of course, I did not sleep in the same room," Smith primly told her constituents, instead using her office couch ten minutes away. There she bathed, dressed, and ate for the duration and, although assisted throughout by Lewis, concluded that "what a woman Senator needs is a wife."[99] Although her colleagues had wives to supply them with clean clothes and food, they nevertheless often appeared on the floor in pajamas, chain smoking, coffee gulping, unshaven, and exhausted, while Smith one day answered three roll calls in three different, fresh dresses. For nine days, a total over 157 hours, from 29 February through 8 March, the Senate was in session and then Johnson worked his miracle, broke the filibuster, and passed what the press characterized as "watered-down" but Smith thought was a "good bill."[100]

Senator Smith's major concern in 1960 was her third campaign for the Senate. Assuming her usual election role of victim under attack, her twenty years in Congress notwithstanding, she began the contest by telling her supporters that this would be her "toughest campaign" and that "she might be beaten."[101] Her reference was not to the Republican primary, where she had always fielded her toughest opponent, because this time the party accepted her seniority and ran no one. Her concern, instead, was for the Democrat whom Edmund Muskie had "handpicked" to run against her in the first general election in Maine not to be scheduled earlier than other states'. The innovative Democrats startled Smith and the nation by nominating a woman and providing the United States with its first all-female Senate contest. For years Smith had argued that women should be in politics; now she ruefully admitted, "I must have overdone it."[102]

In portraying herself as the underdog, Smith characterized her opponent as "a political gem," "likeable," "dynamic," and "articulate."[103] This paragon was Lucia Cormier, a former schoolteacher who had earned both master of arts and doctor of philosophy degrees before winning a seat in the state legislature. There she became Democratic floor leader in the House and represented the party on the national committee. Veteran *Bangor News* columnist Lorin Arnold characterized her as "the most efficient, most sincere, and hardest-working woman legislator ever to grace the legislative scene."[104] Smith was furious when Muskie hosted luncheons in Washington for Cormier, staged a press conference for her, and took her on to the Senate floor to sit in one of the seats so that, Smith said, "she could begin to warm" it up.[105] Warmed up herself, Smith noted which senators supported Muskie's efforts and twelve years later printed their names in her book, *Declaration of Conscience*.

Then Smith began writing "scorching" letters to people all over Maine recounting her support for them and insisting on their votes as repayment. If they had voted earlier for her opponents, she reminded them and said that if they wanted more of her assistance, they would have to support her in 1960. To her supporters she sent alphabetical lists of those who had signed her nomination papers, who had received her assistance, and who had offered their support. Soon these volunteers were organizing rallies, telephoning voters, and mailing brochures, placards, and other campaign literature. In common, the message was that a Cormier-Smith election was "like the office boy and the top executive trying for the same position."[106]

That assessment of Smith's advantage was accurate, but in this instance it was office girl and female executive, and the national press raced to Maine for the story or a possible "clawing, scratching 'cat' fight," as Smith feared. What Smith, advised by Lewis, gave them was a "silent candidate." She refused to make statements for television and radio, turned down offers of free airtime, accepted no invitations for guest appearances and interviews, and attended only functions she considered "social gatherings." The Smith-Lewis reasoning that Cormier would gain in recognition from any press contact Smith had was common political wisdom but seldom carried to this extreme. The usual context was for a well-known incumbent to avoid debate with an unknown opponent, and that possibility Smith refused to consider even when *Bangor News* reporter Don Larrabee offered to arrange a national, not just state, encounter. She saw debates as "bloodletting," where the "incumbent inescapably is on the defense," and in this instance where "Lucia would win."[107]

What Smith could not avoid was an active campaign pleasantly waged by a skilled politician, and that was what the younger, attractive, and energetic Cormier did. Of the once stigmatized French-Canadian descent, Cormier proudly campaigned as a French-speaking Catholic in border towns and built a solid constituency there. Her other area of strength was urban labor, and she spent a great deal of time visiting factories. The Democratic party had politicized these two groups in opposition to the traditional Republican constituency of timber, paper, textiles, and shoe manufacturers, and Cormier benefited from it. Her theme was that she "cared" for the poor, the aged, workers, and women, and Smith was stung to the quick. As Smith heard Cormier's campaign, Cormier "cared and I did not. She accused me of having a callused attitude toward the aged, of being cold and arrogant and unsympathetic," and "of insulting the intelligence of Maine voters." Lewis recorded each of Cormier's "attacks and taunts," prepared a response for Smith, and "indexed and tabbed" the charges and rebuttals in a three-hole looseleaf notebook. Then they waited.[108]

Smith did not attend the Republican convention in 1960, instead using the month Congress was in recess to tour Maine. From 7 July through 6 August, thirty-one days, she drove over five thousand miles, stopping in each of the state's sixteen counties. "I was extremely pleased with what I found—a happy and prosperous Maine," she said. "It seems to me that generally throughout the state business and economic conditions are the best they have ever been."[109] In contrast, Cormier stressed hard times in Maine. She saw a decline in jobs with the textile industry moving South to cheap labor, the shoe industry facing cheap foreign competition, and the state's young people leaving for better jobs elsewhere.

Instead of acknowledging the reality of Cormier's assessment and then having to accept responsibility, Smith applied her "things are the best they have ever been" theme to her strong suit, military preparedness. Nationally, Senator John F. Kennedy of Massachusetts was running for the presidency against Vice President Richard Nixon with the "missile gap" accusation that the Eisenhower administration had allowed the Soviets to develop a nuclear advantage. Using her positions on Armed Services and Space, Smith defended the administration and reassured Mainers. "Our beloved country," she said, "has gone far ahead of Russia. The missile gap . . . has vanished" because of the "spectacular success of the Polaris missile submarines," which were built at the Kittery Naval Yard and directed by the communications center at Cutler, Maine. "I am proud of my country—and I have unbounded faith in my country."[110] "Not only have we gone ahead of Russia," she said in another statement, "but we have gone ahead of her in a big way."[111]

Smith waited until the Sunday before the election to debate Cormier on WCSH-TV in Portland. Armed with Lewis's notebook, she "paid special attention to my clothes and grooming," and planned to answer each of Cormier's accumulated accusations. Then, she said, "there would be little time left for Miss Cormier to launch new attacks."[112] Although Cormier bore no relationship to Joe McCarthy, used no ugly rhetoric toward Smith, and spent considerable campaign time denying that Jimmy Stewart was financing her campaign, Smith's opening statement was vintage victim on the defensive:

Although she [Cormier] has repeatedly characterized me . . . as being cold and arrogant, not caring about the older persons and the working people, of insulting the intelligence of Maine voters, ridiculing my voting record, implying that I was afraid to debate, chiding me for my independence of thought, and making other attacks on me—I have never made an attack on her or voiced criticism of her.[113]

Smith was delighted with the debate and considered it "ladylike" but not the "powder puff" contest many had expected.[114] Certainly her moral sledgehammer was effective because she won with the highest vote in the history of Maine, 255,478, which was 96,000 more votes than Cormier received. Smith's 61.6 percent of the total vote was the highest percentage won by any other U.S. senator in 1960, and she returned to Washington politically stronger than ever.

Her sanctimony increased also, and she determined that Edmund Muskie should be chastised for actively supporting Cormier. Her censure was public and involved a dramatic departure from Senate protocol. When the new session began on 3 January 1961, Smith startled her colleagues by refusing to be escorted down the aisle by Muskie to be sworn for a new term. Instead, she took the arm of newly elected Maurine Newberger, Democrat of Oregon, and for the first time in history two women walked down the Senate aisle to begin serving simultaneous terms. "An historic occasion" was Smith's public explanation for slighting her colleague from Maine, and Muskie, who was not informed of her plan, refused to comment.[115] "Speculation is not a good thing to indulge in," he said, "when you're dealing with Margaret's sensitivities."[116]

With John Kennedy in the White House and a Democratic majority in Congress, Smith acquired a good Republican characteristic: outspoken criticism of the administration. Unlike her Republican colleagues, who were awed by John Kennedy's youth, energy, and charisma, Smith knew him as the interloper in her 1954 campaign, the inactive chairman of her Reorganization Subcommittee, and "an angry young man" whom she had witnessed physically threatening a committee staff member.[117] Consistent with her growing reputation for holding grudges, Smith sought vengeance in humor. In a banquet address to some eight hundred members of the National Federation of Republican Women on 16 April 1962, Smith danced the "Kennedy twist." The twist was the new dance of the early 1960s, and there had been considerable press coverage of its infiltration of the White House. Smith used the play on words to illustrate the issues on which Kennedy had "talked one way as candidate but acted the opposite as President," or did the "Kennedy twist." As heavy-handed in her use of humor as always, she cited Kennedy's campaign criticism of summitry and his presidential summit in Vienna with Soviet premier Nikita Khrushchev. This inconsistency Smith called the "Kennedy twist" "to the tune of a Viennese waltz." The contradiction between the candidate's calling for the overthrow of Fidel Castro in Cuba and the president's failing to authorize use of air support in the 1961 Bay of Pigs invasion she referred to as the "Kennedy Twist . . . done in agony to a Cuban beat."[118]

The White House was not amused and had both the power and will to retaliate. First, Smith's junior senator began receiving advance notification of federal projects benefiting Maine for which Muskie could then receive credit by releasing the news to the press. The first time this happened was in Smith's area of expertise, national defense, and concerned a $60 million contract for the Kittery Naval Yard to build nuclear-powered submarines. After Smith read Muskie's news release in the paper, she sent a telegram to the president to say that she "resented this very obvious playing politics with national defense. I remind you that you are the President of the United States and the Commander in Chief of the Armed Services rather than the head of the Democratic Party."[119] When Smith complained to the press about the slight, she took a beating with Maine coverage about her "ego," "outbursts," "going off the deep end," and "lacking humility."[120] Instead of backing off, Smith took on the press in her segment of the monthly Sunday night radio address, "The Maine Delegation Reports." As scathing as she had been on the "Kennedy twist," she accused the *Portland Press-Herald,* the *Evening Express,* and the *Sunday Telegram* of "heaping scorn and ridicule on me."[121] With her thin skin revealed, the White House continued to pierce with other news leaks to Muskie while press secretary Lawrence O'Brien promised to discover the source of the leaks for her.

That was for openers. A more studied insult from the White House came when President Kennedy decided to travel to Maine. Traditionally presidents visiting states invite that state's two senators and the district's congressman to accompany him, but the White House invited only Edmund Muskie. Smith had offered use of her new vacation house at Cundys Harbor to the president as soon as she learned of his plans but received no response to her invitation until the day of his departure. Presidential aide Kenneth O'Donnell sent a note declining but saying nothing about accompanying Kennedy on *Air Force One* to the Brunswick Naval Air Station. Refusing the insult, Smith arranged for a navy plane to fly her to Brunswick ahead of the presidential party, but not before she answered the last roll call vote and told the Senate what had happened. She feared that the smaller naval plane would not arrive at Brunswick before the base was closed to protect the arrival of the president. "But I am sure," she told the Senate, "that the President and everyone will understand fully that my official Senate duty to answer roll call votes and to remain here to do what I was elected to do . . . takes priority." Covered if she failed, Smith then raced with Lewis to the air field and to Maine. Urged on, the pilot revved the plane to where Smith feared it would vibrate to pieces, but she arrived five minutes ahead of *Air Force One,* raced again to the receiving line, and said to Muskie as he escorted the president, "Hi, Ed! What took you so long?"[122]

Senate majority leader Mike Mansfield, shocked by Smith's treatment, remonstrated with the White House but was not able to heal the breach. Instead Smith accelerated her attack, and the arena Smith selected was her usual Cold War stomping ground of defense. Although she had been correct during the 1960 campaign in denying the existence of a missile gap, President Kennedy went ahead in 1961 and increased defense spending by some $6 billion. Creating a missile gap that significantly favored the United States, Kennedy authorized the construction of five times the number of intercontinental ballistic missile Minutemen that Eisenhower had considered necessary. With this advantage, Kennedy switched from the previous policy of threatening the Soviet Union with massive nuclear retaliation to a new strategy of flexible response employing both nuclear and conventional weapons. Smith preferred Eisenhower's brinkmanship and believed Kennedy was weakening American defenses and encouraging Soviet advances with his "lack of will" and "unwillingness to use the power of the United States."[123]

Her office informed the press that she planned to make a major foreign policy speech on 21 September 1961, a speech that would be as important as her Declaration of Conscience. With more confidence than she had displayed on the earlier occasion, Senator Smith addressed her remarks "specifically to the President of the United States." Ominously she declared that "everywhere Communists press forward stronger. Khrushchev, vowing to take over the world for communism, and acting with all the confidence of a winner, threatens to put an end to civilized survival." Given American military superiority, Smith said her purpose was to ask, "What has happened that permits Khrushchev to act as he does? Is it conceivable," she continued, "that Khrushchev could assess that the will of the American people has collapsed?" The president had "played" into Soviet hands by "turning to an emphasis on conventional weapons" and convincing the premier that "we do not have the will to use that one power with which we can stop him. We have the nuclear capability but not the nuclear credibility." Smith concluded, "How much longer can we afford to lose? When will we start to win? Where will we draw the line?"[124]

After the humiliating defeat of CIA-trained Cubans at the Bay of Pigs, Kennedy was vulnerable to charges of weakness, and although he did not mention Smith by name, he told a United Nations audience a few days later that he would not hesitate to use nuclear weapons if necessary. Privately the president told friends that he was "stung" by her remarks, but that people who argued like her were "ignorant" and ignored the fact that he had to weigh 30 to 40 million casualties in a nuclear war.[125]

Soviet radio commentators referred to Smith as "that bloodthirsty little woman" and remembering that she had wanted to use the atomic bomb in China, added that she "was having another attack of cannibal instinct." Then Khrushchev wrote that Smith was "blinded by savage hatred" and added that he found it "hard to believe how a woman," if she is not "the devil in a disguise of a woman, can make such a malicious man-hating call." The Soviet premier was writing to the British Labour party, which had asked him to halt nuclear testing. He could not, he replied, while Americans were "inflaming war passions." Disdainfully, Smith responded, "Khrushchev isn't really mad at me; I'm not that important. He is angry because American officials have grown more firm since my speech."[126] Nina Khrushchev supported her husband and called Smith a "warmonger," whose "threats are made to destroy our homes, to kill our husbands, and to take the lives of our children." The senator suggested that Mrs. Khrushchev have a "heart-to-heart talk with her husband and tell him to start acting for peace by doing two specific things—stopping the evil, open-air nuclear explosions completely and tearing down the wall that divides Berlin."[127]

Smith had her supporters in the Congress, in the military, and among civilians as the continuing national debate over the Cold War escalated. Cold warriors like Smith looked through World War II eyes and demanded unconditional surrender by the Soviets to America's uncontested military superiority. In opposition to these hawks, other analysts saw the Soviet Union's acting defensively against the United States and favored the Kennedy policy of flexible and controlled response. Avoiding military confrontation, the administration held on to West Berlin while the Soviets built the Berlin Wall and kept Americans out of Laos in order to accept a Soviet offer to neutralize the nation.

Smith saw these accommodations as retreats and, one year from the day of her 1961 speech, goaded the president again. Maintaining that the outlook for the United States had "deteriorated steadily" to such a "disturbingly low level" that Khrushchev had stated that the "United States would not fight to defend itself," Smith called for the use of the concept of "counterforce" to meet every Soviet advance. Smith expected that the administration's response would be that it could not "risk provoking the communists," "promoting an arms race," or "increasing the likelihood of war." Spokesmen for the administration would argue, she continued, "that in a nuclear war there could be no winner. With all the emphasis at my command, I disagree. We can win."[128]

As Bill Lewis saw it, "it took only one month to prove the validity of" Smith's thesis of counterforce.[129] On 22 October 1962 President Kennedy startled the nation and much of the rest of the world by going on television to tell of Soviet missile installations being constructed in Cuba. Gravely, Kennedy said that he was quarantining Cuba and threatened use of nuclear weapons if the missiles there were not dismantled. For the first time in the Cold War, the United States took the world to the brink of nuclear annihilation, and, as Margaret Chase Smith had predicted, the Soviet Union backed down and agreed to remove the missiles.

Although hardliners were jubilant, others saw the president as acting rashly in response to political charges of weakness and risking world destruction over a negligible threat that did not change the vast military superiority of the United States. When Smith and Lewis learned that "the real reason why Kennedy could stand eyeball-to-eyeball with Khrushchev and demand and get removal of the missiles from Cuba was the nuclear superiority that we had over Russia," they manifested no chagrin that their attack on the administration for weakening American defenses had been in error. Instead they credited the nuclear superiority to Eisenhower, ignoring Kennedy's buildup, and criticized Kennedy again for proposing "to downgrade to parity with that of Russia."[130] As misguided, Smith ignored the determination of the Soviet Union after its humiliation in the Cuban missile crisis to escalate its arms buildup. The president understood that Smith had presidential intentions of her own for 1964, and when asked what he thought of her as a presidential candidate, said with a grin to a laughing male-dominated press corps that she would be a "formidable candidate."[131]

A month later President John Fitzgerald Kennedy was assassinated. As the nation and much of the world contemplated the implacable reality of death, Margaret Chase Smith in the Senate chamber unpinned the rose on her lapel, crossed the aisle to the Democratic side, and laid it in silent tribute on the desk that her brash, glamorous adversary had used.

Her gesture received considerable praise and became a symbol of the putting aside of political differences and uniting in the face of a national tragedy. The gesture also revealed the underside of Smith's politics of conscience, because the initiative was not hers, born of some charitable regret over the loss of a young man's life. Instead, the action was stage-managed, not by Lewis, who was no more forgiving than Smith, but by Mike Mansfield, who genuinely mourned the president's death. He suggested that Smith pay tribute to Kennedy by surrendering her rose, and immediately seeing the political value of the gesture, she complied and received the praise.[132] Politics of conscience not only made Smith sanctimonious but also painted her human acts of pettiness and hypocrisy in bold relief.

Chapter Seven

THE WILTED ROSE

"To run or not to run."

"Margaret, do we have to discuss that again?"

"We need to decide, Bill. Now that the president is dead, Goldwater doesn't need me on his ticket."

"Did you read the reporter who said Oswald shot you down also?"

"For the vice presidential nomination, maybe, but not for the presidential. Tell me again why I should run and why I shouldn't."

As quick and organized as ever in his thinking, Bill Lewis answered his closest friend and boss in numerical order of importance. She should run, first, because she offered a choice between Nelson Rockefeller and Barry Goldwater and, second, because she would be pioneering for women. She should not run because she lacked both money and organized support, and she might miss roll call votes. Also, third, there was "the humility of expected crushing defeats."[1] He meant "humiliation," but the word, much less the experience, was too alien to contemplate. "Humility" was a virtue they courted as integral to Smith's public persona.

Smith decided at least to take advantage of the press speculation about her entering the February New Hampshire primary by accepting an invitation to speak at the Women's National Press Club on 27 January 1964. She would announce her decision then.

"What is your decision?" Bill asked.

She had not decided and coyly asked him to write her a speech with two endings: one in which she announced that she would run and the other where she would not.

The press packed the many-chandeliered ballroom of the Mayflower Hotel to hear Smith read Lewis's remarks in her usual quiet-to-boring style. She

emphasized the mail from fifty states asking her to run for the presidency.
"Now I try to be serious without taking myself too seriously—but this mail
was not what I had seriously expected. Frankly, it had its effect."[2] With her
audience assuming now that she had been bitten by the long-lived and ever-
active presidential bug, Smith listed the reasons she should run. To the ear-
lier rationale, Lewis had added more political experience and independence
than the other candidates but still used numerical order.

Denting the certainty of her listeners that they knew her intention, Smith
switched to the reasons she should not run. Here Lewis had added the sexist
reasoning that "no woman should ever dare to aspire to the White House—
that it is a man's world and that it should be kept that way—and that a
woman on the national ticket . . . would be more of a handicap than a
strength." Smith also listed "that as a woman I would not have the physical
stamina and strength to run."[3]

Soberly, Smith concluded that "as gratifying as are the reasons advanced
urging me to run, I find the reasons advanced against my running to be far
more impelling." A collective groan came from the primarily female audi-
ence, but Smith spoke over it. "So because of these impelling reasons against
my running, I have decided that I shall enter the New Hampshire primary."[4]

Margaret Chase Smith was not the first woman to run for the presidency. She had been preceded by Victoria Claflin Woodhull in 1872 and Belva Lockwood in both 1884 and 1888. Smith's predecessors had been candidates for the obscure Equal Rights party, and no one, including the nominees, took their campaigns seriously. Both were feminists, and their dominant motivation was to voice women's issues, particularly the need for suffrage, from a national platform.

Smith, in contrast, maintained that her equally obscure campaign for the 1964 Republican nomination for the presidency was serious. "I would not have been in it if I hadn't been serious," she affirmed in defiance of near universal skepticism, which undoubtedly included Lewis's.[5] Both Senator Barry Goldwater of Arizona and New York governor Nelson Rockefeller had well-financed, well-organized campaigns underway. Smith had an unspecified number of letters suggesting that she run; an offer of support, later withdrawn, from former governor Wesley Powell of New Hampshire; and one visit from "a group of young men legislators from Illinois," who turned out to be Young Republicans.[6]

Earlier in 1963 there had been press speculation that, if nominated, Goldwater would select Smith as his vice presidential candidate. Goldwater had publicly stated that he was not opposed to a female running mate, but the closest he came to specifying Smith was when he joked with her about all the publicity she had received in her attacks on President John Kennedy. "Why don't we reverse the ticket," Goldwater said, "and you be the candidate."[7] He did not take her response, "It's all right with me. I'm ready," seriously, and later he added that "nobody ever approached me in a serious way about taking her as vice president."[8] In reference to whether Goldwater viewed her presidential candidacy seriously, he said, "No, frankly, I never did," but added in response to whether Smith took her campaign seriously, "Many, many people do that. Lord, I guess everybody in the Congress thinks they ought to be president."[9]

Other than Smith, the one person of note who credited her initiative with the possibility of victory was Vermont senator George Aiken. Before announcing, Smith and Lewis had dinner with Aiken and his administrative assistant and, later, wife, Lola Pierotti. The highly respected Republican dean of the Senate said that he believed Smith could win the New Hampshire primary in a three-way race with Rockefeller and Goldwater, and he told the press so. Aiken sat in the front row during her speech to the Women's National Press Club, and Smith said that he "just hollered when I said I would run."[10]

Smith viewed her candidacy in the New Hampshire primary as a test of how the voters would respond to a candidate "without campaign funds," "with a professional party organization," who "refused to absent herself from official duties," refused "to purchase political time on television," and who "will campaign on a record rather than on promises."[11] In other words, Smith would run for the presidency as she had always campaigned in Maine and hope that the eighteen thousand more women than men in New Hampshire would work in her favor.

Determined to complete the backlog of work in her office before leaving for New Hampshire, she stayed at her desk until 9:00 P.M. on a Saturday evening, left Washington at 4:00 A.M. Sunday morning 9 February for a twelve-hour drive to Pittsburg on the Canadian border, and was out campaigning at 6:30 A.M. on Monday. The temperature was 28 degrees below zero, but Smith turned out in short boots, short skirt, short coat, and no hat. With no entourage, no scheduled appearances, no headquarters, and no known supporters, she walked into stores, restaurants, banks, radio stations, and newspaper offices and introduced herself. More startled than not, those approached responded to her charm. "People can be awfully nice to you and still not vote for you," Smith observed with more political savvy than her harebrained campaign manifested.[12]

"She had never had any real hope of winning," Lewis alleged, "but she had not anticipated such deep disappointments."[13] She came in fifth to Lodge, who won, followed by Goldwater, Rockefeller, and Nixon. When Clare Boothe Luce was asked if Smith's coming in fifth meant that women would not vote for a woman, Luce responded only if Harold Stassen's placing last as a male meant men would not vote for a man. Then Luce announced that she was supporting Goldwater and maintained that "Smith's chances for the Presidential nomination are closer to zero than the New Hampshire weather."[14]

Lewis characterized Smith's prospects in the next primary in Illinois as "dim and grim."[15] The young men who had urged her to run were now "ambivalent," Lewis believed, because of possible "repercussions and reprisals" from Goldwater's organization.[16] Smith spent two weekends and $85 of her own money in the state and lost to Goldwater. Surprisingly, she received 30 percent of the vote, which to Lewis meant that "she had literally crashed Goldwaterland."[17] Smith credited her showing as a "victory for every woman in America," and Art Buchwald suggested that she affirm that if elected she would appoint fifty men to high posts in the government.[18]

The only other primary Smith entered was in Oregon, and there she came in fifth again. Supporters put her name on ballots in Massachusetts, Texas, and Pennsylvania, and in those states she retained her lock on fifth place.

Press coverage of Smith's campaign varied from treating it as a joke to puzzling over her intentions. "See Margaret Chase Rocky, See Margaret Chase Barry, See Margaret Chase Smith," one reporter wrote, and on "Face the Nation" reporters refused to believe the presidential nomination was her goal.[19] May Craig's retort to skeptics was, "You don't know her."[20] Not one reporter indicated a belief that she would succeed, and *Time* dismissed her decision to run as "frivolously feminine."[21] A December 1963 Gallup Poll gave her a 4 percent preference nationally for the nomination and last place to the other five mentioned candidates. Other journalists observed that she was, at sixty-six, the oldest of the candidates and, if elected, would be second to Eisenhower as the oldest president. Reporter Richard Warren of the *Evening Star* worried about Senator Smith's being menopausal. "The female of the species," he wrote, "undergoes physical changes and emotional distress of varying severity and duration which have an effect on judgment. Her cause is hopeless," he concluded, "and makes a travesty of the women's rights cause."[22]

For most reporters Smith's venture was a colorful footnote to an ugly campaign. UPI's Mike Posner said that he "gave it quite a ride:" "I wrote the daylights out of that story; I rode it hard because to me it was an interesting story."[23] The more informed members of the press pointed to the risk Smith was running in becoming a nuisance to the Republican leadership. National Committee chairman William E. Miller had tried to keep her out of the New Hampshire primary, Senate leader Everett Dirksen had been publicly angry at her entering the Illinois primary, and Governor Mark Hatfield tried to keep her out of Oregon. Sherman Adams called Smith the phantom candidate. When Smith refused to end her obviously failed candidacy, the convention chairman, Senator Thurston Morton of Kentucky, angrily said that "three people will be nominated for President—Goldwater, Scranton, and that G— D— Margaret Chase Smith."[24] When Aiken told Morton that Smith could add "two million votes to the ticket," Morton said, "If she proves in the primaries that she can bring us the suffragettes and the old maids, she's in."[25]

The high point of the campaign for Smith came at the Maine state convention when delegates to the national convention were instructed to support Smith as long as she remained a candidate. For the first time in her long public career, Smith was publicly moved to tears.

Before she stepped off a TWA airliner on Sunday afternoon, 12 July 1964, in San Francisco, Smith had attended only one other national Republican convention. That had been after her first election to the Senate in 1948. Now she had sixteen delegates pledged to support her tilt at the presidential windmill. Fourteen of her delegates were from Maine; the other two were George Aiken and the North Dakota delegate, John Rouzie. Mert Henry, who was an alternate on the Maine delegation, flew to the convention with the other state delegates and with the Massachusetts delegation. They arrived in San Francisco before Senator Smith's flight from Washington and decided to wait for her. "What happened," Henry grinned, "was her plane was delayed a couple of hours and most of the Maine delegation and some from Massachusetts . . . stayed in the bar too long. She got a very enthusiastic demonstration when she arrived."[26] In addition to the inebriated well wishers, a band played "Hello, Maggie," and a small crowd of "Rosebuds" waved "Smith for President" signs.

Goldwater had the votes for nomination, and everyone knew it. His supporters sported black eye makeup and said, "I'd rather fight than switch," but Smith went through the charade of trying to change their minds and considered herself courageous for doing so. Governor John Reed of Maine thought the convention was "tumultuous" because of the Goldwater "mania" and believed the delegates "treated Nelson Rockefeller very shabbily." Henry agreed and said that it was a "nasty convention," because the "ultraconservative element" was "a very raucous, nasty group of people. I saw them mistreat one of the blacks who had been an assistant secretary of labor," and Henry saw newsman John Chancellor "picked up and bodily thrown out of the convention."[27]

Instead of staying away from the Cow Palace while Aiken nominated her, Smith proudly sat in her box with friends and listened. Aiken began by confessing that he could not promise cabinet appointments, government contracts, or lavish entertainment in exchange for delegates voting for his candidate. For a while he had thought he could at least take delegates out for coffee on the contributions that had been received. "Then do you know what happened?" he asked, "Do you know what my candidate pulled on me? She took every big check—every little check—every $10.00 bill—every $1.00 bill and every penny and sent them straight back to where they came from."[28] While his audience smiled, Aiken lamented, "Our entertainment fund is shattered. Our demonstration wallet collapsed. Our conscience is intact."[29] That was Margaret Chase Smith's theme, and Aiken sang all the lyrics: integrity, respect, courage, experience, and common sense. Only smear was omitted.

With the convention packed with Goldwater supporters, the Maine delegation for Smith worried about staging a demonstration after her nomination. "So we made a deal," Henry said, with the supporters of William Scranton, Hiram Fong, and other contenders that "we would all demonstrate together for each of the candidates other than Goldwater."[30]

Smith's demonstrators took to the aisles while the convention band played "Drink a Toast to Dear Old Maine" and "Everything's Coming up Roses," and a card section flashed, after some reorganizing, "Hello, Maggie." Other delegates joined in and gave Smith their respect and good wishes, if not their votes, and Mert Henry said, "The Goldwater people could never figure out quite what was going on." Even Smith's old foe, Horace Hildreth, who was a Goldwater supporter, "was a good sport and carried a poster in the Margaret Smith demonstration," Henry remarked.[31] While Maine governor John Reed, Representative Frances Bolton, and two others gave seconding speeches, diehards tried to get the Goldwater forces to ask each of their pledged delegations to cast one vote for Smith "in honor of women nationally."[32] "They were curtly rebuffed," Lewis said.[33] The supporters of Governor Scranton did announce their willingness to have Smith as a vice presidential nominee, but it was too late.

To avoid embarrassment, Smith left the hall while the roll call vote was underway. She came in second to Goldwater's 883 votes with 27 votes and ahead of Henry Cabot Lodge, Jr. Most notable among her scattered new votes was one from Massachusetts from her old friend, former Speaker of the House of Representatives Joe Martin. The reason Senator Smith did so well was that the Maine delegation refused to change its vote to Goldwater, as most of the other delegations that voted for losing candidates did. Smith captured headlines the next day despite her loss because she spoke out in opposition to Goldwater's statement that "extremism in defense of liberty is not a vice."[34] She referred back fourteen years when she had spoken out, she said, "against extremism in my Declaration of Conscience speech and I have not changed my mind since then."[35]

What was it all about, this doomed campaign that placed two of her vaunted characteristics—common sense and experience—in doubt? When it was all over, Smith had another first. She was now the first woman to be nominated for the presidency at the convention of a major party. When a Goldwater supporter, in Smith's words, "sneered at a Smith supporter" and said, "You're wasting your time,"[36] the Smith supporter replied, as Smith often repeated the story, "You're only running, I'm making history."[37] That left the most important issue of all. Where were her female supporters during this campaign on their behalf? Most of the 59.4 million female voters were in opposition to her candidacy is the answer. Psychologist Dr. Joyce Brothers maintained that women were "irrationally prejudiced" against a woman president,[38] and the press made much of Desilu Productions president Lucille Ball's saying, "No! It's a bad idea. The boss should be a man."[39] Actor

Van Johnson added, "What! A woman president? You're teasing."[40] One of the many negative letters Smith received from women said, "We would not vote for you if you were the last candidate on earth . . . you are a very vain person. And not much for looks either."[41] Aiken's experienced assistant, Lola Pierotti, believed "the trouble with women . . . is that they are harsher against their own than they should be."[42] Press comments quoted from women supported Pierotti: "It's the funniest thing I ever heard of"; "She'll never make it. No woman could"; "I've never heard of such a thing"; "She'll make a fool of herself"; and "I don't think members of my sex should be president" are a sampling.[43] Columnist Ralph McGill, earlier the highly respected editor of the *Atlanta Constitution,* thought Smith's haphazard candidacy "set the course of women back several decades."[44]

Criticism was to be expected, but so were positive comments, yet they were glaringly absent. Senator Maurine Neuberger did say that she was "delighted that Mrs. Smith has chosen to assault this last frontier," but her comment was striking in that other elected women did not make similar public remarks.[45] Most notable in their absence were the Business and Professional Women's Club; the 232 female delegates at the convention, a larger number than ever before; and female convention officials like assistant national chairman Elly Peterson, parliamentarian Katharine St. George, secretary Mrs. C. Douglass Buck, and treasurer Mrs. J. Willard Marriott. Not only did female Republican leaders fail to support Smith, "two of her most trusted staff members," Lewis said, both females, resigned because of their increased work load.[46]

Illinois supporter Vi Dawson organized a small group of women for the primary and proclaimed herself national chairman of the Smith-for-president forces. Dawson came to San Francisco for the national convention and joined with Marion Otsea, chairman of the Smith California Committee. Donna Wright, who organized the floor demonstration for Smith, was the only other woman credited by Lewis for aiding her campaign. Still, Smith concluded, "I've never had a feeling of regret. I hope it gave courage and incentive to women," while acknowledging that her support had not come primarily from women and never had.[47] More accurately, when asked if her purpose had been to encourage women in public life, she said, "I'll be candid. I ran because I would like to be President of the United States."[48]

Aside from women in the military, Smith had not championed females during her long congressional career. She had given token support to the equal rights amendment, occasionally encouraged women to enter politics, and voted for some female legislation, but she had never been a feminist senator. Only when women's issues and her own agenda corresponded, as with military women and her work on the Armed Services Committee, had she assumed a leadership role. Otherwise her feminist relevance was symbolic, and her firsts were more for herself than for inspiring other women. In earlier women's history, pioneering queen bees, as the reference was, had commonly been self-motivated, but Smith was now in the 1960s, and an impassioned feminist movement was underway. Sisterhood was the new ethic, with its expectations of camaraderie, sharing, and mentoring, and yet, in this climate, as well as in the first women's histories being published, Smith and her presidential campaign were nonevents.

Smith was also a no-show in reference to the significant women's legislation of the 1960s, including the 1963 Equal Pay Act and 1964 Civil Rights Act, which were before the Senate during her presidential campaign. Although she was specifically invited to join the National Organization for Women, founded in 1966, she refused. "She felt that if she joined the organization," Lewis said, "that might put her in a position of conflict of interest. Therefore, she wouldn't join and they didn't like it."[49]

In contrast, the fourteen other women in Congress agreed with Michigan representative Martha Griffiths, who repeatedly told the men on Capitol Hill that it was "a new world."[50] During the 1960s the number of white women completing high school increased by 34 percent, and for black women the increase was 20 percent. College-educated women rose a dramatic 160 percent, or 60 percent more than men. By the end of the decade 43 percent of female adults worked outside the home and comprised 38 percent of the workforce. Women were the head of household of 43 percent of poor families, and 66 percent of employed women in the United States were single, separated, or divorced.[51]

Other congressional women—among them Maurine Neuberger, Edith Green, Patsy Mink, Edna Kelly, Katharine St. George, and even Frances Bolton—railed against the labyrinthine legislation that discriminated against women. Without Smith, these women succeeded in remedying some social security, tax, banking, and insurance inequities. Led by Edna Kelly and Edith Green, their great coup came in 1963 when they amended the Fair Labor Standards Act with the Equal Pay Act. At the same time that other congressional women were fighting for equal pay legislation, Smith had compensation battles of her own underway. Her first concern was for the retirement pay of retired army and air force officers, which had been threatened under a recent comptroller-general's restriction on dual compensation. Then she resurrected the equal pay issue for workers at the Kittery shipyard, but in reference to the Equal Pay Act for women, Smith said, "I never could quite understand by what interpretation or whose interpretation would there be equal pay for equal work."[52] Unlike Smith's special interests concerns, the Equal Pay Act prohibited sex discrimination in wages, affected the lives of millions of women, and led to another advance the next year with Title VII of the Civil Rights Act. Title VII was the equal employment opportunity provision, which, as it was originally written, prohibited discrimination on the basis of race, color, religion, and national origin. Martha Griffiths masterminded the addition of the word *sex* to the provision in order to end prejudice against the hiring of women. Once Griffiths led her amendment through the House, she monitored its progress in the Senate and credited Smith only with supporting it privately in the Republican Conference and voting for it.

Smith stepped aside again in the 1970 congressional debate over the equal rights amendment when for the first time in forty-seven years the steely-eyed Griffiths forced the amendment out of the Judiciary Committee with a discharge petition and secured House passage with an astounding 350 to 15 vote. Always on the alert for a possible bandwagon, eighty-three senators, Smith among them, signed as sponsors of the ERA under the leadership of Eugene McCarthy of Minnesota and Birch Bayh of Indiana. For one breathholding moment feminists, still denigrated in the press as women libbers, dared to believe that dream was about to become reality. Majority leader Mansfield, for once demonstrating LBJ-style leadership, used a procedural technicality to keep the bill before the full Senate and thus avoided ERA opponents Sam Ervin of North Carolina and Ted Kennedy of Massachusetts on the Judiciary Committee. Refusing to be steamrolled, Ervin insisted on hearings, laced with prestigious opponents, and, then aided by Kennedy and AFL-CIO lobbyists, introduced an amendment to prevent the drafting of women into the armed forces. Although Ervin used the draft as a divisive issue to defeat the ERA, the tactic landed the controversy in Smith's one arena of feminist activity: women in the military. Refusing the opportunity to become the Senate's Martha Griffiths, Smith stood by as her colleagues voted thirty-six to thirty-three to exempt women from the military, an amendment the House was unlikely to accept. To be certain the ERA was dead, the determined Ervin succeeded in adorning the corpse with a second amendment permitting prayer in public schools. Accurately, the *Wall Street Journal* concluded that the reason the ERA failed in 1970 was that "there was no Senate equivalent of Martha Griffiths, ready to push and nag and— if need be—fight dirty. Margaret Chase Smith . . . took little part in pushing it."[53] Not until 1972 did both the House and the Senate pass the ERA, and then Griffiths, Massachusetts representative Margaret Heckler, and New York representative Bella Abzug worked the Senate floor. When Griffiths sat on the day of the vote, she pointedly used Edmund Muskie's desk. With the eventual failure of the equal rights amendment to be ratified, Smith, when asked if she still considered the ERA a good idea, replied, "I think we already have it. Civil rights law gives equal rights to the sexes."[54]

As controversial as the women's movement was, there was widespread support for economic fairness. Women workers in Maine were aware of their lower pay, and May Craig provided the documentation showing more female laborers in manufacturing in the state than male. That was true in Skowhegan as well, and women's salaries in manufacturing were lower than men's. Craig did not mention Smith in her reports on women's issues.

Ironically, as Smith reached the height of her seniority and influence, the times passed her by. She was of the female suffrage generation that believed women could reform politics because of their inherent moral superiority. As skillfully as any bricklayer, Smith had erected a political edifice of conscience mortared with personal integrity and crowned with political courage. Astoundingly, she had never been faulted for dishonesty, anything approaching bribery, or use of her position for personal gain. By her own standards she had succeeded admirably. "The greatest compliment that has come to me," Smith said late in her career, "is that I was always a lady in the Senate, although I was as firm as any man around the table when it came to legislation on an issue I was particularly interested in."[55] Smith prided herself on never asking for or receiving special privileges and advised all other women in politics to do the same.

Maurine Neuberger was Smith's one experience with another female senator, and, after escorting Neuberger down the aisle for her swearing in, their relationship was more of a nonexperience. "She let Maurine know right away that there was going to be no tea-partying," a colleague of the two observed. "She seemed to balk at the idea of being linked together as 'just we girls.' "[56] Another senator comparing the two said that Smith "takes herself very seriously," but "Maurine Neuberger takes a lot of good-natured kidding from us men."[57] By press consensus Smith was "upright, almost stiff."[58]

Given the pejorative connotations of feminism that many people had in the 1960s and 1970s, Smith's deliberate separation from the women's movement made some political sense. Alienating the press, which she also did, made none. An extreme sensitivity to criticism became Smith's Achilles heel early in her career, a vulnerability that many held Lewis responsible for nurturing. The most extensive of Smith's files are under the heading of "Press Relations," and they contain hundreds and hundreds of letters, many drafted by Lewis, remonstrating the press for inaccuracies, criticisms, and opposing interpretations. To illustrate, Lewis wrote a letter for Smith's signature to Lewiston reporter Jack Toomey, referring to her critics as a "hate-gang," "the ones who have always attacked me—Fulton Lewis, Jr., Ruth Montgomery, the *Bangor News*, etc."[59] In the biographical files Lewis wrote on hundreds of Smith's acquaintances, he characterized Toomey as a "very loyal friend of Senator Smith."[60]

In a profile on columnist John O'Donnell, Lewis wrote that O'Donnell was a "bitter and constant critic and enemy of Senator Smith."[61] Lewis called George Sokolsky a "rabid McCarthyite" who "has attacked Senator Smith on several occasions."[62] Under "Publishers–Anti" Lewis listed twenty-two times that press figures as diverse as David Lawrence, Victor Lasky, and Austine Hearst had referred to Smith. These biographical entries were often contradictory in that both positive and negative references were included, but it was the inconsistency that bothered Lewis. Either the person was invariably loyal to Smith or went on the enemy list. Lewis wrote to columnist Jack Anderson to compliment him and added, "Perhaps there is something unusual in my saying this since I have always regarded you as being unfriendly to Senator Smith."[63] Indeed, a year earlier Lewis had written over Smith's signature that "Mr. Anderson has long been making misrepresentations against me and he will continue to do so."[64] Fulton Lewis, Jr., was another reporter on whom Lewis frequently commented, saying that he "repeatedly libeled Senator Smith with vicious lies. What made him so mad was that she ignored him like a minuscule gnat nipping at an elephant."[65] Lewis, writing for Smith's signature, characterized Robert Novak as having a "deprecating and unfriendly attitude toward her."[66]

Lewis kept files on specific publications as well as on reporters. For *Time-Life* Publications Lewis collected article excerpts in reference to Smith, one of which referred to her as "cold, calculating, and thorny."[67] Another reported her concern that the "Eisenhower Administration did not pay enough attention to the only woman in the Senate."[68] Other carefully culled references had Smith "unforgivingly sore," maintaining "pursed-lipped silence about her intentions," and being motivated by "pique."[69] The *Chicago Daily Tribune,* according to Lewis, was "maliciously against Senator Smith," and Smith referred to it as "inaccurate and irresponsible with respect to her."[70] She frequently commented on a 1947 editorial that referred to her as a man but of which the editorial staff had no memory. Smith retorted that the staff "apparently have poor memories—or convenient loss of memory—that they are apparently as faulty in their memories as in their facts."[71] Richard E. Warren, publisher of the *Bangor Daily News,* became so concerned about the "bitterness which exists in your heart" about his paper that he engaged in lengthy correspondence with Smith to remedy the situation.[72] Smith curtly responded with an enumerated eleven-item list of differences and concluded that she would "show just as much friendliness and cooperation as the *News* does."[73]

Lewis and/or Smith felt the same way about the *Saturday Evening Post,* which they wrote had "a record of 'hatchet' jobs on me."[74] Smith particularly resented a "snide" article Maxine Cheshire wrote for the magazine about her during her 1960 campaign.[75] Lewis, Maine congressman Stanley Tupper said, gave Cheshire a "tremendous tongue-lashing" for coming to Skowhegan and asking people about Smith.[76] Referring to Cheshire as a "Washington gossip reporter," Smith said that the experience was notable because of Cheshire's "penchant for standing close to me eavesdropping" and for her "saccharine praise of me."[77] "Brace yourself," Lewis told her. "That spoken sugar is going to turn to vinegar in print."[78] "It did," Smith concluded.[79] To an objective reader the article is colorful and balanced, but balance appeared to be the problem. Those reporters who escaped Smith's and Lewis's criticisms were "loyal" and "good friends," not balanced in their reporting. Lewis wrote that Jack Toomey was "a contrast" to "our Fair-weather friends,"[80] and Smith thanked Josephine Ripley for her "loyal friendship."[81] Before Ruth Montgomery became objective in her reporting, Lewis, writing for Smith, referred to her as "our good friend."[82] Frances

Hapgood of the Gannett papers was another whom Smith, writing over her own initial, appreciated for her "loyal friendship."[83]

Commonly the correspondence corrected presumed inaccuracies or interpretations and often intemperately. Smith wrote to the editor of the *Overseas Weekly* that an article about her had been "a deliberate, personal smear against me."[84] In another letter Smith wrote, "The publication *Family Week* lied."[85] On another occasion Lewis wrote Drew Pearson a five-page, single-spaced letter correcting a column and concluded that Pearson's writing was "reminiscent of 'guilt by association' and 'trial by accusation' tactics."[86]

Over the years Smith's primary concern with the press involved the Gannett papers in Maine and their Washington correspondent, May Craig. The senator's initially friendly relations with both changed, not coincidentally, when Lewis assumed direction of her office. He saw it differently and wrote for Smith, "As friendly as Guy and Mrs. Gannett were to me, it seems that their children are just as unfriendly."[87] Smith believed that the Gannett daughter, Jean, and her reporters, Dwight Sargent and Pete Damborg, were "against" her and had an "obvious desire to see me destroyed politically."[88] Jean Gannett Williams Hawley, whom Lewis derided as "Jean Gannett many names," had another explanation.[89] As a young woman learning the business, she visited Washington and made "courtesy calls" on Maine's congressional delegation.[90] Because of her father's relationship with Smith, Hawley assumed that she had a "closeness" to Senator Smith but was quickly disabused of the assumption.[91] Smith "lambasted" her and said that "your papers have been cruel and not kind to me. I was dumbfounded, and I said, 'Senator, I do not know what you are talking about. I think we've been very supportive of you.' . . . From then on our relationship was not very friendly."[92] Lewis saw Hawley as "unfriendly and opposed to Senator Smith and a very ardent supporter of Senator Muskie."[93] This "anti-Smith pro-Muskie . . . policy of the Gannett chain," Lewis believed, was the work of Hawley "under the recommendations of Dwight Sargent . . . and Peter Damborg . . . with enthusiastic support from May Craig."[94]

Smith had ended her personal relationship with Craig during her first Senate term, but of necessity their professional dealings continued. Hawley believed the friendship ended because Smith concluded that Craig "was not favorable to her," and Craig was "quite hurt emotionally and deeply because Margaret didn't want to have anything more to do with her."[95] Smith wrote Craig that she considered "your Maine in Washington column one of the meanest reporting jobs ever done on me."[96] Craig had reported that Smith had attended a cocktail party without mentioning that the Muskies and other officials were also there. Smith assured Craig that she did not drink and was there only a short time. Craig responded that there was "nothing naughty in you being there" and expected the others to complain because she had not mentioned them.[97] Worse than that, Smith tried to have Craig fired. "Is there any chance that you might someday replace May Craig as the Washington correspondent?" Smith wrote Frances Hapgood, a Gannett employee, in 1957.[98] "I would like to see that happen. But I wouldn't dare mention it myself."[99] Smith came close to mentioning it herself when she wrote to the general manager of the Guy Gannett Publishing Company, Robert B. Beith, to complain about Craig. "The unfriendliness of your Washington correspondent toward me," Smith wrote, "has been evident for a long time . . . but it is going too far for your correspondent . . . to repeatedly carry false statements about me."[100]

Relations declined further when Craig went public with the widely rumored feud between Smith and Edmund Muskie. Specifically, Craig's strident pen wrote that the Maine congressional delegation did not meet in September 1962 because of "hard feelings" between the two senators.[101] Smith wrote Craig a three-page, single-spaced letter maintaining that there were no "hard feelings" between Muskie and herself,[102] and the next day Craig responded, "I regret the error."[103] Refusing to let it go, Smith, referring to herself as a "former member of the press," read a statement on the floor of the Senate in condemnation of "criticism based upon misrepresentation" as "negative, destructive and unworthy of the traditions of journalism."[104] Then she reminded Craig and her other critics, although not by name, that "several years ago when serious misrepresentations were made against me by a writer-reporter and a publisher, I sued them for libel."[105] In denial of the feud allegation but inadvertently in illustration of it, Smith wrote Muskie a four-page, single-spaced letter in which she concluded, "Mrs. Craig is guilty of a flat misinterpretation."[106] Then Smith took the issue to the January 1963 delegation meeting, which the press covered, because she considered Craig's column "a matter of printed reflection on the integrity of the delegation—on the two Senators. This misrepresentation is grave. But the indicated attitude of the writer is even more grave. I feel deeply that Mrs. Craig has no right to imply that we are fighting over petty things to the detriment of Maine interests."[107] While agreeing that the story was in error, Muskie saw it as speculative, "not deliberate misrepresentation."[108] Still unhappy, Smith used her 10 March 1963 congressional report on WGAN-Portland to elaborate on Craig and the issue, as she saw it, of "managed news."[109]

In a 29 March 1963 editorial the *Portland Press-Herald* defended Craig and alleged that over the years Smith had changed "until now she has become super-sensitive to honest errors, unintended slights, and objective criticism. The conviction grows that Senator Smith would like to see published . . . only news and comment that meet her approval." The editorial expressed the paper's regret that Smith had reached a "state of mind" where she saw the "slightest difference of opinion as hostility." Personally Craig did not respond, but increasingly her columns began, "Senator Edmund Muskie said today . . ."[110]

With the headline "Maggie vs. May," *Newsweek* picked up the story and referred to Smith's "claws being out of the sheath" against Craig over WGAN.[111] The account trivialized the incident but quoted Smith as ordering "no press release be sent to Mrs. Craig's desk."[112] Smith's comment on the article was that "my enemies call me Maggie."[113] According to Gannett reporter John Murphy, "Everybody called her that. Certainly not to her face. That's the way she was always known to me in the newspaper business."[114]

Lewis called Don Larrabee, the *Bangor Daily News* correspondent in Washington, to tell him that Craig was "persona non grata in this office from now on."[115] Lewis also called reporters to read "chapter and verse of things she'd written that he said showed she wasn't a reliable reporter."[116] Larrabee believed Lewis "did it deliberately I think to embarrass and hurt her."[117] By this time, Craig was, depending on one's perspective, either a Washington monument or a Washington joke. The younger generation did not know about her fight for female press rights, her being the first woman to cover the London blitz and liberated Paris, and her flying the Berlin Airlift. Instead, at presidential press conferences they saw a tiny old lady in flowery hats and funny suits being the butt of John Kennedy's humor or Lyndon Johnson's patronizing. Miss May's mind was still sharp, her questions dodge-proof, and her repartee with presidents tart, and she was certain to be called on. When Craig retired in 1967, Larrabee succeeded her and rode the same roller coaster with Smith and Lewis that she had. He started out as confidant, with Lewis calling him to read "letters he'd written to other reporters in which he was critical of the things they had written."[118] Then Larrabee wrote what he considered an accurate and laudatory reference to the Smith-Lewis relationship's being "the greatest love story ever seen in Washington" and received their unfailing condemnation. Larrabee's reference was to "the essence of true love," "of people needing each other and working together, and depending on each other."[119] "This was the friend that he turned out to be," Senator Smith said, still angry in 1988. "But Don did that and he was a very dishonest man and still is as far as I know."[120]

Another cherished affront from the press was what Smith and Lewis both referred to as the "Damborg mission."[121] The Gannett papers sent Peter Damborg to photograph the house in which Smith and Lewis lived. As Hawley recalled, the photographer was to get photos of all the houses of the Maine congressional delegation. Smith and Lewis assumed the story was to suggest that they were living together instead of sharing the same house, as they had for years. "It was not deliberately done as an invasion of privacy," Hawley said, but their reaction was "fiery."[122] In the backlash, Congressman Tupper believed that Damborg almost lost his job over the inference because he was the first to print the innuendo.[123] Larrabee remembered that there "was a lot of gossip and talk," but "nobody ever wrote about those things very much in those days."[124] Larrabee and Bill Caldwell were among the few people, and probably the only reporters, to be invited to the house. "It had more privacy than most houses in Silver Spring," Caldwell thought,[125] and neither he nor Larrabee saw anything to convince them of anything more than a convenient living arrangement for two people who shared a life of work together. *Press-Herald* reporter John Murphy said Larrabee nonetheless became convinced that they were "husband and wife" and that he would eventually "find a record that Maggie and Bill Lewis had been married."[126] The record was never found, for the good reason that they were not married, but Mike Posner said that "everybody in the Senate talked about them anyway." "There was no secret about their living arrangement"; "it was common knowledge," and "it was always titillating," according to Posner. "These dirty old men," as he flippantly referred to the senators, "were always whispering about Bill Lewis and what was his real relationship to Maggie. I have no idea if they were sleeping together or not." Posner remembered that "once I walked in the office" and "there was this shouting match going. It was Bill Lewis, knowing there were reporters present, really bawling her out. I mean it was embarrassing for us," because "it was like a marital spat."[127] The gossip was there, but aside from the "Damborg mission," which resulted in nothing more than a published photograph of the house as Smith's home, nothing was written in the press about her relationship with Lewis. Smith was aware of the "miserable stories" in circulation and believed the Damborg mission was "to sniff around to see if they could find something." Surprisingly, "I never had it come up in my campaigns," she said.[128]

A near unanimous consensus emerged from reporters in both Washington and Maine that Smith had abysmal relations with the press, unlike those of any other senator, and that Lewis was responsible. Larrabee, who next to Craig knew them best, believed Lewis convinced himself that "most of the men were out to do her harm and to hurt her in various ways, and he was going to make sure that they didn't." Then Lewis's "paranoia controlled her thinking," because he "instilled it in her. If he decided someone was against her, she believed it. He obviously convinced her that he was the only person in the world that could keep her from harm."[129] "I'm not sure Margaret Chase Smith ever really trusted anyone except Bill Lewis," Posner agreed; "he built the Margaret Chase Smith image, and they both wanted it to remain sacrosanct."[130] "She was always very sensitive," Don Hensen added, "almost as though she felt she should be beyond criticism."[131] "An assumed slight would send Maggie into a frenzy," Dwight Sargeant told John Murphy who thought the general feeling was that Smith was "hyper-sensitive to criticism."[132] "The guys around here had no use for her," Bill Caldwell learned when he went to work for the Gannett papers. "She's a pain, she gets upset on the least thing, she's vindictive," he heard but "had never seen that side of Margaret" until later. He learned that "if anybody, that included the newspapers, was not a hundred percent for Margaret they were Lewis's enemy," and Caldwell believed Lewis was a "spiteful man of tremendous loyalty to Margaret."[133] Posner saw Smith as "vindictive" also; "she held a grudge, and I'll tell you Margaret Chase Smith never forgot. She never forgot."[134] Making this catch-22 for reporters, John Murphy added, was that "Maggie's sources were myriad. All these old ladies in Maine love Maggie, and they would feed her reports and rumors. She had a network out there." Then a reporter would "receive a letter from the Senator and no matter what you've written and no matter what you've professed publicly," Smith would up-braid because "I've been told that you were heard to say such and such."[135]

The result was the formation of the Order of the Wilted Rose by those who had been stung by Smith's criticisms. Columnist George Dixon first brought the "clandestine organization," as he called it, to the public's atten-tion. He said that the membership requirement was "being chewed out by Smith," and although members did not carry cards or parade, Smith con-sidered the group "tinged with subversion." That had to do, Dixon went on, with her "persecution complex" and her "sense of what was due her."[136] Writer Peggy Lamson believed that members of this "unofficial society" had once been "quite close" to Smith but had "for one reason or another fallen from grace."[137] Although most members were reporters, Dixon said that the "ex officio membership" included all of the Maine congressional delegation, many Republicans, and Richard Nixon as the "best known member, because he had been chewed out so often it was a wonder he didn't look like a beaver dam."[138] According to reporter Len Cohen, the group should be open to anyone who had received one of Smith's "waspish letters,"[139] but there was concern about the society's becoming too large. Lewis considered the "snide attitude" of the Order of the Wilted Rose "despicable," and believed "ev-eryone should be proud that Senator Smith was sensitive and did take ex-ceptions to attacks on her character."[140]

For all of her problems with women and the press, Smith's 1966 campaign for a fourth term showed that the bloom was still on the rose. As in 1960, the Republicans did not field a primary opponent for her, and the Democrats had difficulty finding someone foolhardy enough to run. The sacrificial lamb selected was state senator Elmer H. Violette, a Van Buren attorney and conservationist who had been active politically since 1921. His fellow Dem-ocratic candidate, Peter Kyros, remembered Violette as a "wonderful man" with "this sweet style and gentleness" who ran "a homespun campaign."[141] "I had my eyes wide open . . . when I entered the race," he said; Smith is "the greatest vote getter in Maine history, but in an election anything can happen."[142] What immediately happened was that the Republican candidate for the Senate flew into Maine with the Democratic president on *Air Force One* to begin her campaign. In Portland, Smith emerged, to the delight of photographers, directly behind Lyndon, Lady Bird, and Lynda Bird Johnson and set off a flurry of speculation about the senator's relationship with the president. While Johnson was briefly photographed with Violette, the real story was that the president had pledged not to campaign against Smith, "his long time personal friend."[143] Press speculation about their "intriguing relationship" varied from "love story" to "political marriage" and did Smith as much good as her three-term record.[144] Mrs. Johnson said that "there is a bond between them, a great respect and liking,"[145] and her press secretary, Liz Carpenter, believed LBJ "flattered a lot of women. He liked women. A slight flirtation . . . with Helen Douglas or Margaret Smith might have been part of the mannerism that goes with Southern men."[146] Once President Johnson called Senator Smith to say, "I just wanted to call you and tell you I loved you. I don't have anything to talk to you about except that I missed seeing you. . . . You're my sweet girl and a mighty big patriot . . . and I had one minute and wanted to spend it telling you so."[147]

Toward the end of the campaign Violette commented gently that lately Smith had not been "active" for Maine and complained about her "brief visits to Maine."[148] As mild as the complaints were, Smith was "delighted that he had changed his tactics so drastically" and called Violette's "charges" "false and malicious."[149] She rebutted the criticism with her well-honed "Don't Trade a Record for a Promise" speech and illustrated her service to Maine with her "all-time voting attendance record," which was nearing 2,400 consecutive votes.[150] Her record was as impressive in terms of staying close to the people of Maine because she claimed a visit to the state each month for the past 104 consecutive months—nearly nine years. Smith won easily with 59 percent of the vote, but so did the Democratic candidates for governor and Congress. The Democratic conclusion about the Republicans in the 1966 election was, "Boy, are these guys in a bad way."[151]

During the campaign there had been speculation, probably encouraged by Lewis, that Smith intended to seek the chairmanship of the Senate Republican Conference after her reelection.[152] Indeed, many reporters saw her running more for the chairmanship than for her assumed reelection to the Senate. Leverett Saltonstall of Massachusetts was retiring from both the conference chairmanship and the Senate, but Smith demurred, "If I took that position, I should have my head examined."[153] Conservative senator from New Hampshire Norris Cotton wanted the position, but Smith's nominator of choice, George Aiken, promoted her for the position. In keeping with Senate tradition, Aiken, immediately after the election, circulated letters to Republican leaders asking for their support for Smith as conference chairman. Positive responses were immediately forthcoming from Gordon Allott, Clifford Case, Edward Brooks, Jacob Javits, John Sherman Cooper, and John J. Williams.[154] Typical of their replies, Edward Brooke, Saltonstall's successor, said that he had long admired Smith's "dedication, her independent judgment, and the constructive Republicanism which has characterized her service."[155] With this support going in, Aiken had no difficulty in having Smith unanimously elected.

A woman had never before or since held the position for either party, and Smith saw it as her entry into the leadership group. "I was accepted. I was a part of the United States Senate," she said. "I was in the inner circle."[156] Others saw the position more as an honor than evidence of leadership or power. Smith as chairman presided at the rare party caucuses, but the real power resided in the Policy Committee where Gordon Allott presided over a select group of sixteen senators, nominated and elected by the conference. Still, as Maine senator and Senate majority leader George Mitchell said in 1989, "You don't rise to become chairman of the conference without being a person of significance and influence."[157] At the same time Maine's Republican senator, William Cohen, pointed out that a perquisite of the conference chairman was representing the Congress at White House meetings, which were held every Thursday during Smith's last term. By any measure, in a system based on seniority, Smith's election to a fourth term, her elevation to conference chairman, membership on the Policy Committee, ranking minority position on Armed Services and Space and third on Appropriations made her a Senate power. All the more as Senator Robert Dole observed, "When you do your committee work, you have influence," and Smith remained diligent toward her responsibilities.[158]

As frequently happens with legislators who survive the brutal election process and grow old in Washington, history seemed to pass Margaret Chase Smith by just as she reached her long-sought goal of seniority. She watched as her friend, majority leader, and president, Lyndon Johnson, left Washington in disgrace and Joe McCarthy's old friend, Richard Nixon, replaced him in the White House. Helpless, she saw the Senate come under the ineffectual leadership of Mike Mansfield of Montana and the Republican party decline with its rancorous division into conservative and moderate-to-liberal wings. Most distressing as a member of the latter group, she realized that her and their "fierce individual independencies" kept them from "uniting behind one clear leader."[159]

At first Smith tried to develop a power base with her position as chairman of the Republican Conference. Long a dormant organization, the conference seldom met and never other than for organizational purposes. Smith proposed weekly meetings for an exchange of views; she specifically wanted to establish a party consensus on the Vietnam War. Of the thirty-five Republicans, only Jacob Javits of New York supported her, and the best Smith accomplished was a Tuesday luncheon meeting. Although she considered these mini-conferences "one of the nicest things I've seen happen," they were sporadically attended and eventually ended.[160] Smith also used the conference in an effort to end what she referred to as "unwarranted incursions" by some committees into the jurisdiction of other committees.[161] Her initial effort was "mostly ignored," according to conference staff member Sam Bouchard; she tried again and "got more attention but it still didn't get done."[162] Another of her conference initiatives was to have Bouchard document the absenteeism on roll call votes for each senator and to use what Bouchard called "the public school grading system where below seventy was not passing" to rank individual senators.[163] Smith published the results with a proposed constitutional amendment that members of Congress below 10 percent attendance be expelled. Bouchard said that there were "ten senators that would have been expelled and another ten who would have gotten a D."[164] Speaking from the all-time record of 2,941 consecutive roll call votes, Smith justified her initiative by maintaining that "the United States Senate is in trouble" because of the "chronic absences" of "presidential candidates," "moonlighters," and "prima donnas." "No wonder the American public is so fed up with Congress" and "those Senators who are dedicated" are discouraged, she chided.[165]

Predictably the report produced general consternation among her colleagues, a great amount of publicity (some twenty-five thousand letters to Smith alone), and no action. Policy Committee chairman Gordon Allott, among those embarrassed, not only "hated her guts because of that study," according to Bouchard, he also saw to it that the conference returned to its former dormancy.[166]

Smith fared better on her other committees, especially Space, where Sam Bouchard was also on the staff and maintained that chairman Clinton P. Anderson of New Mexico treated her as co-chairman. On other committees, Bouchard had observed that minority members were "barely kept informed and most kept in the cold," but Anderson "didn't make a move without her, always kept her informed . . . and they made decisions together."[167] Space was the committee of choice during the 1960s, because John Kennedy had declared space America's New Frontier and made its conquest part of the Cold War. Early Soviet successes had launched a space race between the two nations, and ever the cold warrior, Smith agreed that U.S. honor required being first to land a man on the moon with Project Apollo. Victory came in 1969, cost $24 billion, and generated criticisms that the money could have been better spent in poor states like Maine to generate jobs, improve education, and care for the poor and elderly. With Anderson, Smith successfully lobbied colleagues for further funding and made difficult choices like voting for the space shuttle and against mass transit programs, increased funding for Project Head Start and food stamps, and unemployment compensation for migrant farmworkers. She justified her commitment to the space program because it gave the United States "unprecedented preeminence" over the Soviet Union and "practical benefits" in weather forecasting, international communications, defense, and environmental protection.[168]

On Armed Services, Smith continued to defend the military, which in turn protected Maine's defense industries. Being a cold warrior was both a matter of conscience for her as well as good politics. Here she was in the unique position of also being on Appropriations and, specifically, a member of Appropriations' Subcommittee on Defense. These assignments gave Smith a powerful voice on both defense policy and defense spending. She opposed reducing American forces in Europe, ending military aid to Greece, prohibiting U.S. aid to foreign police, and reducing technical aid abroad. "The day of reckoning is approaching," Smith said in 1971 in an attempt to increase the defense budget; "the balance of military power is shifting to the Soviet Union."[169] Both Richard Russell, Democrat of Georgia, and John Stennis, Democrat of Mississippi, as successive chairmen of the committee, agreed with Smith on the Cold War and on defense appropriations. The ever-genteel Stennis said that Russell talked to him about Smith's willingness "to do her part, go her part of the way, and make her part of the sacrifices. You relied on her work and took her representations as correct facts," Stennis learned; "I knew when Margaret put her foot down on the facts, as we used to say that's what the facts were." In part, these powerful chairmen disarmed Smith by making her their confidante, but as Stennis saw it, he had "to have someone that he could talk to and learn facts and get confidential information from, and I was always free to go to Senator Smith and discuss the facts with her."[170] In deference to Smith's independence, Stennis added that "she almost frightened me to death in a tie vote matter on several occasions." On other issues he added, "She resisted all drives on her to desert me in debate."[171]

Over the years Smith became increasingly sensitive to being "indiscriminately maligned" along with the other members of Armed Services as " 'tools' and 'puppets' of the military-industrial complex."[172] In rebuttal to the old chestnut that she never saw a new weapon that she did not like, she actively opposed the antiballistic missile system (the ABM) from 1967 through 1969. Although she had initially followed the lead of both the Johnson administration and Richard Russell, whom she considered a "great man" who had "pretty much brought" her "up," and voted for deployment of the ABM, she changed her mind publicly.[173] For the next six months the ABM was the greatest national security controversy since the 1941 draft, which had passed by one vote, her's, Smith had claimed. Increasingly convinced that the presumed Soviet ABM system might "be decoys of classic deception designed to motivate us to a very costly defense system," she voted with the minority in committee against the Safeguard ABM in 1968.[174] By the time the ABM reached the floor in 1969 in the defense procurement bill, Nixon was president, Stennis chairman, and both were fervent supporters of the system.

As the senior Republican on Armed Services, Smith did not want to take the lead in opposing the new president but saw no way to vote against just the ABM except to propose what she called a "fish or cut bait" amendment.[175] On 6 August 1969, Smith quietly but firmly defended her amendment before a tense Senate and in so doing maintained control of the floor for four hours. "In all my years," one senator told Bill Lewis, "I have never seen one Senator dominate the Senate floor as long as she did. And to think it would be the only woman in the one hundred Senators!"[176] In her brief defense Smith stated that the American offensive arsenal, not defensive technology, had preserved the peace during the twenty-five years of the Cold War. As quickly as armaments were developing, she believed the ABM would be "an obsolete white elephant" by the time it was deployed, "a self-deluding Maginot Line."[177] She preferred supporting the new laser technology that scientists were already reporting would be less costly and more effective than the ABM. Appreciating both the controversy of her decision as well as Nixon as adversary, Smith dramatically ended by affirming her belief "in America," "in our form of government," "in free enterprise," and in "our American way of life. The ABM is not an acid test of patriotism."[178]

As the other anti-ABM senators crowded around Smith, Mansfield observed that he had "never seen so many men so publicly woo one woman."[179] More tartly, ABM supporter Barry Goldwater asked Lewis if he were "sure there wasn't a witch somewhere in Margaret's New England ancestry."[180] Stennis became so angry that, Smith said, "he shouted out at me, the only time he ever did."[181] On the final vote, after minor wording changes to secure more support, Vice President Spiro Agnew took the gavel, all one hundred senators took their seats, and the clerk began the roll call. Smith's friend Clinton Anderson had told her, "Margaret, I'm with you," but right before the vote, ABM supporter Henry Jackson, Democrat from Washington, turned him around, and the vote ended fifty to fifty, with Agnew breaking the tie in favor of the ABM.[182] Possibly balancing the defeat, Mike Mansfield said, "Margaret Chase Smith is a first-class Senator. She has a mind of her own."[183]

All this time Smith had been on the periphery of the 1960s upheaval. Feminist or not, she was once again the only woman in the Senate and a valuable political symbol for the women's movement. Since the war between the generations began on the battlefield of civil rights, she was for a time on the ramparts and voted for the Civil Rights Act of 1964, the Voting Rights Act of 1965, open housing legislation, and equal enforcement of integration in the North and South. When blacks took the reins of the movement from whites and black power, black pride, and Black Panthers led to riots in Watts, Newark, and Washington, D.C., Smith stepped back and voted against busing by federal court order, withholding federal aid for not busing, and funding to integrate all metropolitan schools. Since her values had been forged on Maine's puritan anvil, hammered into her psyche by the Great Depression, and painted red, white, and blue by World War II-become-the-Cold War, Smith was on record early for the war in Vietnam.

As far back as 1953 Smith had lectured all over Maine on U.S. responsibility in Indochina. At a time when most Americans could not locate the nation on a map, Smith applied Cold War reasoning that as the fall of China had led to North Korea's invasion of the South, so the Korean War would lead to Indochina. She approved the $400 million the Eisenhower administration had given to the French to suppress the Indochinese rebellion against colonialism and had no difficulty separating French imperialism from "the cynical and brutal Red Imperialism."[184] Accepting the Cold War domino theory, Smith said that "if Indochina falls to the Reds, Burma, Thailand, Malaya, and Indonesia would not long remain free."[185] She justified American interest in Indochina by stressing its production of rice, four-fifths of the world's rubber, half of the world's tin, and various strategic minerals. Although she supported American involvement in Indochina, she saw it was a "calculated risk" and "for a period the length of which will test our patience."[186]

French failure the next year led to increased American support for Ngo Dinh Diem's government in South Vietnam and Chinese sponsorship of Ho Chi Minh in North Vietnam. By the time John Kennedy became president, the South Vietnamese had rebelled against Diem's repressive policies and had the assistance of Ho Chi Minh's Vietcong. Already an entrenched Kennedy critic, Margaret Chase Smith faulted the president's limited escalation of more aid and advisers for Diem when his own administration officials, General Maxwell Taylor and Walt Rostow, called for American ground troops. In Smith's opinion, Kennedy was "either unrealistic" or "deliberately withholding or misrepresenting the facts" and, whichever, she feared the area's loss to communism.[187] She did not protest when Kennedy approved the CIA-sponsored overthrow and assassination of Diem in November 1963 right before his own assassination. Although Smith had visited with Diem years earlier in her around-the-world trip for CBS, she waited two years before referring to his death as "one of the greatest tragedies" in Vietnam and remembering his oppressive government as "stable."[188]

In her 1964 presidential campaign Smith took a "pull out or fight" position and considered a trip to Vietnam because she continued to fear Americans did not have the facts on what was happening.[189] By then Lyndon Johnson had increased Americans there to 15,000 and aid by $50 million, but his defense secretary, Robert McNamara, referred to the U.S. presence in Vietnam as a "training operation" from which troops would be withdrawn by the end of 1965.[190] Smith saw a "quagmire" instead and feared the lack of official information was because Americans were losing a "hot war." In radio broadcasts in Maine she asked what her listeners thought.[191] She received "the grand total of four letters" but continued to criticize the administration for withholding vital information from her defense committees even though McNamara was now warning of "a long and hard war."[192]

In August 1964 in an atmosphere of national crisis, Smith listened to President Johnson tell Congress that North Vietnamese torpedo boats had attacked the *U.S. Maddox* in the Gulf of Tonkin and, without questioning his interpretation of dubious events, voted with the majority for the Gulf of Tonkin Resolution to enlarge the war. Smith credited Johnson with "at long last" adopting a "firm policy" but believed if he had done so earlier the nation would not be in such a "deplorable mess."[193] Smith advised Johnson to declare a "national emergency, call up the Reserve and the National Guard, invoke price and wage controls, and go all-out for complete victory."[194] Instead, in 1965 LBJ authorized the use of ground troops in Vietnam, the bombing of North Vietnam, and greater funding, all of which resulted in a policy of steady escalation to half a million soldiers, expanded bombing, and an eventual $123 billion being spent on the war. To Smith, this was inadequate and marked the transition of Johnson from "bold leader" to "reluctant leader."[195] Lewis was harsher in his judgment and bluntly saw it as a "lack of political courage" on Johnson's part. "He didn't have the courage to do the hard things that should have been done," Lewis said, "no question in my mind."[196]

Johnson's decisions also led to a student revolt, which disturbed Smith more than the war. At first she believed that "our enemies—the Communists" were "playing an important role in organizing and directing these youngsters"[197] and said so on the floor of the Senate, to the derision of those who were marching on Washington. Increasingly offended by the students' long hair, rock music, love beads, promiscuity, and drugs, Smith said, "How tragic are such misguided youth" and drew attention to "stalwart young Americans" who were leading traditional lives.[198] "Smart aleck draft card burners" especially disturbed her, but she did not want them arrested because in their "warped and distorted way of thinking, arrest would place them all the more in the role of a martyr."[199] Instead, Smith wanted them drafted and placed with those who were courageously fighting.

"I have been publicly supporting your policy on Vietnam," Smith wrote to President Johnson, and what she was saying was that "we have no choice but to stay in"; to pull out would be "to leave a country and people to the mercy of the communist enemy."[200] Smith supported Johnson on Armed Services, Appropriations, and the new CIA Subcommittee. Always a hawk, she was now part of the warriors' circle of Russell, Stennis, Symington, and Jackson and met with them in committee behind closed doors more often than not to receive secret briefings on the war. They supported Johnson's orders to bomb Hanoi and Haiphong and increased the Defense Department's request for $17 million by $167.9 million in 1966. "If more is needed to supply our forces there," Smith said to the press, "I am confident the committee is prepared to provide it."[201]

"But voices are growing louder and louder" in opposition to the war, Smith observed. " . . . Not only is the President in trouble—our country is in trouble."[202] For her the riots, protests, and defiance of the law were "reminiscent of the destructive emotional divisions of the McCarthy Era."[203] As those opposed to the war increased in number both inside and outside Congress, Margaret Chase Smith remained consistent (or hidebound, depending on one's perspective) and supported the mining of Haiphong harbor, increased bombing in North Vietnam, use of defoliant chemicals, and bombing of supply lines in Cambodia.

Smith believed the nation had returned "to those days of the smears," but what she encountered at Colby College on 9 May 1970 was altogether new and "the most unpleasant experience of my entire career."[204] Students across the nation had gone on strike after American incursions into Cambodia, and at Kent State University in Ohio National Guardsmen had opened fire on unarmed student protesters, killing four and wounding eleven. Sixteen striking schools in Maine united for a rally that Smith misunderstood to the extent of accepting an invitation to speak in defense of the war. Face to face for the first time with antiwar sentiment, which had shocked her on television, Smith said students shouted "invectives, insults, and even obscenity at me."[205] "Not until then did the full impact of youthful antagonism against our nation register with me," she added with naiveté, which the students saw as ignorance.[206] Asked how her mail was running on Cambodia, Smith turned to Lewis and audibly asked, "Bill, how has the mail been running on Cambodia?"[207] That she did not know, or presumably care, that her prized correspondence was six to one in opposition further antagonized the students, especially those who had been urged to write their senators instead of demonstrating. Compounding the difficulties of the encounter, another student asked how President Nixon could be trusted when he lied about American troops in Laos. Smith authoritatively denied that there were U.S. soldiers in Laos, only to have a Bowdoin student stand and explain how he had been wounded and half the men with him killed in Laos in 1969.

"There she was," *Maine Times* editor John Cole witnessed, "the highest ranking Republican on the Armed Services Committee, and she seemed to have almost no idea of what was happening in the war, and no idea how the students felt about it. It was just a sad performance by an old lady out of touch with reality."[208] To Smith the students were a "small minority" who supported "assault, arson, obscenity, trespass, and even murder," and what they needed was a "positive response" that the nation was "the greatest country in the history of the world."[209]

On 3 February 1972 Lewis sat down with Smith at 8:00 P.M. and handed her a memo that he had written on whether she should run for a fifth term. On the memo he had two columns, one headed with a plus sign and the other a minus sign. Under the reasons for announcing for reelection Lewis listed "Prestige—Stature, *Credibility,* Affection, *Sympathy—Resentment,* Established Following, *Potential Money, Stature Organization, Not Quitting, Potential Pres. of Senate, Continuing Causes.*" Under the minus column Lewis had "*Eyes, Age, Lewis, Muskie,* Primary—General, Money, Defeat, New Activity."[210]

That Lewis listed eyes as the first reason for Smith not to run was an indication that the macular degeneration that nearly blinded her later had begun. Blurring of the central vision with peripheral sight unaffected was the result, and Smith went to great lengths to be sure no one noticed. In the privacy of her office, she used magnifying lenses and telescopic aids to read, but the rate of the deterioration was unknown and the possibility of eventual blindness feared.

Smith was seventy-four years old, she would be seventy-five when the next term began and eighty-one when it ended. Age was the liability of the seniority system she prized, and the entire Senate leadership was its victim. Allen Ellender, Democrat from Louisiana, was eighty-one and chaired Appropriations; John McClellan, Democrat from Arkansas, was seventy-six and head of Government Operations; North Carolina Democrat B. Everett Jordan at age seventy-five led Rules and Administration; and John Sparkman, Alabama Democrat, chaired Banking, Housing, and Urban Affairs at age seventy-two. Stuart Symington, Missouri Democrat, was seventy-one; Strom Thurmond, Republican of South Carolina, was sixty-nine; and James Eastland, Mississippi Democrat, was sixty-seven. Although ageism had not yet developed as a reform, Smith had elderly colleagues who had decided to retire with dignity and not risk the humiliation of defeat, among them were Clinton Anderson, seventy-six, Len Jordon, seventy-three, and John Sherman Cooper, seventy.

Her health was notably absent from Lewis's list, although she had undergone hip replacement surgery in 1968 and 1970. Smith had never been in a hospital before and assumed "if you had a pain someplace you just put up with it."[211] The second surgery received more publicity because it involved total hip replacement with a new procedure. For some time after both surgeries, Smith was physically disabled, and the Senate built its first ramps to accommodate her wheelchair. She progressed to crutches and then to a cane with an elephant on its handle, which Barry Goldwater gave her, and for the first time she used the Senate pool for an hour before its regular opening time for physical therapy.

By 1972, Smith's recovery was complete, and her health was not a consideration for running, but overnight Lewis's health was. On 9 December 1971 Lewis drove Smith to Walter Reed for her scheduled checkup, and there he had a heart attack. For reasons of their own, they did not inform the press, but since the Senate was in session, she began missing votes. Her office turned away inquiries for two weeks before reporter Don Larrabee told Smith's brother-in-law, Spike Bernier, who was managing the office, "Look, this thing is building up. I can't talk to Bill. I can't talk to her. I've got to find out where she is. The papers are demanding it up in Maine. They want to know."[212] That afternoon the telephone in Larrabee's office rang, and Smith said, "This is Margaret. I'm at Walter Reed Hospital. Bill has had a heart attack and I want to be with him." "She wasn't sobbing," Larrabee noted, "but she was very emotional. She said I know you've been trying to reach me, but I can't leave here. I don't know what I would do without him." Larrabee asked if he could quote her, and "she said she didn't care; it didn't matter." To him it mattered because, "Good god, this was the first time she had come right" out and said that "she felt that devoted to him."[213]

For all of his interest in their relationship Larrabee had never informed Mainers of Lewis's influence on her. Now he wrote, "The name of William C. Lewis, Jr., may not have been a household word in Maine these past 23 years. In Washington it is synonymous with Sen. Margaret Chase Smith. . . . Lewis is treated with all the courtesy, honor and respect accorded the Senator herself. He is universally recognized as her alter ego without whom no major decision has been made for almost a quarter of a century."[214] Startled Mainers and fascinated Washington folk followed Larrabee's accounts for weeks. Smith took the room adjoining Lewis's, cared for him day and night, right through Christmas until he was better, and she could bring him home to recuperate. Larrabee considered it his "greatest story" but was surprised that Smith "wasn't bothered" by it and "seemed to feel it was fine."[215]

The "Lewis" on the minus list for running was whether his health would allow it. When Larrabee asked Smith about announcing, "She said if he wants me to run I'll do it. He was going to make that decision and she would do what he felt best."[216]

The reason that "Muskie" was on the minus list, Larrabee believed, was that Muskie was a good possibility for the 1972 Democratic presidential nomination. He was likely to carry Maine and probably the state Democratic ticket, and Smith did not want to lose because of Muskie, of all people.[217] Another interpretation was that if she lost, Muskie would be senior senator, and Smith could not countenance that either.

While Smith and Lewis contemplated their list of positives and negatives, a newcomer to Maine, Robert Monks, began campaigning for her seat. Monks was by any standard the antithesis of Smith: a young thirty-eight year old from old money, Harvard Phi Beta Kappa, Harvard Law School graduate, successful businessman, good family man, and dynamic campaigner. On the assumption "that people Senator Smith's age had not typically run for office again," Monks began traveling Maine in 1971 to acquaint himself with political and business leaders, women's groups, unions, and young people.[218] Some fifty thousand eighteen and nineteen year olds could vote for the first time in 1972, and, using professional campaign techniques, Monks had extensive polls showing that young newcomers in Maine were most likely to vote for him. Another poll showed three to one that Smith "had been around long enough" and "shouldn't run again."[219] Among Republicans Monks uncovered "an almost universal desire for Senator Smith to go" and an "enormous number of individual grievances," "just slight after slight," and the sentiment that Smith was "extremely vindictive."[220] Monks went to Washington in the spring of 1971 to meet with Smith and Lewis with the intention of telling them his plans but said that "candor got lost in politeness."[221] He left the meeting with the sense that what he had been hearing in Maine was accurate and that "they spent their time keeping score, who said what to whom about what, and Senator Smith would call people if she thought they weren't being sufficiently loyal to her or supportive of her."[222] Although he had been told that he "should be very careful," Monks sent Smith seventy-four highly publicized roses on her seventy-fourth birthday on 14 December 1971.[223] Assuming Lewis's heart attack earlier that month had taken them out of the race, Monks announced for the primary on 12 January 1972.

"Had Monks waited another month before he made his announcement," Smith said, "he would have had it like that, because I would not have been a candidate."[224] She would not, however, be forced into not running, and what Monks failed to poll was whether disgruntled Republicans in Maine would vote for him against Smith. They wanted her out but by retiring as an honored senior stateswoman, not by being defeated in a computer-run, expensive campaign waged by a brash, young, inexperienced outsider. On 8 February 1972, Smith ended weeks of intense speculation by stating from the Senate floor her intention to run and noting particularly the "gratifying extent to which young people have expressed confidence in me."[225]

Smith had not had a primary opponent since 1954, and she made sure the comparison between Robert Jones and Robert Monks was obvious. Although Monks's family had been in Maine since 1790 and he had been born there, he had been reared, educated, and employed in Massachusetts. Both his and his wife's families maintained summer homes in Maine, which they had frequently used, and in 1970 Monks moved to Cape Elizabeth, but to xenophobic Mainers he was "from away."

Massachusetts carpetbagger or not, what Monks said was accurate, and that was that in Maine the Republican party was in decline, with a Democratic governor, Democratic congressmen, and a Democratic senator whom early polls favored for a presidential nomination. Monks wanted to revitalize the party by recruiting young, energetic, and innovative members, and he offered his telephone banks, computer lists of voters, and dynamic leadership to local Republican candidates. Again, he heard in response criticisms of Smith's failure as state party leader, because she had her own network, would not campaign for other candidates, refused to host fund raisers, did not have an office in Maine, and seldom visited the state. A towering six-foot-six, ruggedly handsome, exuding energy and charm, Monks overnight flashed like a bolt of lightning from obscurity to prominence and promised to make rebuilding the party his "first priority."[226]

As accurate was Monks's emphasis on Maine's declining economy, a thirty-two-year decline that he contrasted with Smith's thirty-two-year rise to prominence in Congress. Although Smith was the ranking Republican on Armed Services, Maine was forty-third among the states in defense contracts and forty-sixth in funds distributed by the Department of Defense. Despite her top position on Appropriations, Maine was forty-seventh in federal expenditures.[227] In 1970 taxpayers in Maine, Monks pointed out, paid $741 million to Washington but received only $688 million in federal spending, which made the state one of only sixteen to get back less than it paid. In 1972

Maine also ranked thirty-seventh in reference to its large number of poor people and had twice the national average of people living in substandard housing. The state's per capita income was almost 20 percent below the nation's average, and unemployment was higher than the national average.[228]

Monks saw Maine at an economic crossroads where dozens of the state's traditional industries—shoe factories, textile mills, canneries, paper mills, and tanneries—had closed and new businesses had to be established. To do that he founded AIDE (Assistance for Industrial Development and Expansion), established sixty thousand new jobs as his goal, and promised to visit the executives of the top one hundred industries in the nation to persuade them to locate facilities in Maine. Monks did not hold Smith responsible for Maine's decline, but the implication was clear that she was not protecting the state, concerned herself more with national and international affairs, and lacked the vigor to remedy the state's problems. "Nothing wrong with her but father time" was as critical of Smith as Monks got.[229] Because his computers had a "Senator Smith macro," her "pattern of smears and enemies" in past campaigns, he was not surprised when she used the tactic against him.[230] He noted only that she resorted to this attack from the beginning, not at end as was her habit, but believed that was because for the first time since 1948 Smith was frightened.

"I thought Maine had finally been split off from Massachusetts," Smith said. "What are we doing having Massachusetts people run for the Senate."[231] In another press statement Smith insisted Monks "came to the state two years ago with nothing to do. He has money and time. I have neither."[232] When Monks graciously said in Falmouth, where he shared a platform with Smith, that if he lost he would support her in the general election, she responded that she could not make the same pledge because she intended to win. Referring to Monks's "Madison Avenue campaign," Smith told a Bangor audience that "even if I had unlimited finances, I would not attempt to win through the expenditure of vast sums of money."[233] In West Bath Smith took off her white gloves and refuted Monks's "petty lies," "unpleasant claims, accusations, and rumors," and "despicable tactics."[234] "Some of these rumors are getting ghoulish," she said. "I hear that I'm feeble, frail and failing. They're saying I'm not going to live through the next term."[235] A Senate seat should not be "put up for auction to the highest bidder," Smith continued, although she was "delighted to see" people come to Maine "even if only for political ambition."[236] Smith particularly resented a rumor that Lewis had one foot in the grave and believed that the "major effort to purge her" came from "non-Maine outsiders" who were "extreme liberals."[237]

She handled the age and health issues by campaigning as vigorously as she always had. Returning only on weekends in order to remain in Washington while the Senate was in session, she visited her friends across the state. "I can see this little woman," reporter Bill Caldwell said. "She's so small, probably had to sit on a damn cushion and drive this blunderbuss of a car all up and down those northern Maine roads."[238] Friends maintained that people half her age could not keep her schedule, and her aide Sam Bouchard said that he "almost had to run to keep up with her."[239]

With greater impact, Smith began announcing dozens of federal grants to Maine: more than $1 million for fifty units of low-rent housing in Portland, nearly $2 million to prevent traffic accidents, over $90,000 for Head Start, more than $74,000 for occupational health and safety.[240] A second list of grants included $355,000 for a senior citizens' housing center, $234,000 for programs for the aged, $1.3 million for law enforcement, and $280,000 for an antipoverty program.[241]

In March, Smith's *Declaration of Conscience* was published and reminded Mainers of her national prominence and, as the book cover read, her "courage, dedication and integrity."

By now Monks knew that he was in trouble and had been "extremely stupid" to emphasize his computer campaign because the technology was "hostile and threatening" and "exacerbated the perception of myself as an outsider."[242] He also believed that he had not handled the outsider issue well "by being defensive about it" and "talking about having grandparents born there."[243] In seeming rebuttal to Smith's book, friends of Monks arranged for freelance writer Berkeley Rice to publish an article titled, "Is the Great Lady from Maine out of Touch?" in the *New York Times Magazine* on 11 June 1972, eight days before the primary election. Although Smith considered the article a smear, the content was reasonably balanced. Rice used as bad a photograph of Smith as had ever been published, one that had her looking her age, when she and several newspapers had been using younger photographs during the campaign. The article referred to her as a "national institution," "the conscience of the Senate," and "a reflection of the traditional virtues of Maine." But Rice also referred to *Declaration of Conscience* as a "curious history of threats, intrigues, defections, and disloyalty. She describes at great length the minutest details of petty snubs, slights and discourtesies. Her book presents a world sharply divided into friends, traitors and enemies with the lady Senator always vindicated."[244]

Monks also had the good fortune while "he was in the desert" to find "an oasis": Stanley Tupper, former Republican congressman from Maine who had broken with Smith.[245] Tupper was one of Smith's traitors because he had supported Rockefeller in 1964, and in 1972, during the campaign, Smith tried to prevent the civil service promotion of Tupper's former aide Wayne Johnson to state director of federal housing. "For no other reason than the fact that she disliked me," Tupper said, "there was no other reason for it," she opposed a qualified "man who had lost his leg to cancer and overcome all kinds of handicaps."[246] Tupper spoke out against Smith saying, "The day when she can depend upon the three R's of roses, recipes, and roll calls may be at an end."[247] Wayne Johnson became a sympathetic cause for many, and he won his appointment, which made Smith look not only petty but powerless. "Her accomplishments have been in the past," Tupper told the press. "I think we need two very active United States Senators."[248] At other times Tupper had argued that Maine had three senators, because he had seen at first hand the control Lewis had on Smith. "I remember one time she was in my automobile in front of the old Augusta House . . . talking to me, front seat, friendly conversation," Tupper said. "Bill Lewis came down the steps of the Augusta House shouting to her to get out of the car. . . . It shocked me, . . . and it was the first instance when I realized this man was much more than an administrative assistant."[249]

With all his promise, Monks went from a flash of lightning to a flash in the pan. When Election Day came, he could not overcome his handicap of breeding, wealth, youth, and success. Smith defeated the sophisticated and expensive campaign ($147,000 to her $2,700) with better than 66 percent of the vote (76,702 to 38,398), not that she was in Maine to celebrate. She had voted absentee, returned to Washington, answered four roll call votes, and listened to the returns in her office between committee meetings. The next morning when she attended an Armed Services meeting, John Stennis held up Smith's arm and hailed "the champion of all champions."[250] As pleasing for Smith, Edmund Muskie's presidential quest, seemingly invincible, had shuddered to a humiliating conclusion, but ahead was the challenge of William Dodd Hathaway, an astute politician, proven vote getter and a popular opponent with little money of his own.

Forty-eight years old, Hathaway had been in the army air corps during World War II, shot down over Romania, and a prisoner of war. With a Harvard Law School degree he moved to Maine in 1953 to practice with Frank Coffin, who with Muskie began the Democratic resurgence the next year. Hathaway was politically involved from the beginning and was elected to Congress in 1964. His early contact with Smith convinced him that "she wasn't as strong as most people thought," and he observed the "excessive control" Lewis (whom he called "sour apple") had on her.[251] Hathaway went over to the Senate to see Smith once, waited until she came to the cloakroom after a vote, and had Lewis angrily join them to tell her, "You shouldn't have voted that way."[252] Discouraged in the House, although chairman of four subcommittees, Hathaway had a call from a friend who told him with some authority that Smith likely would not run in 1972. Hathaway began polling in Maine before Monks and learned to his surprise that voters thought of Smith as in her fifties or sixties and when told her age responded 50 percent to 50 percent as to whether they would vote for her. Those odds were good enough for Hathaway to leave a near-certain fifth term in the House and announce for the Senate.

Although Hathaway outspent Monks, he did so quietly while publicly maintaining a spartan campaign office in Portland staffed by volunteers. Whether deliberately or not, he campaigned like Smith: traveling the state by car, visiting each of the state's 495 towns at least once, shaking hands, listening to the problems of people, and telling them how much he liked Maine. People responded well to Hathaway—a big, quiet-spoken, solid, reassuring man and a Mainer. Most of the $196,000 he spent was on television ads, something new for the state; the commercials were not polished, but Hathaway believed they convinced people that he was working hard for the job.

Lewis said that Smith was "rightly warned" that she should use television ads also, but the senator responded, "If I have to compromise my principles and my policies of not spending vast sums of money or becoming politically indebted to wealthy non-Maine contributors in order to win, to do so would make me unhappy for the rest of my life. I would rather adhere to my principles and policies and lose than to win the other way."[253]

In contrast, Smith campaigned less for the general election than she had for the primary and said in an early Rockland press conference that she did not plan to discuss the issues but, as always, to run on her record. Columnist Donald Hansen called this "Popeye" tactic, "I yam what I yam," and credited Hathaway for his "candor, frankness and open discussion of issues."[254]

Hathaway accused Smith of taking the people of Maine for granted, but that was as critical as he got. Democratic leaders, including Muskie, told him, "You're not going to win because you're not attacking her. You've got to attack her, you've got to attack her."[255] "I just thought it was poor strategy to criticize a woman," he said.[256] Even on the age issue he refused to comment; "you can't do that with a woman," he believed, because voters would think, "Hathaway's picking on a poor old woman and that's not fair."[257] Smith kept the issue alive for him by becoming increasingly defensive and referring to "irresponsible and false statements" being made about her age and health.[258] Two that she often repeated was that Democratic governor Kenneth Curtis had said that she was "approaching 80 years of age" and that the National Committee for an Effective Congress, which endorsed Hathaway, said that she was "not in good health."[259]

Smith wrote to Portland reporter Bill Caldwell that she was "restraining" herself "against this campaign of lies against me . . . but how long I will refrain from not hitting back with vigorous denunciation is questionable."[260] "The Hathaway forces even spread word that I was dying of cancer and had several heart attacks," Lewis believed. "TV panelists even asked Senator Smith what she was going to do when I died before another full term."[261]

As much a blow to Smith in the general election as the *New York Times*'s "hatchet job" had been in the primary, Ralph Nader's Congress Project released a study on her in August. Although Lewis characterized the study as "vicious,"[262] Nader's researchers documented their statements, used government statistics extensively, and presented a more objective than not account of her long career. That the report mentioned Lewis as "surrogate senator,"[263] quoted reporters on Smith's being "ultra sensitive,"[264] and stated as Smith's response to Maine's problems as "pretty well satisfied and happy with things as they are"[265] led her to conclude that Hathaway was responsible for the study. He was not. Nader's project involved a study of all congressmen, but Smith refused to be interviewed by his researchers, and Hathaway believed Nader "just got his back up at her"[266] and issued the report during the election. To Smith the report was "obviously biased." "The political timing, intent, and prejudice of that report is quite obvious," she told the press.[267] Although Mainers were as unlikely to read Ralph Nader as the *New York Times,* press coverage of both in the state was extensive and did not help Smith.

Neither was Smith aided by politically active feminists in Maine. The co-founder of the National Organization for Women in Maine, Ramona Barth, sought out Smith at a campaign tea in Alma to ask her to join, but Smith refused. That snub led Barth to accuse Smith of being "an elitist" who represented "everything women in the liberation movement women want to eliminate."[268] Announcing to the press her commitment to "nagging and bugging" Smith "to confront the fundamental issues of women's liberation," Barth said that the senator would "prove herself to be a token woman if she tunes us out and takes no stands."[269] Smith's indirect response was that she supported equal rights for women but disapproved of "the extreme exhibition of bra-burning as degrading to the cause of women."[270] Not satisfied, Barth called for Smith's defeat and supported Hathaway, who campaigned that his "record of voting on women's issues was better than Mrs. Smith's."[271] Lewis later checked out Barth and learned that she was in her seventies, a minister's wife, mother, and grandmother. The worst his informant turned up was that Barth "never looks too tidy and neither does her house."[272]

Founded in 1971, the National Women's Political Caucus also failed to support Smith in the election, and there is no explicit reference in the files of the Business and Professional Women, her traditional support group, about organizing on her behalf.

On the eve of the election Smith received a cruel and unexpected blow from the *Somerset Reporter* in Skowhegan, her home town, and the paper on which she had once worked. "We feel it is time for a change," the *Reporter* stated editorially; "perfect attendance and seniority are not enough. At 74 Mrs. Smith can no longer possibly have the stamina necessary to keep pace with the grueling daily schedule demanded of a United States senator."[273]

Washington politicos from the president down failed until the end to appreciate the jeopardy of Smith's position. The last week of the campaign Nixon indicated that he could fly to Maine to campaign for her, but neither Lewis nor Smith thought it necessary, not understanding the possibility of disaster themselves.

And so the end came on 7 November 1972 with Smith and Lewis at home in Skowhegan to hear the election results with friends. There they learned first that Hathaway carried Skowhegan and Somerset County, and then embarrassed acquaintances began to drift away. At midnight NBC projected Hathaway as the winner. Unbelieving, Smith and Lewis alone sat up until 3:00 A.M. when neither found it possible to sustain belief any longer because Hathaway had 53.2 percent of the vote, 224,270 to Smith's 197,040. Smith said that Lewis, without saying a word to her, went back to his apartment at one end of the house while she, feeling that she had failed him, retired to her bedroom at the other end of the small house overlooking the Kennebec River. The next morning, a day as cold, foggy, and dismal as their moods, the two rose early, and at 9:00 A.M. Lewis released Smith's first statement of political defeat to the press while she remained secluded. Without naming Hathaway, Smith congratulated and wished him well in one brief sentence. Then she expressed her gratitude to the people of Maine for "letting" her "serve and represent them for more than 32 years. I am even more grateful to my loyal supporters who worked their hearts out for me. I regret having let them down."[274]

Smith then left to stay at her sister Evelyn's house while Lewis, grimfaced, turned away the press and received callers. That night, still without speaking to the press, Smith quietly left Skowhegan with Lewis for the long drive back to Washington. There Smith continued to refuse the hordes of reporters who came to the house and office, and press speculation grew that she had "collapsed," was "very much injured" by her loss, had taken "reelection for granted," was "bitter," "angry," "in shock," and had become a "virtual recluse."[275] Undoubtedly she was all of the above, but pride would not allow the admission, and she had her staff respond that she did not have the time for individual interviews because she had to vacate her office by 3 January. "I had been there for all those years; I had all those files in the office, in my storerooms; I had all those different offices to clean out," she said.[276] A secretary told the press that she had seen Lewis in his work clothes carrying empty boxes into the office, and Sam Bouchard came over to help the staff pack up. Soon the hallway outside was stacked high with government-supplied cartons, but only one worker in the building reported having seen Smith "dart" into her office. Another one told Don Larrabee, whose calls and knocks had gone unanswered, that she had seen "Strom Thurmond banging on all the doors to her office, and shouting 'Margaret' " with no response, and George Aiken said "he hadn't been able to talk to her."[277] "Some of their old friends in the Senate were telling me that they couldn't get to her and were worried about her," Larrabee wrote for his paper and persisted in his efforts.[278] Finally Lewis answered the telephone and told him, " 'You're never going to talk to her again.' I said, 'Bill, for heaven sakes, all I wrote was what everybody was saying,' " but Lewis accused, " 'You've turned on her,' " and hung up.[279]

Smith found solace in answering her mail, mostly sympathy notes, and wrote that she was "not hiding out or bitter."[280] To Hathaway she wrote, "May you have the very best in the years ahead," but when he responded, "I know how sad and disappointed you must feel" and asked to come by to visit, she did not respond.[281]

No one had predicted Hathaway's victory—not even Hathaway, who "had a good feeling about it. Expected a victory, no."[282] Hathaway's victory, one that gave Maine two Democratic senators for the first time since 1913, almost got lost in the sympathy for Smith. "My mother told me I ought to be ashamed of myself," the states's new senator said. "My wife is carrying a gun; my daughter is circulating a recall petition, and my sister has been kicked out of women's lib. I expect to win the misogynist of the year award."[283]

When one of her well-wishers asked Smith what she intended to do, she responded tersely, "Retire."[284]

Conclusion: Retirement

Nervously, she put on the new blue dress and jacket that had been hand-made for her, added her pearls, and combed her thinning white hair. Then she pinned on a fresh red rose that matched the one on the invitations and began the drive to the Augusta Civic Center. Her good friend and attorney Mert Henry was with her, and she knew he would take good care of her, but she could not help but worry. At the civic center she and Mert formed a receiving line, and when people began coming, she felt the old metamor-phosis begin. The frail, half-blind woman with the widow's hump straight-ened, smiled her magical smile at each of her well-wishers, radiated her special warmth, and established a bond so seemingly real that in a minute they were calling her Margaret.

Margaret Chase Smith stood in the receiving line for nearly two hours, greeted five hundred guests, and worried her doctor, who asked if she wanted a chair. "No, no." The old politician was reborn and having a great time at her ninetieth birthday party. Seemingly immune to the glare of television lights and the popping of flash bulbs, Smith received cordial handshakes, fervent embraces, and shy kisses. Finally, Governor John McKernan and Senator William Cohen escorted her to the blue-draped head table, and mak-ing the dinner bipartisan, the rarest of political occasions, Senators George Mitchell and Edmund Muskie followed. The atmosphere was festive, the affection for Smith palpable, and after she blew out the one candle on her huge cake and said her wish was that the speeches be brief, those present laughingly sang "Happy Birthday, Margaret."

If not brief, the speeches were laudatory and humorous. Mitchell said that organizers had instructed the processional to the head table to enter and turn right, but as the governor's constituents had noticed, McKernan entered and turned left and had to be straightened out. In turn, Cohen told Mitchell, who was coming up for reelection, that Smith had informed him that although she did not feel up to running for the presidency, she was considering another race for the Senate. McKernan surprised Smith by saying that he had been born in 1948, the year of her election to the Senate, his mother had worked in every one of her campaigns, and his first political act had been as a student to introduce Smith when she spoke at his school.

Pride permeated the gathering; those present were proud of Smith, of Maine, and of their elected officials, and they were generous with their applause. There was some grumbling because Vice President George Bush sent his regrets and televised greetings at the last minute and some concern when Senator Muskie spoke. Alert with squared chin raised, Smith became still as Muskie reminisced on their twelve years in the Senate together. He referred to Smith as plain-spoken but did not mention their rivalry; instead he surprised all by saying that Smith had motivated his entry into politics. As a law school student, he had watched Smith's first House race and concluded that if she could win, then he as a Democrat in a Republican state might have a chance. So ingratiating was Muskie that deliberately or not he became Smith's co-honoree, and speakers praised him also. Mitchell referred to Congress's naming one of the state's federal buildings for Smith and the other for Muskie, and McKernan called the two of them the twin towers of Maine.

Mistakenly, speakers referred to Smith as the first woman senator and the first woman elected in her own right to the Senate, but no one was in a mood to quibble. As though by common agreement, there was not one public mention of Bill Lewis, not even by Smith. Instead, there was praise for Margaret Chase Smith.

Speakers called Smith a "trailblazer," "a state icon," and "courageous," and President Ronald Reagan sent his greetings.[1] Mitchell said Smith was one of the greatest citizens in the state's history, and Congresswoman Olympia Snowe maintained that Smith was the first to prove that women could and should serve in public life. "She represents the best that is in all of us," Governor McKernan concluded.[2]

To all of this Smith smiled and responded when it was finally her turn, "I'm wonderful. I know it."

Margaret Chase Smith waited three months after her defeat before she talked to a reporter and six months before she returned to Maine. Cautiously, she invited the cheerful-to-brash but always charming Gannett reporter Bill Caldwell to Silver Spring and visited with him from noon until 7:00 P.M., long enough "to set the record straight," she said.[3] "If I have any bitterness, I am bitter to those who since my defeat are saying that I am sick, lonely, a recluse or an embittered old lady in hiding. None of that is true at all."[4] Nor was it accurate that after thirty-two years in Congress, she was leaving "unnoticed and unmourned," as had been reported in the press.[5] As proof she had Bill Lewis show Caldwell two six-inch-thick stacks of telegrams from well-wishers in the government and read a few aloud. The visit was relaxed to the extent that Smith and Lewis proudly took Caldwell through their home with the understanding that he would write about their living arrangement. With Lewis driving and Smith and Caldwell in the back seat, they also got out of the house and around the neighborhood for awhile. Then when Lewis was out of the car for a minute, Caldwell said to himself, "Here's where you get your courage up and ask her the question that nobody else has. . . . So I turn to her, expecting to get my face slapped and said, 'Why did you never marry?' She turned to me with those big blue eyes and sort of smiled and said, 'He never asked me.' . . . Suddenly, there was the woman and not the senator."[6]

With some difficulty Smith and Lewis returned to Skowhegan in May 1973 for her to give the four commencement addresses that she had scheduled before life as she had known it ended. Lewis spent his time opening 175 cases of her papers that he had sent from Washington. Several universities had expressed interest in receiving her files, but she and Lewis had decided to renovate her Skowhegan home into a library and house them there. Turning their lives-in-search-of-purpose to the creation of a monument, the two organized a prestigious board of trustees chaired by former NASA director James Webb to solicit contributions. Sensing an opportunity to mend political fences, Robert Monks and supporters of his sent donations, only to have them returned with letters from Smith that began, "In view of your attitude in the primary. . . ."[7]

The remainder of their prodigious energies turned, as Lewis wrote Bill Caldwell, to "What would Senator Smith do?"[8] Instead of retiring "to the rocking chair to which some critics would sentence her," she decided to become "an academician."[9] There had been press speculation that she might be appointed to the Supreme Court, named secretary of defense, nominated for governor, or appointed chief of the Strategic Arms Limitation Treaty team, but none of the rumors had materialized into offers. The one firm invitation that Smith received was to become a visiting professor for the Woodrow Wilson National Fellowship Foundation, which after the "Colby affair" seemed a strange offer to accept. She enjoyed the visits Lewis had arranged as trial runs to speak at the University of Alabama School of Law, Washington and Lee, and several other colleges. Not Vietnam but Watergate was the political backdrop for her campus appearances, and honesty in government had long been her forte.

Smith's arrangement with the Woodrow Wilson Foundation began in 1973 and lasted until 1976. She agreed to visit eight colleges a year for a week each for an honorarium of $1,500 per week. The money was to "be paid to me," Smith specified, "as General Lewis has no objective other than to assist me. He also does not desire any billing or listing."[10]

With ease Smith metamorphosed into the role of elder stateswoman, answered respectful questions from students, and received accolades from professors with memories of McCarthy. Lewis, now introduced as Major General William C. Lewis, Jr., shared the classroom as he once had the Senate and wrote again to Caldwell what a "strenuous but exciting, stimulating and really wonderful" year they had enjoyed.[11] Along the way Smith enlarged her collection of honorary doctorates, seventy-one by the end of her congressional career, to ninety by her ninetieth birthday.

Gradually Smith traded the classroom for the board room. Lilly Endowment, Inc. of Indianapolis first invited her to join its board of directors, and Freedom House of New York followed. Soon she was on the boards of Sun Life Insurance in Baltimore, the United States Supreme Court Historical Society in Washington, and the Pennsylvania Medical College Board in Philadelphia.

During this peripatetic period Smith and Lewis frequently visited the business management college, Northwood Institute, where Smith lectured, received an honorary degree, and was given its Distinguished Woman Award. The association led Northwood to offer administration of a Margaret Chase Smith Library Center in exchange for her papers, house, and its fifteen acres. Believing that institutional sponsorship was essential for the future, the original James Webb–led board agreed, and Northwood celebrated Smith at its home offices in Midland, Michigan, with a lavish dinner for five hundred guests including Senators Strom Thurmond and Nancy Kassebaum of Kansas.

Work on the library began in 1979 with Northwood's building a sizable addition to Smith's home to house her papers and memorabilia. Dr. James MacCampbell of the University of Maine assumed responsibility for sorting her papers while the construction was underway.

All of this time Smith and Lewis continued to live in Silver Spring and returned to Maine and Skowhegan infrequently for library business. The anti-Smith sentiment that had flared in the 1972 election continued and in 1974 manifested itself in an ugly incident. The Skowhegan Board of Voters Registration removed Smith's name from their list of eligible voters on grounds of nonresidency. The media picked up the story and broadcast it nationally, and Smith found herself back in the position of being a victim falsely accused.

Caroline Huff, wife of Skowhegan photographer Lyndon Huff, had the misfortune of being the appointed chair of the Board of Voters Registration at the time the Maine secretary of state directed the boards to update their voting lists by removing nonresidents. The criterion established by the secretary of state was that a permanent resident was one who slept in the voting district most of each year. A meticulous woman, Huff specifically asked the secretary of state about Smith, and he replied, "If she does not sleep here, her name comes off the voting list."[12] Believing that she had the support of the Skowhegan Board of Selectmen, Huff said she "followed the rule book to the letter" and informed Smith in a registered letter under her signature, because "nobody else would dare cross Margaret Chase Smith."[13]

Considering the action "an act of disenfranchisement,"[14] Smith wrote her friend Paul Maureau that "the Skowhegan incident is so shocking that it has been difficult for me to hold my tongue."[15] She and her library board began to "wonder about keeping the Library in Skowhegan in such a . . . hostile environment."[16] On grounds that she had voted in Skowhegan since she was of an age to vote and paid taxes there, Smith appealed the decision of the Board of Voters Registration. Not only was the appeal turned down, but an inquiry into Smith's taxes began. "She's never paid any taxes up here," Huff said. "As many years as that woman's lived in that home she never paid any taxes."[17] At this point, Smith turned the matter over to her attorney, Merton Henry, who learned that the basic law was "that residence is a matter of intention" and that sixty days notice had to be given to remove a person from the voting list.[18] Given the bad publicity and dubious legal grounds, the Board of Selectmen unanimously overturned the decision of the Board of Voters Registration and restored Smith's right to vote. The library was given tax-exempt status, and the charge of $1,611.50 in unpaid taxes was quietly dropped. Huff resigned, and said, "I'm telling you if I had it to do over again, I'd say forget the whole thing."[19]

As the Margaret Chase Smith Library neared completion, the senator and general spent more time in Skowhegan but preferred their homes in Cundy's Harbor on the Maine coast. By the time Northwood had scheduled the dedication of the library for August 1982, MacCampbell, advised by Lewis, had Smith's papers in order and ready to be indexed when they were moved to the library. The driving force behind the library, Lewis was liaison with Northwood, in on every decision made about the facility, and looking forward to its completion. He personally planted trees on the large lawn that extended to the banks of the Kennebec, free of logs now but still a powerful river. Under Lewis's guidance, the purpose of the library had been enlarged to a conference center, where the free enterprise system as well as good government could be taught. Lewis envisioned a library for scholars, a museum for visitors, a classroom for schoolchildren, and seminars for adults. He wanted for Smith a memorial where the two of them would be actively involved and influential, a power base the likes of which no other congressman has ever had.

In May 1982 for what must have seemed like the thousandth time Lewis drove Smith from Silver Spring to Maine to inspect again the progress on the library. The trip was always long and tiring, but now Lewis was sixty-nine and Smith eighty-four, and the weather was unseasonably warm. They were pleased with the construction but decided to go on to Cundy's Harbor. Lewis, who always required a project, wanted to lay some carpet in his house, although Smith had told him it was too hot and the carpet too heavy for him to manage alone. Nonetheless, while Smith rested in her adjacent house, Lewis on 26 May completed his project and sat down on his couch to rest. Three hours later a neighbor found him dead. He apparently died, Smith said, "without stress or pain, a smile on his face as though he was happy with his accomplishment."[20] The physician she called said that cardiac arrhythmia caused Lewis's death.

For Smith, Lewis's death was more traumatic than that of Clyde Smith or her beloved mother, Carrie. Months later she wrote that "it all came so suddenly and it was such a shock that I am still having trouble in realizing what happened."[21] Smith wanted Lewis buried at Arlington National Cemetery with full military honors and arranged for a plot for herself beside him. The Northwood staff made the arrangements and issued a press release that quoted Smith as saying, "Public officials are only as good as the people they surround themselves with. General Lewis is the premiere example of this— a person of great vision, judgment, incisiveness and integrity."[22] The funeral service was held 1 June 1982 in the chapel at Arlington with a shattered Smith in attendance. Smith did not participate in the service but listened as Northwood's Dr. R. Gary Stauffer gave the eulogy and friends like Harold Gosselin, Merton Henry, James Webb, and Richard Wels served as honorary pallbearers. Then Smith stood alone by the grave to receive condolences. One friend referred to Lewis as Smith's "compagnon de coeur,"[23] and another told her that Lewis "was content and honored to serve as your chauffeur, your factotum, your memory bank. He almost visibly expanded in recollection of the glorious Washington years. . . . It requires a very large spirit to take his sustenance from reflected light."[24] Since 1948 Smith and Lewis had lived in tandem, and his death nearly destroyed her.

She created what Bill Caldwell called "this little altar" to Lewis in a back room at the library and placed Lewis's office furniture, photographs, and awards there.[25] The August dedication of the library took place as scheduled but added to her sorrow because she and Lewis had looked forward to it together, and he was not there to share in her triumph. Smith moved back to Skowhegan and gradually transferred needs that Lewis had fulfilled to the Northwood staff, particularly to MacCampbell, who was now director of the library. Her new schedule was to arise early, with a housekeeper assisting her with dressing, make herself a spartan breakfast, and then dictate replies to her correspondence to a secretary. She continued to spend considerable time on her mail when it arrived and on the telephone with acquaintances, and at noon one of the staff, usually MacCampbell, who became a pale Lewis, drove her to Charriers, a local restaurant, for lunch. Afternoons were harder to fill unless there was a class of schoolchildren coming, an Elderhostel group arriving, or a friend visiting. Occasionally there were board meetings or speaking opportunities out of town that involved traveling with a companion, frequently Georgia McKearly, the physical therapist who had helped Smith with her hip replacements. There were also honors to be received, more of local or state relevance but still welcomed diversions. Skowhegan named its two bridges and an elementary school after Smith, its chamber of commerce presented her with a certificate of merit, and the high school made Smith an honorary member of the National Honor Society. The governor declared Margaret Chase Smith Day in Maine when the library was dedicated, and the next year the legislature voted a Joint Resolution in Recognition of the Honorable Margaret Chase Smith. Nationally Smith received an Outstanding Woman in Government Award from the United States Jaycee Women, one of the Twelve Smartest Women Living in America from the Book of Knowledge, and one of the Best Coiffeured Women from the Helene Curtis Guild of Professional Beauticians.

As many firsts as she had accomplished in her lifetime and as many awards as she had received, she increasingly needed recognition as validation for her life. None of her awards could have been more pleasing than the Presidential Medal of Freedom, which President George Bush bestowed on her in 1989.

Smith lived to see Nancy Kassebaum from Kansas replace her in 1979 as the only female senator until Barbara Mikulski joined her in 1987. Then, in 1993 five more women were elected to the Senate, and for the first time in history there were seven women senators at once. Making it eight, Olympia Snowe replaced George Mitchell in 1994. In 1984 Smith also witnessed the first woman nominated by a major party for the vice presidency. That Geraldine Ferraro was a Democrat and did not win did not obscure the fact that she had accomplished what Smith had tried to do. Even Smith's consecutive voting record was finally broken by Senator William Proxmire of Wisconsin.

Second only to being female, Smith had always argued that she could not progress beyond the Senate because she was from Maine, a state with few electoral votes. In unspoken rebuttal, she lived to see not only Edmund Muskie's serious campaign for the presidential nomination but also his nomination for vice president. In addition, Smith watched Democratic senator George Mitchell from Maine become the Senate's majority leader. Considered by many to be a Mainer, although, in keeping with Smith's reasoning, he claimed Texas residency, George Bush reached the White House.

Controversy continued to find Smith. Despite being one of the few senators to live on her salary and retiring from the Senate as poor as when she entered, in 1988 Smith's congressional pension became the first to exceed $1 million. In 1988 Smith's pension was $88,715; in 1972 her last congressional salary had been $42,500; and during her retirement she had received $1,034,914 in pension benefits. In a poor state like Maine, Smith's pension was astronomical, and not only did Mainers value frugality, Smith had made it one of her career trademarks. In retirement Smith did not rebut the criticisms; instead, she continued to live the simple life. Clothes, jewels, furs, cars, and other symbols of conspicuous consumption had never interested her and still did not.

Even Smith's retirement was controversial to many. The consensus was that she should have sought a national forum from which she could have had more impact. Her champion Bill Caldwell characterized his assessment of her retirement as "harsh" and said that he considered her retirement "very sad" because she "clutched at these boards she sits on . . . which are apt to be antediluvian outfits." "I think she's lonely" in the "cocoon" of the library, and she "[has not] made the kind of contribution to national opinion or even the opinion of Maine that a woman of that experience and that power could have done."[26]

Increasingly feeble and all but blind, Smith began to experience memory loss in the early 1990s. On 21 May 1995 she suffered a stroke and was hospitalized. Smith lapsed into a coma and when she did not recover consciousness, her staff moved her home as she had instructed. She lingered comatose for eight days before dying in her bedroom on 29 May 1995 at age ninety-seven. In an interview with the author in Skowhegan on 21 October 1987, Smith said that she had made arrangements to be buried in Arlington National Cemetery next to Bill Lewis. Whether or not she changed her mind is not documented, but her staff decided to have a memorial service for her in Skowhegan on 16 June 1995 at the Margaret Chase Smith Library. Her ashes remain in the library.

Smith remains, as she had begun, a daughter of Maine. She was as independent, reclusive, taciturn, candid, hardworking, and suspicious as any other Mainer. Indeed, as the state's most famous citizen Smith symbolized Maine and its citizens' cherished attributes and values. These characteristics, more than anything else, were responsible for Smith's longevity in the Senate and overcame what might have been the liabilities of being female and a liberal Republican. Smith's success in the world outside Maine was not only vindication for the state's virtues but brought honor to all Mainers. When Smith received most valuable senator awards, most admired woman, honest politician, economy champion, Americanism awards, or honorary degrees, Maine was honored because Smith exemplified the state.

Smith enforced this perception of herself as a Mainer by maintaining personal contact with as many of the state's citizens as she could. She was never a part of the state's elite whether measured by the Republican leadership or by the great paper and timber interests. Despite seniority, she insisted on being the outsider, preferably the smeared victim, in each campaign so that Maine's average citizen could rescue her. For that reason she traveled alone by car and stopped at every backroad service station, grocery, and café she could. For that reason she did not ask the attendant, clerk, or waitress for votes but asked instead, "What can I do for you?" For that reason she answered every letter the day she received it and had her volunteers say, "Write Margaret Chase Smith if you want to get something done." Mainers did write their personal requests year after year, and today Smith's papers are filled with them. People continued to write for assistance even after she retired, and her replies became increasingly acerbic. In one instance she wrote, "Having been voted out of office by the voters nearly five years ago, I no longer have any authority or influence. . . . I regret this very much because it was such a pleasure to be able to use my power and influence as a Senator to help the people of Skowhegan and Maine. But apparently not enough of those I had helped thought enough of me to go to the polls to vote for me."[27]

Smith never forgot that she was in Washington to work for Maine. Her national stature enhanced her appeals to hundreds of businesses to locate their plants and offices in Maine. Being on the Armed Services Committee, Smith succeeded in making the military payroll in Maine second only to the paper industry's. As the state's textile mills moved to the South and imports ruined its shoe industry, Smith championed tourism, as controversial as it was, and advertised Maine nationally as a vacation resort for both summer and winter.

So what conclusions does one draw about Maine's daughter? Certainly she was not the first person to enter Congress with limited education and experience or the first to parlay native intelligence and ability into a lengthy and distinguished political career. Congress often attracts and, with its seniority system, trains and protects limited individuals until they grow into the job. Interestingly, these representatives commonly run as anti-Congress, anti–big government, and anti-establishment, as Smith did. She was never a part of the regular Republican party in Maine or in Congress and seldom a team player, much less a part of the leadership. Instead, she commonly ran against and voted against the party establishment, and Smith, as symbol of her independence, never revealed how she intended to vote ahead of time. Instead, she made her party and its leaders wait, and she cast her vote in a hushed chamber, watched through the press by the nation and sometimes the world. Taught by the maverick Lewis, Smith associated independence with power in an arena where the rules required members to trade votes, do favors for each other, and support the leadership in order to gain power personally and for their constituents. For thirty-two years Smith railed against the party structure and transcended the Republican party in Maine and in Congress. She fitted herself into the Maine-stream of the United States and developed a national constituency, but for what profit? Her hopes for a presidential or vice presidential nomination were stillborn, no legislation bears her name, and despite her seniority she never chaired a committee.

What we are left with is gender. Margaret Chase Smith was female, and that characteristic primarily defined her career. Had she been male, her life, including the Declaration of Conscience, would be indistinguishable from that of hundreds of other congressmen. Since she was female, as soon as she entered the Senate she was politically unique and a candidate for the history books, as all politicians yearn to be. Smith did not deal easily with being female in the ultimate gentlemen's club. Of her generation, she wanted to be treated like a lady by her colleagues, but she also desired power, influence, and respect. To that end she tried to overcome gender rather than champion it, which meant that she became antifeminist while, like many other professional antifeminists, doing everything that feminists want all women to have the opportunity to do. Smith's demeanor was commonly ingratiating and quiet spoken, which reassured her fellow senators that she posed no threat and inspired them gallantly to open doors, pull out her chairs, and assist her. Disarmed, colleagues were surprised when Smith revealed the iron fist in the white glove, and they blamed Lewis. Certainly Lewis isolated Smith, taught her to trust only him, and fiercely protected her, but Smith used Lewis as a political lightning rod who received criticisms for her actions. The senator was not clay in Lewis's hands; instead she was tremendously ambitious, independent, and needy. What she needed was Lewis's knowledge, experience, and toughness, and she knew that she needed those characteristics in a male, not a female like May Craig. Smith isolated Lewis too, and once joined in purpose, the furtherance of her career, they lived together a life circumscribed by work. They worked every day, every night, on weekends and holidays; their lives were consumed with work, and the result was a political marriage made possible because Smith was female. Always the soldier-gentleman, Lewis could justify spending his life in her service and assisting her work on behalf of the military and the nation.

Stymied by the seniority system, by being a member of the minority party, and by being female, Smith, with Lewis's guidance, exaggerated her New England characteristics to transform Maine's daughter into America's heroine. The image came out of the 1948 senatorial campaign when Smith fought the Maine Republican leadership and economic establishment, but the Declaration of Conscience gave the image national prominence. The declaration was Smith's finest hour and arguably her only hour; it was her most heroic act and the most frightening event of her life, not one to be repeated. Others spoke out against Joseph McCarthy before and after Smith, but Smith was a female challenger, and that made all the difference. Certainly her speaking out was an act of political courage, but in retrospect Smith and Lewis may have seen it as an act of miscalculation. Regardless, for one brief moment, vulnerable and trembling, she did the right thing and rightly garnered the nation's praise.

With McCarthy's downfall, conscience became the cornerstone of Smith's image, and Smith became the conscience of the Senate. The difficulty was that conscience is not relevant to all political issues or all political opponents, and when Smith and Lewis justified their actions on the grounds that they were right, they often moved to sanctimonious expediency. The image had limits. When Smith and Lewis translated the responsible, hard-working senator into one who never missed a vote, for example, they came perilously close to activity as meaningless as Hattie Carraway's knitting in the Senate chamber. Smith wanted to do good; as in our finer moments we all do, but the complexity of life led her to rigidity, intolerance, a need for enemies, and masochism as good politics.

Maine's daughter and America's heroine accomplished a great deal as a woman who pioneered politics for her gender more successfully than any of her predecessors, contemporaries, or successors. Smith, a role model for women before the phrase was coined, proved that gender is not a barrier to public service. Her accomplishments are as striking today as they were in her own time, and she remains the most influential woman in the history of American politics.

NOTES

CHAPTER 1

1. Margaret Chase Smith (hereafter MCS) Interview with author, 19 July 1988.

2. MCS Files, Genealogy folder, MCS Papers, MCS Library Center, Skowhegan, Maine.

3. Charles E. Clark, *Maine, A Bicentennial History* (New York: W. W. Norton, 1977), 3–5. *Wabanaki* was Anglicized to *Abnaki*.

4. Ibid., 5–6.

5. Lawrence C. Wroth, *Voyages of Giovanni da Verrazzano* (New Haven: Yale University Press, 1970), 140–41.

6. Clark, *Maine,* 44–45.

7. Smith maintained that the Chases' departing New Hampshire to settle in Ohio eventually produced Salmon Portland Chase, U.S. senator, secretary of the treasury, and chief justice of the Supreme Court. Salmon Portland Chase is erroneously identified in one MCS paper in the Genealogy file as governor of Maine. In fact, Salmon Chase was born in New Hampshire on 13 January 1808, left New England for Ohio in 1820, and was the first Republican governor of Ohio. He claimed Aquila Chase as his first American ancestor, as does MCS. See Albert Bushnell Hart, *Salmon Portland Chase* (Boston: Houghton Mifflin, 1899), 1–4.

8. MCS Files, Genealogy folder, MCS Papers.

9. MCS interview with author, 13 July 1988.

10. Certificate of baptism, Notre Dame de Lourdes, Skowhegan, Maine; John Murray interview with author, 21 September 1988. When MCS learned that I had received the baptismal certificate, she wrote to say that she was sending a copy of her birth certificate giving "the correct names of myself and my mother and father." This certificate has the spellings used in the text. MCS to Wallace, 11 August 1989; Birth Certificate, State of Maine, Office of the Clerk of Skowhegan, 21 March 1952.

11. MCS interview with author, 13 July 1988.

12. Ibid.

13. Ibid.

14. Wallace Bilodeau interview with author, 15 September 1988; Evelyn Chase Williams interview with author, 7 July 1988.

15. MCS interview with author, 13 July 1988.

16. Bilodeau interview.

17. MCS interview with author, 13 July 1988.

18. Ibid.

19. Ibid.

20. MCS interview with author, 23 September 1988.

21. Ibid., 27 July 1988.

22. Ibid., 19 July 1988.

23. Ibid.

24. Ibid.

25. Ibid.

26. Scrapbook, Vol. 459, p. 7, MCS Papers.

27. Lyndon Huff interview with author, 3 November 1988.

28. Scrapbook, Vol. 1, p. 11.

29. MCS interview with author, 23 September 1988.

30. Lillian Demo interview with author, 24 September 1988; Bilodeau interview; Peter Mills interview with author, 14 September 1988; Huff interview.

31. Demo interview; Huff interview.

32. MCS interview with author, 19 July 1988.

33. Ibid.

34. Ibid., 13 July 1988. Gladys Wilson married a state attorney general and was herself elected to the legislature after MCS was in Congress. When the two met again under these circumstances, Smith said that Wilson "came over and put her arm around me and told me what a dear, sweet student" she had been. "I could have slapped her face."

35. MCS interview with author, 13 July 1988.

36. Ibid.

37. Lewis Brown interview with author, 22 June 1988.

38. MCS interview with author, 13 July 1988.

39. Brown interview.

40. Ibid.

41. MCS interview with author, 13 July 1988.

42. Ibid.

43. Ibid.

44. Statements and Speeches, Vol. 6, p. 114, MCS Papers.

45. *Independent-Reporter,* 3 January 1916.

46. Ibid., 23 March 1916.

47. MCS interview with author, 19 July 1988.

48. Ibid.

49. United States Capitol Historical Society, *Washington Past and Present* (Washington, 1987), 42–46.

50. Emery Dyer interview with author, 6 July 1988.

51. MCS interview with author, 19 July 1988.

52. Ibid.

53. Ibid.
54. Brown interview.
55. MCS file, 1916 Lever folder, MCS Papers.
56. MCS file, Class of 1916 folder, MCS Papers.
57. *Independent-Reporter,* 29 June 1916.
58. Scrapbook, Vol. 8, p. 32.
59. *Independent-Reporter,* 23 June 1916.
60. Brown interview.
61. *Independent-Reporter,* 29 June 1916.
62. Ibid., 19 April 1917.
63. MCS interview with author, 27 July 1988.
64. *Independent-Reporter,* 27 December 1917.
65. Ibid., 17 April 1919.
66. Ibid., 29 June 1916.
67. MCS interview with author, 27 July 1988.
68. Ibid., 19 July 1988.
69. Ibid.
70. Scrapbook, Vol. 374, p. 141.
71. MCS interview with author, 19 July 1988.
72. *Independent-Reporter,* 13 October 1926.
73. Scrapbook, Vol. 374, p. 141.
74. *Morning Sentinel,* 30 August 1988.
75. Carrie Chase to MCS, 22 July 1924, MCS file, MCS Papers.
76. Evelyn Chase to MCS, 22 July 1924, MCS file, MCS Papers.
77. Clyde Smith to Mrs. Richardson, 23 December 1920, Clyde Smith file, Correspondence folder, Clyde Smith Papers, MCS Library Center.
78. Clyde Smith to Lena M. Dyer, 23 December 1920, Clyde Smith file, Correspondence folder, Clyde Smith Papers.
79. Carrie Chase to MCS, 22 July 1924, MCS Files, MCS Papers.
80. MCS interview with author, 27 July 1988.
81. Ibid., and 23 September 1988.
82. Ibid., 27 July 1988.
83. Ibid.
84. Ibid.
85. Business and Professional Women's Club, MCS Papers.
86. *Independent-Reporter,* 14 October 1926.
87. MCS interview with author, 19 July 1988.
88. "Only One Skowhegan" folder, MCS Papers.
89. MCS interview with author, 19 July 1988.
90. Ibid.
91. Ibid., and 23 September 1988.
92. Huff interview.
93. MCS interview with author, 27 July 1988.

CHAPTER 2

1. *Maine Legislative Record—Senate,* 5 April 1923, 1113–16.

2. Lyndon Huff interview with author, 3 November 1988.

3. Clyde Smith Papers, Margaret Chase Smith (hereafter MCS) Library Center, Skowhegan, Maine.

4. Scrapbook, Vol. 8, p. 40, MCS Papers.

5. Ibid., Vol. 7, p. 6.

6. Ibid., Vol. 8, p. 40.

7. MCS interview with author, 22 September 1988.

8. MCS speech to the Republican Women's National Conference, 11 May 1955, George Arents Research Library, Syracuse University, Syracuse, New York.

9. Scrapbook, Vol. 288, p. 27.

10. MCS interview with author, 27 July 1988.

11. *Lewiston Weekly Journal,* 3 May 1934.

12. Ibid., 12 September 1934.

13. MCS interview with author, 23 September 1988.

14. Peter Mills interview with author, 14 September 1988.

15. Frank Graham, *Margaret Chase Smith* (New York: John Day Company, 1964), 26.

16. 1932 Trip folder, Clyde Smith Papers, MCS Library Center.

17. *Somerset Reporter,* 13 May 1934.

18. Campaign for Governor folder, Clyde Smith Papers, MCS Library Center.

19. MCS interview with author, 23 September 1988.

20. Clyde Smith Papers, MCS Library Center.

21. Duford to Farley, 22 July 1936, Clyde Smith Papers, Collection 0F300, Box 19, Franklin D. Roosevelt Library, Hyde Park, New York.

22. MCS interview with author, 23 September 1988.

23. "Mainesay," *Waterville Sentinel,* January 1990.

24. MCS *Declaration of Conscience* (Garden City, N.Y.: Doubleday, 1972), 65.

25. Clyde Smith Papers, MCS Library Center.

26. "Mainesay."

27. Ibid.

28. Anecdotes folder, MCS Papers.

29. Scrapbook, Vol. 1, p. 12.

30. Ibid., 2.

31. Scrapbook, Vol. 2, p. 56.

32. U.S. Congress, House, Representative Smith speaking for the wage-hour bill, 75th Congress, *Congressional Record,* Vol. 84, p. 2822.

33. Ibid., Vol. 83, p. 7308.

34. John Reed interview with author, 1 September 1988.

35. Annabel Paxton, *Women in Congress* (Richmond: Dietz Press, 1945), 36–37.

36. Anecdotes folder, MCS Papers.

37. Scrapbook, Vol. 5, p. 97.

38. Ibid., 74.

39. Scrapbook, Vol. 1, p. 12.

40. Clyde Smith to Dr. John A. Kolmer, 1 December 1938, Clyde Smith Papers, MCS Library Center.

41. Anecdotes folder, MCS Papers.

42. Scrapbook, Vol. 2, p. 52.

43. Ibid., p. 53.

44. Ibid., Vol. 5, p. 43.

45. Ibid., Vol. 4, p. 9.

46. "Mainesay."

47. Scrapbook, Vol. 5, p. 95.

48. Anecdote folder, MCS Papers.

49. Ibid.

50. MCS interview with author, 23 September 1988.

51. Scrapbook, Vol. 5, p. 74.

52. Dr. Paul Dickens to Clyde Smith, 18 August 1939, Clyde Smith Papers, MCS Library Center.

53. Scrapbook, Vol. 2, p. 55.

54. Ibid., 56.

55. Dr. Paul Dickens to Clyde Smith, 6 April 1950, Clyde Smith Papers, MCS Library Center.

56. MCS interview with author, 23 September 1988.

57. Ibid.

58. Ibid.

59. Scrapbook, Vol. 6, p. 108.

60. MCS interview with author, 23 September 1988.

61. U.S. Congress, House, Representative Oliver, speaking, 76th Congress, 3d session, 8 April 1940, *Congressional Record,* Vol. 86, p. 4196.

62. Lyndon Huff interview with author, 3 November 1988.

63. Scrapbook, Vol. 6, p. 103.

64. U.S. Congress, House, 76th Congress, 3d session, *Congressional Record,* Vol. 86, p. 2557.

CHAPTER 3

1. Alice Fleming, *The Senator from Maine, Margaret Chase Smith* (New York: Dell, 1969), 42–43.

2. Scrapbook, Vol. 6, p. 113, Margaret Chase Smith (hereafter MCS) Papers, MCS Library Center, Skowhegan, Maine.

3. Miscellaneous Speeches and Statements, 1925–1945, p. 67, MCS Papers.

4. Ibid., 32.

5. Ibid., 23.

6. "Mainesay," *Waterville Sentinel,* January 1990.

7. Scrapbook, Vol. 10, p. 6.

8. Miscellaneous Speeches and Statements, p. 35.

9. Ibid., 43.

10. Scrapbook, Vol. 10, p. 6.

11. Ibid.

12. Ibid., p. 4.

13. Ibid., p. 27.

14. Ibid.

15. *Boston Sunday Globe,* 2 June 1940.

16. MCS interview with author, 21 October 1987.

17. Scrapbook, Vol. 181, p. 90.

18. Ibid., Vol. 10, p. 8.

19. Miscellaneous Speeches and Statements, p. 30.

20. Primary, 17 June 1940 folder, MCS Papers.

21. Miscellaneous Speeches and Statements, p. 58.

22. Scrapbook, Vol. 10, p. 8.

23. Ibid., Vol. 7, p. 84.

24. Ibid., Vol. 10, p. 27.

25. Ibid.

26. Ibid.

27. Ibid., Vol. 12, p. 143.

28. Ibid., 109.

29. Ibid., 50.

30. Ibid., Vol. 14, pp. 106–7.

31. *Washington Post,* 20, 29 December 1940.

32. Frank Graham, *Margaret Chase Smith, Woman of Courage* (New York: John Day, 1964), 36.

33. Scrapbook, Vol. 16, p. 15.

34. *Washington Post,* 7 January 1941.

35. U.S. Congress, House, 77th Congress, 1st session, State of the Union, *Congressional Record,* Vol. 81, p. 44.

36. Graham, *Margaret Chase Smith,* 36.

37. Scrapbook, Vol. 14, p. 6.

38. Graham, *Margaret Chase Smith,* 35.

39. Scrapbook, Vol. 21, p. 1.

40. Ibid., Vol. 18, p. 11.

41. Ibid., Vol. 12, p. 121.

42. George E. Allen, "Told in Washington," *Washington Post,* November 1953.

43. MCS oral history interview, 18 February 1975, Sam Rayburn Library, Bonham, Texas.

44. Ibid.

45. Scrapbook, Vol. 275, p. 13.

46. Don Larrabee interview with author, 9 February 1989.

47. Ibid.

48. John Murphy interview with author, 21 September 1988.

49. Bill Caldwell interview with author, 21 September 1988.

50. Murphy interview.

51. Larrabee interview.

52. Liz Carpenter interview with author, 13 November 1990; Marion Martin file, MCS Papers.

53. Scrapbook, Vol. 18, p. 125.

54. Ibid., 113.

55. Ibid., 126.

56. Ibid., 16.

57. Ibid., Vol. 19, p. 43.

58. Ibid., 65.

59. Fleming, *Senator from Maine,* 50–51.

60. Peggy Lamson, *Few Are Chosen: American Women in Political Life Today* (Boston: Houghton Mifflin, 1968), 11.

61. Eliot Janeway, "The Man Who Owns the Navy," *Saturday Evening Post,* 15 December 1945.

62. MCS interview with author, 21 October 1987.

63. Fleming, *Senator from Maine,* 51.

64. Ibid., 49.

65. Scrapbook, Vol. 38, p. 162.

66. Warren G. Magnuson oral history interview, Lyndon Baines Johnson Library, Austin, Texas.

67. Scrapbook, Vol. 266, p. 117.

68. MCS interview with author, 23 September 1988.

69. Ibid., 21 October 1987.

70. Statements and Speeches, Vol. 2, p. 55.

71. Scrapbook, Vol. 29, p. 45.

72. Ibid., Vol. 23, p. 170.

73. MCS interview with author, 23 September 1988.

74. Ibid.

75. Ibid., 21 October 1987.

76. Ibid., 23 September 1988. Lyndon Johnson was equally impressed with Lewis and, in Smith's words, "tried to lure him away from Carl Vinson." Lewis refused, and Johnson, Smith said, "never forgave anyone who said 'No' to him." Johnson Administration file, Smith's Statements about President Johnson folder, MCS Papers.

77. Scrapbook, Vol. 23, p. 103.

78. Statements and Speeches, Vol. 2, p. 391.

79. Lewis to Vinson, 19 November 1973, Carl Vinson folder, Lewis Correspondence-General, William C. Lewis Papers, MCS Library Center.

80. Smith to Nunn, 30 May 1984, Sam Nunn folder, Georgia Congressional Delegation file, MCS Papers.

81. Scrapbook, Vol. 28, p. 15a.

82. Ibid., Vol. 30, p. 6.

83. Ibid., Vol. 28, p. 149.

84. Ibid., 155.

85. MCS interview with author, 21 October 1987.

86. Statements and Speeches, Vol. 2, p. 14.

87. Miscellaneous Speeches and Statements, p. 101.

88. U.S. Congress, House, 78th Congress, 2d session, 9 March 1944, *Congressional Record* 97:2455.

89. Statements and Speeches, Vol. 2, p. 391, Vol. 6, p. 102; MCS interview with author, 21 October 1988.

90. MCS interview with author, 21 October 1987.

91. Ibid.

92. Statements and Speeches, Vol. 1, n.p.

93. MCS, "Report Covering Various Assignments Pertaining to the Women in

the Naval Services," 24 November 1944, in *Naval Affairs Committee Hearings and Reports, 1943–1946*, 2487–92.

94. Statements and Speeches, Vol. 2, p. 466.

95. Scrapbook, Vol. 27, pp. 117–18.

96. MCS *Declaration of Conscience* (Garden City, N.Y.: Doubleday, 1972), 85–86; Mary V. Stremlow, *A History of the United States Marines, 1946–1977* (Washington: History and Museums Division, Headquarters United States Marines, 1986), 15–16.

97. Stremlow, *A History of the United States Marines*, 11, 16.

98. Smith, *Declaration of Conscience*, 87.

99. Smith to Andrews, 14 February 1948, Lewis Papers, MCS Library.

100. Statements and Speeches, Vol. 9, p. 251.

101. Smith, *Declaration of Conscience*, 89–91.

102. Ibid., 93.

103. Ibid., 94–95.

104. Ibid., 94.

105. Ibid., 95–96.

106. MCS interview with author, 21 October 1987.

107. Smith, *Declaration of Conscience*, 71–72.

108. Ibid., 73–74.

109. Ibid., 77–79.

110. Scrapbook, Vol. 50, pp. 124–33.

111. Smith, *Declaration of Conscience*, 85.

CHAPTER 4

1. Margaret Chase Smith, *Declaration of Conscience* (Garden City, N.Y.: Doubleday, 1972), 105.

2. Scrapbook, Vol. 41, p. 160, Margaret Chase Smith (hereafter MCS) Papers, MCS Library Center, Skowhegan, Maine.

3. *Lewiston Journal*, 22 September 1946.

4. Scrapbook, Vol. 277, p. 13.

5. John Reed interview with author, 1 September 1988.

6. MCS interview with author, 23 September 1988.

7. Scrapbook, Vol. 46, p. 51.

8. Smith to Truman, 30 July 1947, Smith to David Miles, and Matthew J. Connelly to Smith, 6 August 1947, Official file, Harry S Truman Papers, Harry S Truman Library, Independence, Missouri.

9. Carrie Matilda Murray Chase, MCS files, MCS Papers.

10. Scrapbook, Vol. 51, p. 9.

11. Ibid., Vol. 151, p. 47.

12. Ibid., Vol. 52, p. 74.

13. "Washington and You," Statements and Speeches, Vol. 5, p. 285, MCS Papers.

14. Maine Critics file, MCS Papers.

15. Scrapbook, Vol. 59, p. 258.

16. Ibid., Vol. 55, p. 4.

17. Oliver Moses file, MCS Papers.

18. 1948 Election file, Contributions Correspondence folder, MCS Papers.

19. Scrapbook, Vol. 54, p. 253.

20. Peggy Lamson, *Few Are Chosen: American Women in Political Life Today* (Boston: Houghton Mifflin, 1968), 12; Hope Chamberlin, *A Minority of Members: Women in the United States Congress* (New York: Praeger, 1973), 142.

21. Scrapbook, Vol. 52, p. 80.

22. Ibid., Vol. 55, p. 42.

23. Ibid., Vol. 54, p. 253.

24. Smear Smith Strategy, Statements and Speeches, Vol. 5, n.p.

25. Bar Association, Statements and Speeches, Vol. 5, n.p.

26. *Bangor Daily News,* 16 June 1948.

27. Answers Used for Questions at Forums During Campaign, Statements and Speeches, Vol. 5, n.p.

28. Scrapbook, Vol. 53, p. 166.

29. Ibid., Vol. 34, p. 179.

30. Material for Donald Robinson, Statements and Speeches, Vol. 13, p. 373.

31. Scrapbook, Vol. 59, p. 18.

32. Ibid., 253.

33. Scrapbook, Vol. 46, p. 89.

34. "What Is a Liberal?" Statements and Speeches, Vol. 5, n.p.

35. Answers Used for Questions During Campaign, Statements and Speeches, Vol. 5, n.p.

36. Statements and Speeches, Vol. 5, p. 146.

37. Scrapbook, Vol. 53, p. 166.

38. Governors of Maine, General Material file, Cross, Burton M. folder, MCS Papers.

39. Correspondence file, 1948 Election folder, MCS Papers.

40. Ibid.

41. Scrapbook, Vol. 55, p. 278.

42. Ibid., Vol. 54, p. 212.

43. Smear Charges and Replies file, 1948 Election folder, MCS Papers.

44. Correspondence file, 1948 Elections folder, MCS Papers.

45. Smith, *Declaration of Conscience,* 458–60.

46. *Chicago Daily Tribune,* 22 June 1948.

47. Smith, *Declaration of Conscience,* 105.

48. MCS interview with author, 12 November 1984.

49. Smith, *Declaration of Conscience,* 106–7.

50. Smear Smith Strategy, Statements and Speeches, Vol. 5, n.p., MCS Papers.

51. Smith, *Declaration of Conscience,* 109.

52. Ibid., 110.

53. Smear Smith Strategy, Statements and Speeches, Vol. 5, n.p., MCS Papers.

54. Correspondence file, 1948 Elections folder, MCS Papers.

55. *Portland Sunday Telegram,* 11 July 1948.

56. Russian Challenge, Statements and Speeches, Vol. 5, n.p., MCS Papers.

57. Scrapbook, Vol. 53, p. 195.

58. Liz Carpenter interview with author, 13 November 1990.

59. Frances P. Bolton file, Radio Transcript folder, MCS Papers.

60. Merton Henry interview with author, 29 September 1988.

61. Scrapbook, Vol. 59, p. 258.

62. Ibid., Vol. 57, p. 129.

63. Ibid., Vol. 65, p. 85.

64. Ibid., Vol. 58, p. 202.

65. Ibid., Vol. 61, p. 178.

66. *Saturday Evening Post,* 11 September 1948.

67. Recipes file, MCS Paper: "Wash 1½ cups blueberries. Drain thoroughly. Sift 1½ cups flour with ½ teaspoon salt, 3 tablespoons sugar, and 3 teaspoons baking powder. Beat one egg and mix with ¾ cup milk. Stir in flour mixture. Add berries and 3 tablespoons melted shortening. Mix well and pour into greased muffin tins until ¾ full. Bake in 400° oven for 20 minutes for 9–12 muffins."

68. Scrapbook, Vol. 63, p. 3.

69. Ibid., 28.

70. Ibid., Vol. 66, p. 192.

71. Ibid.

72. Ibid., Vol. 70, p. 181.

73. Ibid., Vol. 69, p. 104.

74. Carpenter interview.

75. Scrapbook, Vol. 67, p. 18.

76. Ibid., 24.

77. Ibid., 26.

78. Ibid., 47.

79. Ibid., Vol. 68, p. 90.

80. Ibid., 81.

81. Ibid., Vol. 69, p. 165.

82. Ibid., Vol. 73, p. 122.

83. Ibid., Vol. 74, p. 45.

84. Ibid., Vol. 80, p. 165.

85. Ibid.

86. Ibid., Vol. 73, p. 158.

87. Don Larrabee interview with author, 9 February 1989.

88. Carpenter interview.

89. Scrapbook, Vol. 74, p. 196.

90. Ibid., Vol. 67, p. 45.

91. Ibid., Vol. 78, p. 247.

92. Ibid., 251.

93. Ibid., Vol. 81, p. 31.

94. Ibid., Vol. 82, p. 79.

95. Cynthia Harrison, *On Account of Sex: The Politics of Women's Issues* (Berkeley: University of California Press, 1988), 31.

96. Scrapbook, Vol. 70, p. 184.

97. Ibid., Vol. 73, p. 173.

98. Lewis Correspondence file, Parents folder, Lewis Papers, MCS Library.

99. Scrapbook, Vol. 82, p. 74.

100. Ibid., Vol. 83, p. 105.

101. Articles by Senator Smith file, *Cosmopolitan* folder, MCS Papers.

102. Peter Mills file, Correspondence folder, MCS Papers.

103. Press Relations file, Guy Gannett folder, MCS Papers.

104. Eisenhower, Dwight David file, Senator Smith's Relationship with Ike folder, MCS Papers.

105. Scrapbook, Vol. 113, p. 82.

106. Margaret Smith for Vice President file, MCS Papers.

107. Scrapbook, Vol. 114, p. 204.

108. Margaret Smith for Vice President file.

CHAPTER 5

1. U.S. Congress, Senate, 81st Congress, 2d session, *Congressional Record, Senate*, 1 June 1950, Vol. 96, Part 6, pp. 7894–95.

2. Russian Challenge, Statements and Speeches, Vol. 5, p. 392, Margaret Chase Smith (hereafter MCS) Papers, MCS Library Center, Skowhegan, Maine.

3. Ibid.

4. Scrapbook, Vol. 50, p. 125, MCS Papers.

5. Statements and Speeches, Vol. 5, p. 393.

6. MCS, *Declaration of Conscience* (Garden City, N.Y.: Doubleday, 1972), 4–5; McCarthy, Joseph R. file, MCS Papers.

7. MCS, *Declaration of Conscience*, 5.

8. McCarthy, Joseph R. file.

9. MCS *Declaration of Conscience*, 7.

10. Holway-Smith Correspondence file, Lady of Maine folder, MCS Papers.

11. McCarthy, Joseph R. file.

12. MCS *Declaration of Conscience*, 7.

13. Ibid.

14. Interview with MCS by Shoalmire, 15 June 1976, MCS Papers.

15. David M. Oshinsky, *A Conspiracy So Immense: The World of Joe McCarthy* (New York: Free Press, 1983), 164.

16. MCS, *Declaration of Conscience*, 7.

17. Ibid., 8.

18. Ibid.

19. Holway-Smith Correspondence file, Lady of Maine folder.

20. MCS interview with author, 21 October 1987.

21. MCS, *Declaration of Conscience*, 10.

22. Ibid.

23. Ibid.

24. Ibid.

25. Ibid., 11.

26. MCS interview with author, 21 October 1987.

27. Scrapbook, Vol. 387, p. 144.

28. MCS, *Declaration of Conscience*, 11.

29. Ibid., 12.

30. U.S. Congress, Senate, 81st Congress, 2d session, 1 June 1950, *Congressional Record*, Vol. 96, no. 108, p. 7884.

31. Ibid., 7885.

32. Ibid., 7888.

33. Ibid., 7891.

34. MCS, *Declaration of Conscience,* 14.

35. Don Larrabee interview with author, 9 February 1989.

36. Holway-Smith Correspondence file, Lady of Maine folder.

37. MCS, *Declaration of Conscience,* 12.

38. Scrapbook, Vol. 384, p. 35.

39. U.S. Congress, Senate, 81st Congress, 2d session, 1 June 1950, *Congressional Record,* Vol. 96, No. 108, p. 8795.

40. Ibid.

41. Ibid.

42. Scrapbook, Vol. 88, pp. 38, 41, 12, 24.

43. *Washington Star,* 6 June 1950.

44. *Hartford Courant,* 2 June 1950.

45. *Washington Post,* 2 June 1950.

46. George Aiken, Papers, Crate 11, Box 1, Folder 13, University of Vermont, Burlington, Vermont.

47. *Washington News,* 2 June 1950.

48. *St. Augustine Record,* 3 June 1950.

49. Scrapbook, Vol. 88, p. 12.

50. *Christian Science Monitor,* 3 June 1950.

51. Scrapbook, Vol. 89, p. 84.

52. *Houston Chronicle,* 6 June 1950.

53. Scrapbook, Vol. 88, p. 68.

54. Ibid., 39.

55. Ibid., 59.

56. Ibid., 62.

57. MCS, *Declaration of Conscience,* 19.

58. Thomas C. Reeves, *The Life and Times of Joe McCarthy: A Biography* (New York: Stein and Day, 1982), 297.

59. Aiken Papers, Crate 11, Box 1, Folder 12.

60. Scrapbook, Vol. 89, pp. 86, 84.

61. *Washington Post,* 6 June 1950.

62. MCS to Lippmann, 1 June 1950, Walter Lippmann Collection, Box 102, Folder 1965, Manuscripts and Archives, Yale University Library, New Haven, Connecticut.

63. Ibid., 23 May 1950.

64. MCS, *Declaration of Conscience,* 20–21.

65. Scrapbook, Vol. 89, p. 99.

66. Ibid., 96.

67. MCS to Grace B. Nuneen, 7 December 1957, George Arents Research Library, Syracuse University, Syracuse, New York.

68. Robert Griffith, *The Politics of Fear: Joseph R. McCarthy and the Senate* (Lexington: University of Kentucky, 1970), 104.

69. Ibid.

70. MCS, *Declaration of Conscience,* 21.

71. Ibid., 22.

72. Ralph Owen Brewster file, MCS Papers.

73. MCS, *Declaration of Conscience,* 22–23.

74. Expenditures in the Executive Departments Committee, Investigations Subcommittee file, Correspondence folder, MCS Papers.

75. Scrapbook, Vol. 95, p. 188.

76. Peter Wiggins, *MCS: A Woman of Courage* (Maine Broadcasting System, 11 December 1987), video recording.

77. Scrapbook, Vol. 95, p. 101.

78. Ibid., 103.

79. *Denver Post,* 2 February 1951.

80. MCS, *Declaration of Conscience,* 24–25.

81. Griffith, *Politics of Fear,* 153.

82. MCS, *Declaration of Conscience,* 25.

83. Scrapbook, Vol. 104, p. 129.

84. Ibid., 86.

85. Ibid., Vol. 281, p. 48.

86. Ibid., Vol. 105, p. 121.

87. Becker to author, 12 December 1989.

88. McCarthy, Joseph R. file.

89. Maryland Senate Election of 1950, Report No. 647, Committee on Rules and Administration, U.S. Senate, 82d Congress, 1st session, Butler-Tydings Case.

90. MCS, *Declaration of Conscience,* 28.

91. Ibid., 29.

92. Ibid., 30.

93. Ibid.

94. Ibid.

95. Committee on Rules and Administration, Privileges and Elections Subcommittee file, General Materials folder, MCS Papers.

96. MCS, *Declaration of Conscience,* 28, 29.

97. Scrapbook, Vol. 107, p. 46.

98. MCS, *Declaration of Conscience,* 33.

99. Griffiths, *Politics of Fear,* 168.

100. MCS, *Declaration of Conscience,* 38.

101. Ibid., 39.

102. Jack Lait and Lee Mortimer, *U.S.A. Confidential* (New York: Crown Publishers, 1952), 53, 88.

103. *U.S.A. Confidential* file, MCS Papers.

104. Ibid.

105. Analysis *U.S.A. Confidential* file, MCS Papers.

106. Ibid.

107. Ibid.

108. Nevada Congressional Delegation file, McCarran, Pat folder, MCS Papers; New Hampshire Congressional Delegation file, Bridges, Styles folder, MCS Papers; Ohio Congressional Delegation file, Bricker, John folder, MCS Papers; Indiana Congressional Delegation file, Jenner, William E. folder, MCS Papers.

109. Lait and Mortimer, *U.S.A. Confidential,* ix.

110. Ibid., 52.

111. Ibid., 351.

112. Ibid., 356.

113. Ibid.

114. Ibid.
115. Ibid., 53.
116. Scrapbook, Vol. 111, p. 13.
117. *U.S.A. Confidential* file.
118. MCS, *Declaration of Conscience,* 38–39.
119. *U.S.A. Confidential* Chronology file, MCS Papers.
120. MCS, *Declaration of Conscience,* 40.
121. Ibid.
122. Ibid., 41.
123. Ibid., 44–45.
124. Ibid., 51.
125. Scrapbook, Vol. 133, p. 139.
126. MCS, *Declaration of Conscience,* 51.
127. McCarthy, Joseph R. file, Chronology folder.
128. Ibid.
129. MCS, *Declaration of Conscience,* 52.
130. Scrapbook, Vol. 131, p. 143.
131. Abrahamson-Smith file, Correspondence folder, MCS Papers.
132. Ibid.
133. McCarthy, Joseph R. file, Chronology folder.
134. Scrapbook, Vol. 131, p. 143.
135. MCS, *Declaration of Conscience,* 52–53.
136. Scrapbook, Vol. 131, p. 143.
137. MCS, *Declaration of Conscience,* 55.
138. 1954 Election file, Jones, Robert L. folder, MCS Papers.
139. Ibid.
140. Scrapbook, Vol. 132, p. 112.
141. Ibid., Vol. 131, p. 143.
142. *New York Herald Tribune,* 5 February 1954.
143. Scrapbook, Vol. 134, p. 156.
144. Ibid., Vol. 135, p. 43.
145. Ibid., 14.
146. Ibid., 8.
147. Ibid., 26.
148. Ibid., 8.
149. Ibid.
150. Ibid., Vol. 134, p. 169.
151. Ibid., 156.
152. Ibid., 169.
153. Ibid., Vol. 135, p. 161.
154. Ibid., 34.
155. Ibid., Vol. 134, p. 156.
156. Ibid., Vol. 135, p. 34.
157. Ibid., Vol. 139, p. 112.
158. Ibid., Vol. 135, p. 38.
159. Ibid., Vol. 138, p. 7.
160. Ibid., Vol. 136, p. 106.
161. Ibid., 70.

162. Ibid., Vol. 138, p. 29.

163. Ibid., 49.

164. Ibid., 21.

165. Ibid.

166. Ibid., 52.

167. Ibid., Vol. 142, p. 138.

168. Robert C. Byrd, *The Senate, 1789–1989: Addresses on the History of the United States Senate* (Washington: Government Printing Office, 1988), 577–80.

169. Scrapbook, Vol. 142, pp. 99, 127, 102.

170. Ibid., Vol. 141, pp. 54, 55, 56, 62.

171. Ibid., Vol. 143, p. 3.

172. Eisenhower to MCS, 22 June 1954, DDE Records as President, PPF946, Smith, Margaret Chase, Dwight David Eisenhower Library, Abilene, Kansas.

173. Scrapbook, Vol. 310, p. 7.

174. Ibid., Vol. 280, p. 48.

175. MCS, *Declaration of Conscience*, 61.

176. Elections 1954 Campaign, Fullam, Paul A. file Summary folder, MCS Papers.

177. Scrapbook, Vol. 148, p. 121.

178. Edmund Muskie interview with author, 7 February 1989.

179. Scrapbook, Vol. 145, p. 158.

180. Ibid., Vol. 144, p. 37.

181. Ibid., 55.

182. Ibid., 37.

183. Ibid., Vol. 146, p. 17.

184. Elections 1954, Fullam, Paul A. file, Summary folder.

185. MCS to Robert W. Hill, 20 March 1954, Publicity file, John Day Company Inc. Publishers folder, MCS Papers.

186. Muskie interview.

187. Elections 1954, Fullam, Paul A. file, Summary folder.

188. Scrapbook, Vol. 146, p. 39.

189. Elections 1954, Fullam, Paul A. file, Summary folder.

190. Scrapbook, Vol. 148, pp. 116, 121, MCS Papers; Elections 1954, Fullam, Paul A. file, Summary folder; Elections 1954 file, Speeches (MCS) folder, MCS Papers.

191. Elections 1954 file, Speeches (MCS) folder.

192. Elections 1954, Fullam, Paul A. file, Summary folder.

193. Ibid. Fullam died and a few months later was given an honorary doctorate posthumously by Colby College. At the same time the college presented MCS with an honorary master's degree, not an honorary doctorate, which she considered a deliberate insult.

194. MCS, *Declaration of Conscience*, 57.

195. Scrapbook, Vol. 148, p. 39.

196. Statements and Speeches, Vol. 30, n.p.

197. Scrapbook, Vol. 158, p. 98.

198. Statements and Speeches, Vol. 12, n.p.

199. Scrapbook, Vol. 150, p. 59.

200. Scrapbook, Vol. 149, pp. 24–28.

201. MCS file, Styles Bridges Papers, New England College, Henniker, New Hampshire.

202. *New Hampshire Sunday News,* 14 November 1954.

203. Scrapbook, Vol. 157, p. 81.

204. Ibid., Vol. 149, pp. 34, 41.

205. Statements and Speeches, Vol. 12, p. 149.

206. Samuel Shaffer, *On and Off the Floor: Thirty Years As a Correspondent on Capitol Hill* (New York: Newsweek Books, 1980), 46.

207. Ibid.

208. Scrapbook, Vol. 151, p. 118.

209. Byrd, *The Senate,* 581.

210. Ibid.

211. MCS to McCarthy, 14 July 1956, Joseph McCarthy file, MCS—McCarthy Correspondence folder, MCS Papers.

212. Conversation Memo, 24 July 1956, Joseph McCarthy file, MCS—McCarthy Correspondence folder.

213. McCarthy, file, Eulogy Resolution folder, MCS Papers.

214. Ibid.

215. MCS, *Declaration of Conscience,* 61.

CHAPTER 6

1. U.S. Congress, Senate, 88th Congress, 1st session, 24 September, p. 17831.

2. Quoted in Frank Graham, *Margaret Chase Smith, Woman of Courage* (New York: John Day Company, 1964), 96.

3. Scrapbook, Vol. 121, p. 166, Margaret Chase Smith (hereafter MCS) Papers, MCS Library, Skowhegan, Maine.

4. Ibid., 154.

5. Rhodes to Bill Lewis, 18 January 1977, Rhodes-Smith Correspondence file, MCS Papers.

6. Scrapbook, Vol. 121, p. 154.

7. Rhodes to Bill Lewis, 18 January 1977, Rhodes-Smith Correspondence file.

8. Scrapbook, Vol. 121, p. 155.

9. Ibid., 154.

10. Ibid., Vol. 12, p. 186.

11. Ibid., 124.

12. Ibid., Vol. 123, p. 31.

13. Ibid., Vol. 122, p. 186.

14. Ibid., 186, 39.

15. Ibid., Vol. 123, p. 39.

16. Ibid., 65.

17. Baruch to MCS, 26 June 1953, George Arents Research Library, Syracuse University, Syracuse, New York.

18. *Investigation of the Ammunition Shortage in the Armed Services, Interim Report, The Preparedness Subcommittee Number 2 of the Committee of Armed Services, United States Senate* (Washington: Government Printing Office, 1953).

19. Quoted in Graham, *Margaret Chase Smith,* 172.

20. Statements and Speeches, Vol. 10, p. 267, MCS Papers.

21. Scrapbook, Vol. 125, p. 165.

22. Statements and Speeches, Vol. 10, p. 163.

23. *Boston Herald,* 29 May 1953.

24. Scrapbook, Vol. 128, p. 170.

25. Quoted in Graham, *Margaret Chase Smith,* 87.

26. Scrapbook, Vol. 125, p. 186.

27. Statements and Speeches, Vol. 10, p. 267.

28. MCS, *Declaration of Conscience* (Garden City, N.Y.: Doubleday, 1972), 216.

29. Ibid., 227.

30. Graham, *Margaret Chase Smith,* 123.

31. Statements and Speeches, Vol. 15, pp. 36, 91, 95.

32. MCS, *Declaration of Conscience,* 228.

33. Quoted in Graham, *Margaret Chase Smith,* 123.

34. Statements and Speeches, Vol. 15, pp. 147–48.

35. Quoted in Graham, *Margaret Chase Smith,* 124.

36. MCS, *Declaration of Conscience,* 228–29.

37. Drew Pearson, "Washington Merry-go-round," n.d., Styles Bridges Papers, New England College, Henniker, New Hampshire.

38. Peter Mills file, Correspondence folder, MCS Papers.

39. Press Relations file, Milton Caniff folder, MCS to Caniff, 11 August 1957, MCS Papers.

40. Ibid.

41. Scrapbook, Vol. 194, p. 42.

42. Quoted in Angele de T. Gingres, *The Best in Congressional Humor* (Washington: Acropolis Books, 1973), 73.

43. Armed Services Committee, Air Force Personnel file, Emmett O'Donnell folder, MCS Papers.

44. Scrapbook, Vol. 211, p. 101.

45. Quoted in Graham, *Margaret Chase Smith,* 135.

46. Barry Goldwater interview with author, 7 June 1989.

47. Scrapbook, Vol. 266, p. 117.

48. *Life,* 29 June 1959, p. 28.

49. Quoted in Graham, *Margaret Chase Smith,* 136.

50. Scrapbook, Vol. 208, p. 168.

51. Statements and Speeches, Vol. 18, n.p.

52. Armed Services Committee, James M. Stewart file, Ruth H. Morrison folder, MCS Papers.

53. Armed Services Committee, James M. Stewart file, Views of Senator Smith on Stewart folder, MCS Papers.

54. Barry Goldwater to Styles Bridges, 3 June 1959, Bridges Papers.

55. Goldwater interview.

56. Lewis eventually received his promotion to brigadier general, and he and Smith frequently commented on his rank's surpassing her own as lieutenant colonel.

57. Quoted in Graham, *Margaret Chase Smith,* 131.

58. Statements and Speeches, Vol. 18, p. 319.

59. Ibid., 317.

60. Armed Services Committee, Kittery-Portsmouth Naval Shipyard file, General Materials folder, MCS Papers.

61. Statements and Speeches, Vol. 16, p. 30.

62. Scrapbook, Vol. 191, p. 26.

63. Ibid.

64. Statements and Speeches, Vol. 16, pp. 152–53.

65. Ibid., Vol. 17, pp. 7–8.

66. Scrapbook, Vol. 176, p. 149.

67. Ibid., Vol. 153, p. 76.

68. Ibid., 81.

69. Ibid., 74.

70. Ibid., Vol. 181, p. 90.

71. MCS interview with author, 21 October 1987.

72. Lewis to Parents, July 1949, Lewis Correspondence file, Parents folder, MCS Papers.

73. Scrapbook, Vol. 198, p. 100. Excluded from a great deal of Washington social life by male-only clubs, Smith, with one exception, publicized that she stayed home by choice. That exception involved her being excluded when the rest of the Republican senators were included. On that occasion Senator Prescott Bush, father of President George Bush, arranged a luncheon for President Eisenhower at Burning Tree, the most exclusive of Washington's male-only bastions. Smith angrily cried foul, and the elder Bush, without understanding why she was angry, belatedly persuaded the club to make a one-time-only exception for her.

74. Statements and Speeches, Vol. 18, p. 89.

75. Ibid., 90.

76. Scrapbook, Vol. 266, p. 117.

77. Ibid., Vol. 203, p. 26.

78. Ibid., Vol. 158, p. 97.

79. Ibid., Vol. 177, p. 66.

80. Ibid., Vol. 173, p. 80.

81. Ibid., Vol. 178, p. 90.

82. Ibid., Vol. 177, p. 111.

83. Ibid., 87.

84. MCS, *Declaration of Conscience*, 205.

85. Ibid.

86. Ibid., 206.

87. Ibid., 205, 207.

88. Ibid., 211, 208.

89. Ibid., 209.

90. Ibid., 210.

91. Ibid., 211.

92. Scrapbook, Vol. 200, p. 20.

93. MCS to Richard K. Warren, 2 February 1956, Press Relations file, *Bangor Daily News* folder, MCS Papers.

94. Muskie interview.

95. Civil Rights file, Smith, "Segregation" folder, MCS Papers.

96. Statements and Speeches, Vol. 20, n.p.

97. Ibid., 138.

98. Quoted in Graham, *Margaret Chase Smith,* 139.

99. Statements and Speeches, Vol. 20, p. 139.

100. Ibid., 331.

101. Quoted in Graham, *Margaret Chase Smith,* 140.

102. MCS, *Declaration of Conscience,* 242.

103. Ibid.

104. *Bangor News,* 28 February 1959.

105. MCS, *Declaration of Conscience,* 242.

106. Graham, *Margaret Chase Smith,* 141–43.

107. MCS, *Declaration of Conscience,* 241–44.

108. Ibid., 247–50.

109. Statements and Speeches, Vol. 21, p. 87.

110. Ibid., 90–91.

111. Ibid., 142.

112. MCS, *Declaration of Conscience,* 250–51.

113. Ibid., 252.

114. Ibid., 253.

115. Quoted in Graham, *Margaret Chase Smith,* 146.

116. Muskie interview.

117. MCS, *Declaration of Conscience,* 290–91.

118. Ibid., 301–4.

119. Armed Services Committee, Air Force Base file, Dow Air Force Base folder, MCS Papers.

120. Scrapbook, Vol. 248, p. 4.

121. Statements and Speeches, Vol. 25, p. 120.

122. MCS, *Declaration of Conscience,* 306–8.

123. Ibid., 260.

124. Statements and Speeches, Vol. 23, pp. 186–205.

125. Scrapbook, Vol. 239, p. 1.

126. MCS, *Declaration of Conscience,* 273–74.

127. Ibid., 274.

128. Statements and Speeches, Vol. 25, pp. 135–49.

129. MCS, *Declaration of Conscience,* 285.

130. Ibid.

131. Ibid., 332.

132. MCS, *Declaration of Conscience,* 310; Frank Graham in *Margaret Chase Smith,* 173, used the rose-on-desk story as his final, dramatic paragraph and proclaimed it symbolically "the key to her political success." Inadvertently, Graham was correct because good stage management was responsible for much of Smith's success.

CHAPTER 7

1. Margaret Chase Smith (hereafter MCS), *Declaration of Conscience* (Garden City, N.Y.: Doubleday, 1972), 362–3.

2. Ibid., 369.

3. Ibid., 370.

4. Ibid., 371.

5. MCS interview with author, 23 September 1988.

6. Ibid.

7. Scrapbook, Vol. 261, p. 37, MCS Papers, MCS Library Center, Skowhegan, Maine.

8. Barry Goldwater interview with author, 7 June 1989.

9. Ibid.

10. Dow Family file, Running for President folder, MCS Papers.

11. MCS, *Declaration of Conscience,* 371–72.

12. Scrapbook, Vol. 293, p. 121.

13. MCS, *Declaration of Conscience,* 376.

14. Scrapbook, Vol. 267, p. 1.

15. MCS, *Declaration of Conscience,* 376.

16. Ibid.

17. Ibid., 378.

18. Scrapbook, Vol. 296, p. 188.

19. Ibid., Vol. 292, pp. 59, 72, Vol. 263, p. 149.

20. Ibid., Vol. 277, p. 13.

21. *Time,* 7 February 1964, 23.

22. *Evening Star,* 3 February 1964.

23. Mike Posner interview with author, 7 February 1989.

24. MCS, *Declaration of Conscience,* 381.

25. Presidential Nomination file, Maxine Cheshire folder, MCS Papers.

26. Merton Henry interview with author, 29 September 1988.

27. John Reed interview with author, 1 September 1988, Henry interview.

28. MCS, *Declaration of Conscience,* 383.

29. Ibid., 384.

30. Henry interview.

31. Ibid.

32. MCS, *Declaration of Conscience,* 388.

33. Ibid.

34. Statements and Speeches, Vol. 29, p. 34, MCS Papers.

35. Ibid.

36. Ibid.

37. Ibid.

38. Scrapbook, Vol. 291, p. 23C.

39. Ibid.

40. Ibid.

41. Ibid., Vol. 300, p. 131.

42. Lola Pierotti Aiken interview with author, 3 October 1988. Pierotti married George Aiken, and in his papers at the University of Vermont is a letter to MCS in which he writes that nominating Smith "remains the highlight of what I have done in public life." To which Pierotti added, "Amen, Lola."

43. Scrapbook, Vol. 290, p. 145.

44. MCS, *Declaration of Conscience,* 377–78.

45. Scrapbook, Vol. 290, p. 137.

46. MCS, *Declaration of Conscience,* 373. A worse calamity followed when

Blanche Bernier Hudon—receptionist, secretary, seamstress, hairdresser—resigned in 1966 at the insistence of her husband.

47. Scrapbook, Vol. 274, p. 36.

48. Ibid., Vol. 268, p. 68.

49. Ibid., Vol. 387, p. 175.

50. Emily George, *Martha Griffiths* (Washington: University Press of America, 1982), 144.

51. Ibid.

52. MCS interview with author, 21 October 1987. In 1947 Smith had unsuccessfully co-sponsored an equal pay bill with Helen Gahagan Douglas.

53. *Wall Street Journal,* 22 December 1970.

54. MCS interview with author, 21 October 1987.

55. Scrapbook, Vol. 380, p. 93.

56. Presidential Nomination file, Maxine Cheshire folder.

57. Ibid.

58. Scrapbook, Vol. 262, p. 118.

59. MCS to Jack Toomey, 29 March 1955, Press Relations, *Lewiston Daily Sun* file, Jack Toomey folder, MCS Papers. The letter bears the original filing code of "TROUBLE" and is marked "l/p" to indicate Lewis drafted the letter for Smith's signature.

60. Ibid. When the MCS Library Center director, James MacCampbell, first became aware of Lewis's profiles, he said, "I must admit I was appalled. . . . I didn't know those summaries existed until one day I ran across a box of them. . . . I talked with her about it, and she thinks they're wonderful." MacCampbell interview with author, 19 September 1988.

61. Press Relations file, John O'Donnell folder, MCS Papers.

62. Press Relations file, George Sokolsky folder, MCS Papers.

63. Press Relations file, Jack Anderson folder, MCS Papers.

64. Ibid.

65. Lewis to Maureau, 17 September 1973, Paul Maureau—MCS Correspondence file, MCS Papers.

66. MCS to Barbara Heckethorn, 13 January 1965, Publishing Company file, Macmillan Company folder, MCS Papers.

67. Press Relations file, *Time-Life* folder, MCS Papers.

68. Ibid.

69. Ibid.

70. Press Relations file, *Chicago Daily Tribune* folder, MCS Papers.

71. Ibid.

72. Warren to MCS, 2 April 1955, Press Relations file, *Bangor Daily News* folder, MCS Papers.

73. MCS to Warren, 5, 25 April 1955, Press Relations file, *Bangor Daily News* folder.

74. MCS to Richard Conarroe, 30 April 1968, Press Relations file, *Saturday Evening Post* folder.

75. MCS, *Declaration of Conscience,* 246.

76. Stanley Tupper interview with author, 22 September 1988.

77. MCS, *Declaration of Conscience,* 246.

78. Ibid.

79. Ibid.

80. MCS to Toomey, 29 March 1955, Dick Toomey file.

81. MCS to Ripley, 10 September 1950, Press Relations file, *Christian Science Monitor* folder.

82. MCS to Estelle Gaines, 28 April 1950, Press Relations file, *Time-Herald* folder.

83. MCS to Hapgood, 31 December 1959, Press Relations file, Guy Gannett file, J. Frances Hapgood folder.

84. MCS to Marion von Rospach, 23 April 1961, Press Relations file, *Overseas Weekly* folder.

85. MCS to Mr. and Mrs. A. C. Larson, 20 November 1972, Press Relations file, *Family Weekly* folder.

86. Lewis to Pearson, 4 October 1963, Press Relations file, Drew Pearson folder.

87. MCS to Edward Carlson, 10 August 1964, Gannett Publishers file, Edward L. Penley folder.

88. MCS to Hapgood, 31 December 1957, Press Relations, Guy Gannett file, Frances Hapgood folder.

89. MCS to author, 20 October 1987.

90. Jean Gannett Hawley interview with author, 21 September 1988.

91. Ibid.

92. Ibid.

93. Lewis to Robert H. Austin, 23 September 1959, Press Relations file, Correspondence General folder.

94. Ibid.

95. Hawley interview.

96. MCS to Craig, 5 May 1955, Press Relations, Craig, May file, Correspondence folder.

97. Craig to MCS, 9 May 1955, Press Relations, Craig, May file, Correspondence folder.

98. MCS to Hapgood, 31 December 1957, Press Relations, Guy Gannett file, Hapgood folder.

99. Ibid.

100. MCS to Beith, 30 August 1961, Press Relations, Guy Gannett Publishers file, Gannett folder.

101. Scrapbook, Vol. 252, p. 9.

102. MCS to Craig, 26 December 1962, Press Relations, May Craig file, Correspondence folder.

103. Craig to MCS, 27 December 1962, Press Relations, May Craig file, Correspondence folder.

104. Statements and Speeches, Vol. 25, p. 129.

105. Ibid.

106. MCS to Muskie, 3 January 1963, Edmund Muskie file, MCS Papers.

107. Scrapbook, Vol. 252, p. 9.

108. Ibid.

109. Statements and Speeches, Vol. 26, p. 191.

110. Scrapbook, Vol. 255, p. 166.

111. *Newsweek,* 8 April 1963, pp. 23–24.

112. Ibid.

113. Ibid.

114. John Murphy interview with author, 21 September 1988.

115. Don Larrabee interview with author, 9 February 1989.

116. Ibid.

117. Ibid.

118. Ibid.

119. Ibid.

120. MCS interview with author, 23 September 1988. Another person who shared Larrabee's sentiments but who escaped Smith's wrath was the legendary doorkeeper of Congress, William "Fishbait" Miller, who referred to the senator's relationship with Lewis as the "most beautiful love story I knew on Capitol Hill." (William "Fishbait" Miller, *Fishbait, The Memoirs of the Congressional Doorkeeper* (Englewood Cliffs, N.J.: Prentice-Hall, 1977), 74.)

121. MCS to Robert Beith, 30 August 1961, and Lewis to Beith, 25 January 1962, Press Relations, Guy Gannett Publishers file, Gannett folder.

122. Jean Gannett Hawley interview with author, 21 September 1988.

123. Stanley Tupper interview with author, 22 September 1988.

124. Larrabee interview.

125. Bill Caldwell interview with author, 21 September 1988.

126. Murphy interview.

127. Mike Posner interview with author, 7 February 1989.

128. MCS interview with author, 21 October 1987.

129. Larrabee interview.

130. Posner interview.

131. Don Hensen interview with author, 21 September 1988.

132. Murphy interview.

133. Caldwell interview.

134. Posner interview.

135. Murphy interview.

136. Scrapbook, Vol. 233, p. 5.

137. Peggy Lamson, *Few Are Chosen: American Women in Political Life Today* (Boston: Houghton Mifflin, 1968), 27.

138. Scrapbook, Vol. 233, p. 5.

139. Ibid., Vol. 296, p. 135.

140. Lewis to Beith, 25 January 1962, Press Relations, Guy Gannett Publishing file, Gannett folder.

141. Peter Kyros interview with author, 10 February 1989.

142. Scrapbook, Vol. 310, p. 142.

143. Ibid., 110, 126.

144. Ibid., 129.

145. Lady Bird Johnson, *A White House Diary* (New York: Holt, Rinehart and Winston, 1970), 414.

146. Liz Carpenter interview with author, 13 November 1990.

147. Quoted in *Houston Chronicle,* 23 September 1993.

148. Ibid., Vol. 311, pp. 35–36.

149. Statements and Speeches, Vol. 33, p. 242; Scrapbook, Vol. 33, p. 24.

150. Statements and Speeches, Vol. 33, pp. 159–60.

151. George Mitchell file, MCS Papers.

152. Scrapbook, Vol. 310, p. 143.

153. Ibid., Vol. 309, p. 94.

154. Republican Conference file, Rules folder, MCS Papers.

155. Brooks to Aiken, 7 December 1966, Republican Conference file, Rules folder.

156. MCS interview with author, 21 October 1987.

157. George Mitchell interview with author, 6 February 1989.

158. Robert Dole interview with author, 8 February 1989.

159. Statements and Speeches, Vol. 30, p. 19.

160. Scrapbook, Vol. 322, p. 73.

161. Republican Conference file, Committee Jurisdiction folder, MCS Papers.

162. Bouchard to Lewis, 21 January 1971, Republican Conference file, Sam Bouchard folder.

163. MCS to Bouchard, 5 October 1971, Republican Conference file, Sam Bouchard folder.

164. Sam Bouchard interview with author, 9 May 1989.

165. Absenteeism file, News Releases folder, MCS Papers.

166. Bouchard interview.

167. Bouchard to Lewis, 21 January 1977, Republican Conference file, Bouchard folder.

168. Statements and Speeches, Vol. 34, pp. 149, 265.

169. *Portland Press Herald,* 6 June 1971.

170. John Stennis interview with author, 23 May 1989.

171. Mississippi Congressional Delegation file, John C. Stennis folder, MCS Papers; Oral History interview with MCS, 15 June 1976, MCS Papers.

172. MCS, *Declaration of Conscience,* 393.

173. Oral history interview with MCS, 15 June 1976, MCS Papers.

174. MCS, *Declaration of Conscience,* 394.

175. Ibid., 396.

176. Ibid., 404.

177. Statements and Speeches, Vol. 36, p. 326.

178. Ibid., 330–31.

179. MCS, *Declaration of Conscience,* 405.

180. Ibid.

181. Oral history interview with MCS.

182. MCS, *Declaration of Conscience,* 411.

183. Ibid., 415.

184. Statements and Speeches, Vol. 10, p. 405.

185. Ibid., 407.

186. Ibid., 442, 408.

187. Scrapbook, Vol. 246, p. 93.

188. Statements and Speeches, Vol. 31, p. 377.

189. Scrapbook, Vol. 295, p. 21.

190. Statements and Speeches, Vol. 28, p. 358.

191. Ibid., 305, 308.

192. Ibid., 361, 358.

193. Ibid., Vol. 30, p. 218.

194. MCS to Jakie Pruett, 29 October 1977, Johnson Administration file, MCS Statements about President Johnson folder, MCS Papers.

195. Interview with MCS, 20 August 1975, Johnson Administration file, Oral History Project folder, MCS Papers.

196. Ibid.

197. Statements and Speeches, Vol. 31, p. 211.

198. Ibid., 336, 211.

199. Ibid., 453; Scrapbook, Vol. 282, p. 108.

200. MCS to LBJ, 5 January 1966, Central Name File, LBJ Library; Statements and Speeches, Vol. 31, p. 337.

201. Scrapbook, Vol. 307, p. 161.

202. Statements and Speeches, Vol. 33, pp. 43–44.

203. Ibid., 44.

204. Ibid.; Berkeley Rice, "Is the Great Lady from Maine Out of Touch?" *New York Times Magazine,* 11 June 1972, p. 52.

205. Statements and Speeches, Vol. 38, p. 25.

206. Ibid.

207. Rice, "Is the Great Lady from Maine Out of Touch?" 52.

208. Ibid.

209. Statements and Speeches, Vol. 38, p. 25.

210. Elections, 1972 file, MCS Papers.

211. MCS interview with author, 28 September 1988.

212. Larrabee interview.

213. Ibid.

214. *Portland Press Herald,* December 1971.

215. Larrabee interview.

216. Ibid.

217. Ibid.

218. Robert Monks interview with author, 9 February 1989.

219. Ibid.

220. Ibid.

221. Ibid.

222. Ibid.

223. Ibid.

224. MCS interview with author, 23 September 1988.

225. Scrapbook, Vol. 351, p. 54.

226. Ibid., Vol. 350, p. 16.

227. Michall Barone, Grant Ujifusa, and Douglas Matthews, *The Almanac of American Politics* (Boston: Gambit Publishers, 1972), 315, 317, 319.

228. Robert Monks file, MCS Papers.

229. Scrapbook, Vol. 348, p. 83.

230. Monks interview.

231. Scrapbook, Vol. 345, p. 53.

232. Ibid., Vol. 351, p. 105.

233. Ibid., p. 72, Vol. 354, p. 67.

234. Ibid., Vol. 354, p. 134.

235. Ibid.

236. Ibid.

237. Ibid., Vol. 351, p. 72.

238. Caldwell interview.

239. Bouchard interview.

240. Ibid., Vol. 345, p. 83.

241. Ibid., Vol. 346, p. 88.

242. Monks interview.

243. Ibid.

244. Rice, "Is the Great Lady from Maine Out of Touch?" 48–49.

245. Monks interview.

246. Tupper interview.

247. Scrapbook, Vol. 356, p. 12.

248. Ibid.

249. Tupper interview.

250. Scrapbook, vol. 357, p. 62.

251. William Hathaway interview with author, 6 February 1989.

252. Ibid.

253. William C. Lewis file, Speeches folder, Lewis Papers, MCS Library.

254. Scrapbook, Vol. 360, p. 72.

255. Hathaway interview.

256. Ibid.

257. Gay Cook and Dale Pullen, *Margaret Chase Smith, Republican Senator from Maine,* Ralph Nader Congressional Project, Citizens Look at Congress (New York: Grossman Publishers, 1972), 12.

258. Elections 1972 file, News Clippings folder, MCS Papers.

259. Ibid.

260. MCS to Caldwell, 6 October 1972, Bill Caldwell file, MCS Papers.

261. William C. Lewis file, Correspondence folder, Lewis to Barnee Breesken, 29 November 1972, Lewis Papers, MCS Library.

262. Ibid.

263. Cook, *Margaret Chase Smith,* 1.

264. Ibid., 2.

265. Ibid., 9.

266. Hathaway interview.

267. Scrapbook, Vol. 361, p. 11.

268. Ibid., Vol. 357, p. 94.

269. Ibid.

270. Memo from Senator MCS (R) Maine, Elections 1972 file, MCS Papers.

271. Hathaway interview.

272. NOW file, Ramona Barth folder, MCS Papers.

273. Ibid., Vol. 361, p. 2.

274. Elections 1972 file, News Clippings folder, MCS Papers.

275. Scrapbook, Vol. 362, pp. 58, 65, 68.

276. MCS interview with author, 23 September 1988.

277. Larrabee interview; Scrapbook, Vol. 362, p. 68.

278. Larrabee interview.

279. Ibid.

280. Election 1972 file, Correspondence (Post Election) folder, MCS Papers.

281. Hathaway file, Correspondence folder, MCS to Hathaway, 11 November 1972; Hathaway to MCS, 12 November 1972, MCS Papers.

282. Hathaway interview.

283. Scrapbook, Vol. 363, p. 26.

284. MCS to Mrs. R. C. Tucker, 1 December 1972, Election 1972 file, Correspondence (Post Election) folder, MCS Papers.

CONCLUSION

1. Margaret Chase Smith (hereafter MCS) 90th Birthday Party, 14 December 1987, videocassette 2, MCS Library Center, Skowhegan, Maine.

2. Ibid.

3. *Maine Sunday Telegram,* February 24, 1973.

4. Ibid.

5. Ibid.

6. Bill Caldwell interview with author, 21 September 1988.

7. Robert Monks interview with author, 9 February 1989.

8. Lewis to Caldwell, 28 June 1973, Bill Caldwell file, MCS Papers, MCS Library Center.

9. Ibid.

10. MCS to H. Ronald House, 23 July 1973, Woodrow Wilson National Fellowship Foundation file, MCS Papers.

11. Lewis to Caldwell, 18 March 1974, Caldwell file.

12. Caroline Huff interview with author, 23 September 1988.

13. Ibid.

14. Scrapbook, Vol. 368, p. 70, MCS Library.

15. MCS to Maureau, 18 June 1974, Paul Maureau file, Maureau-Smith Correspondence folder, MCS Papers.

16. MCS to Donald Atkinson, 29 June 1977, Skowhegan, Maine, Board of Voters Registration file, Correspondence folder, MCS Papers.

17. Huff interview.

18. Henry to Lewis, 17 May 1974, Skowhegan, Maine, Board of Voters Registration file, Correspondence folder.

19. Huff interview.

20. MCS to Mr. and Mrs. Edwin Witzenburger, 25 January 1983, Lewis Death file, Correspondence folder, MCS Papers.

21. Ibid.

22. Senator Smith's Statement for the Press, Lewis Death file.

23. Charles Lombard to MCS, 29 May 1982, Lewis Death file.

24. Janice Turner to MCS, 1 June 1982, Lewis Death file.

25. Caldwell interview.

26. Caldwell interview.

27. Kenneth Gerald folder, MCS to Gerald, 29 October 1977, Armed Services Committee–Army Personnel file, MCS Papers.

BIBLIOGRAPHY

PRIMARY SOURCES

Manuscript Collections

Aiken, George. University of Vermont, Burlington, Vermont.

Baruch, Bernard. George Arents Research Library, Syracuse University, Syracuse, New York.

Bingham, Millicent Todd. Yale University Library, Yale University, New Haven, Connecticut.

Bridges, Styles. New England College, Henniker, New Hampshire.

Dirksen, Everett. Everett McKinley Dirksen Congressional Leadership Research Center, Pekin, Illinois.

Dulles, John Foster. Princeton University Library, Princeton University, Princeton, New Jersey.

Eberstadt, Ferdinand. George Arents Research Library, Syracuse University, Syracuse, New York.

————. Princeton University Library, Princeton University, Princeton, New Jersey.

Eisenhower, Dwight David. Dwight David Eisenhower Library, Abilene, Kansas.

Flanders, Ralph E. George Arents Research Library, Syracuse University, Syracuse, New York.

Hendrickson, Robert C. George Arents Research Library, Syracuse University, Syracuse, New York.

Johnson, Lyndon Baines. Lyndon Baines Johnson Library, Austin, Texas.

Lewis, William C. Margaret Chase Smith Library, Skowhegan, Maine.

Lippmann, Walter. Yale University Library, New Haven, Connecticut.

McIntire, Clifford G. University of Maine, Orono, Maine.

Rankin, Karl Lott. Princeton University Library, Princeton University, Princeton, New Jersey.

Smith, Clyde. Franklin D. Roosevelt Library, Hyde Park, New York.
————. Margaret Chase Smith Library Center, Skowhegan, Maine.
Smith, H. Alexander. Princeton University Library, Princeton University, Princeton, New Jersey.
Smith, Margaret Chase. Margaret Chase Smith Library Center, Skowhegan, Maine.
Somervell, Brehon. George Arents Research Library, Syracuse University, Syracuse, New York.
Stevenson, Adlai E. Princeton University Library, Princeton University, Princeton, New Jersey.
Stokes, Harold Phelps. Yale University Library, Yale University, New Haven, Connecticut.
Thompson, Dorothy. George Arents Research Library, Syracuse University, Syracuse, New York.
Tupper, Stanley. University of Maine, Orono, Maine.

Interviews

Aiken, Lola. Interview with author. 3 October 1988, Burlington, Vermont. Tape recording.
Barth, Ramona. Telephone interview with author. 27 September 1988. Tape recording.
Bernier, Joseph. Telephone interview with author. 20 August 1988. Tape recording.
Bilodeau, Wallace. Interview with author. 15 September 1988, Skowhegan, Maine. Tape recording.
Bouchard, Sam. Telephone interview with author. 9 May 1989. Tape recording.
Brooke, Edward. Telephone interview with author. 5 June 1989. Tape recording.
Brown, Lewis. Interview with author. 22 June 1988, Skowhegan, Maine. Tape recording.
Caldwell, Bill. Interview with author. 21 September 1988, Portland, Maine. Tape recording.
Carpenter, Liz. Interview with author. 13 November 1990, Austin, Texas. Tape recording.
Chase, Richard. Interview with author. 31 August 1988, Skowhegan, Maine. Tape recording.
Cherne, Leo. Telephone interview with author. 27 September 1988. Tape recording.
Cohen, William. Interview with author. 8 February 1989, Washington, D.C., Tape recording.
Crane, Henrietta Page. Telephone interview with author. 15 September 1988, 4 May 1989. Tape recording.
Curtis, Kenneth. Telephone interview with author. 27 September 1988. Tape recording.
Demo, Lillian. Interview with author. 24 September 1988, Skowhegan, Maine. Tape recording.
Dole, Robert. Interview with author. 8 February 1989, Washington, D.C. Tape recording.

Duke, Joe. Telephone interview with author. 3 November 1988. Tape recording.

Dyer, Emery. Interview with author. 6 July 1988, Skowhegan, Maine. Tape recording.

Fridley, Russell. Telephone interview with author. 3 November 1988. Tape recording.

Fulbright, J. William. Interview with author. 10 February 1989, Washington, D.C. Tape recording.

Godley, Gene. Interview with author. 8 February 1989, Washington, D.C. Tape recording.

Goldwater, Barry. Telephone interview with author. 7 June 1989. Tape recording.

Gosselin, H. L. (Hal). Telephone interview with author. 4 November 1988. Tape recording.

Hathaway, William. Interview with author. 6 February 1989, Washington, D.C. Tape recording.

Hawley, Jean Gannett. Interview with author. 21 September 1988, Portland, Maine. Tape recording.

Henry, Merton. Interview with author. 29 September 1988, Portland, Maine. Tape recording.

Hensen, Don. Interview with author. 21 September 1988, Portland, Maine. Tape recording.

Hudon, Blanche. Interview with author. 3 September 1988, Brunswick, Maine. Tape recording.

Huff, Caroline. Interview with author. 23 September 1988, Skowhegan, Maine. Tape recording.

Huff, Lyndon. Interview with author. 3 November 1988, Skowhegan, Maine. Tape recording.

Kyros, Peter. Interview with author. 10 February 1989, Washington, D.C. Tape recording.

Larrabee, Don. Interview with author. 9 February 1989, Washington, D.C. Tape recording.

MacCampbell, James. Interview with author. 19 September 1988, Skowhegan, Maine. Tape recording.

Magnuson, Warren G. Oral history interview. Lyndon Baines Johnson Library, Austin, Texas. Typescript.

Mills, Peter. Interview with author. 14 September 1988, Skowhegan, Maine. Tape recording.

Mitchell, George. Interview with author. 6 February 1989, Washington, D.C. Tape recording.

Monks, Robert. Interview with author. 9 February 1989, Washington, D.C. Tape recording.

Murphy, John. Interview with author. 21 September 1988, Portland, Maine. Tape recording.

Muskie, Edmund. Interview with author. 7 February 1989, Washington, D.C. Tape recording.

Posner, Mike. Interview with author. 7 February 1989, Washington, D.C. Tape recording.

Quinn, Elizabeth. Telephone interview with author. 27 September 1988. Tape recording.

Reed, John. Interview with author. 1 September 1988, Norridgewock, Maine. Tape recording.

Scribner, Fred. Interview with author. 29 September 1988, Portland, Maine. Tape recording.

Smith, Margaret Chase. Interviews with author. 21 October 1987, 13 July, 19 July, 27 July, 23 September 1988, Skowhegan, Maine. Tape recording.

———. Interview by James Kiepper. 25 August 1988, Skowhegan, Maine. Tape recording.

———. Oral history interview by Joe B. Frantz. 20 August 1975. Lyndon Baines Johnson Library, Austin, Texas. Typescript.

———. Oral history interview. 18 February 1975. Sam Rayburn Library, Bonham, Texas. Typescript.

———. Oral history interview by Caroline K. Ehlers. 12 November 1984, University of Maryland, College Park, Maryland. Typescript.

Snowe, Olympia. Telephone interview with author. 5 June 1989. Tape recording.

Stennis, John. Telephone interview with author. 23 May 1989. Tape recording.

Stockwell, Angela. Interview with author. 16 September 1988, Skowhegan, Maine. Tape recording.

Thurmond, Strom. Interview with author. 8 February 1989, Washington, D.C. Tape recording.

Tierney, James. Telephone interview with author. 14 December 1988. Tape recording.

Tupper, Stanley. Interview with author. 22 September 1988, Boothbay Harbor, Maine. Tape recording.

Violette, Elmer. Telephone interview with author. 2 November 1988. Tape recording.

Wagg, Selma. Telephone interview with author. 8 May 1989. Tape recording.

Webb, James. Oral history interview. 10 September, 15 October 1985, National Air and Space Archives, National Air and Space Museum, Smithsonian Institution, Washington, D.C. Typescript.

———. Telephone interview with author. N.d. Tape recording.

Wels, Richard. Telephone interview with author. 3 November 1988. Tape recording.

Williams, Evelyn Chase. Interview with author. 7 July 1988, Skowhegan, Maine. Tape recording.

Documents

Maine Legislative Record, Senate. 1923.

U.S. Congress. House. Committee on Naval Affairs. "Report Covering Various Assignments Pertaining to the Women in the Naval Services." *Naval Affairs Committee Hearings and Reports, 1943–1946.* November 1944.

U.S. Congress. House. *Congressional Record.* 1937–1948.

U.S. Congress. Senate. *Congressional Record.* 1949–1972.

SECONDARY SOURCES

Books

Baker, Richard Allan. *The Senate of the United States: A Bicentennial History.* Malabor, Fl.: Robert Krieger Publishing Company, 1988.

Barone, Michall, Grant Ujifusa, and Douglas Matthews. *The Almanac of American Politics.* Boston: Gambit Publishers, 1972.

Biographical Directory of the United States Congress, 1774–1989. Washington, D.C.: Government Printing Office, 1989.

Brinkley, David. *Washington Goes to War.* New York: Knopf, 1988.

Byrd, Robert C. *The Senate, 1789–1989: Addresses on the History of the United States Senate.* 2 vols. Washington, D.C.: Government Printing Office, 1988.

Caro, Robert A. *The Years of Lyndon Johnson.* Vol. 1, *The Path to Power.* Vol. 2, *Means of Ascent.* New York: Knopf, 1982, 1990.

Chamberlin, Hope. *A Minority of Members: Women in the United States Congress.* New York: Praeger, 1973.

Clark, Charles E. *Maine: A Bicentennial History.* New York: W. W. Norton, 1977.

Coburn, Louise Helen. *Skowhegan on the Kennebec.* 2 vols. Skowhegan: Independent-Reporter Press, 1941.

Cotton, Norris. *In the Senate Amidst the Conflict and the Turmoil.* New York: Dodd, Mead, 1978.

Dole, Bob. *Historical Almanac of the United States Senate.* Washington, D.C.: Government Printing Office, 1989.

Fleming, Alice. *The Senator from Maine, Margaret Chase Smith.* New York: Dell, 1969.

George, Emily. *Martha W. Griffiths.* Washington, D.C.: University Press of America, 1982.

Gingres, Angele de T. *The Best in Congressional Humor.* Washington, D.C.: Acropolis Books, 1973.

Goldwater, Barry, with Jack Casserly. *Goldwater.* Garden City, N.Y.: Doubleday, 1988.

Gould, Alberta. *First Lady of the Senate—A Life of Margaret Chase Smith.* Mt. Desert, Maine: Windswept House Publishers, 1990.

Graham, Frank. *Margaret Chase Smith: Woman of Courage.* New York: John Day Company, 1964.

Green, Mark, with Michael Waldman. *Who Runs Congress?* New York: Dell, 1984.

Griffith, Robert. *The Politics of Fear: Joseph R. McCarthy and the Senate.* Lexington: University of Kentucky, 1970.

Harrison, Cynthia. *On Account of Sex: The Politics of Women's Issues.* Berkeley: University of California Press, 1988.

Hart, Albert Bushnell. *Salomon Portland Chase.* Boston: Houghton Mifflin, 1899.

Hartmann, Susan M. *From Margin to Mainstream: American Women and Politics since 1960.* New York: Knopf, 1989.

Johnson, Lady Bird. *A White House Diary.* New York: Holt, Rinehart and Winston, 1970.

Lait, Jack, and Lee Mortimer. *U.S.A. Confidential.* New York: Crown Publishers, 1952.

Lamson, Peggy. *Few Are Chosen: American Women in Political Life Today.* Boston: Houghton Mifflin, 1968.

McCullough, David. *Truman.* New York: Simon & Schuster, 1992.

Martin, Kathleen A., ed. *Voice on the Kennebec.* Skowhegan: Skowhegan Press, 1983.

Miller, William "Fishbait." *Fishbait, The Memoirs of the Congressional Doorkeeper.* Englewood Cliffs, N.J.: Prentice-Hall, 1977.

Osborn, William C. *The Paper Plantation: Ralph Nader's Study Group Report on the Pulp and Paper Industry in Maine.* New York: Grossman Publishers, 1974.

Oshinsky, David M. *A Conspiracy So Immense: The World of Joe McCarthy.* New York: Free Press, 1983.

Paxton, Annobel. *Women in Congress.* Richmond, Va.: Dietz Press, 1945.

Reeves, Thomas C. *The Life and Times of Joe McCarthy: A Biography.* New York: Stein and Day, 1982.

Riedel, Richard Longham. *Halls of the Mighty: My 47 Years at the Senate.* Washington, D.C.: Robert B. Luce, 1969.

Rowe, William H. *The Maritime History of Maine.* New York: W. W. Norton, 1948.

Scobie, Ingrid Winther. *Center Stage: Helen Gahagan Douglas: A Life.* New York: Oxford University Press, 1992.

Shaffer, Samuel. *On and Off the Floor: Thirty Years As a Correspondent on Capitol Hill.* New York: Newsweek Books, 1980.

Sheed, Wilfred. *Clare Boothe Luce.* New York: E. P. Dutton, 1982.

Smith, Hedrick. *The Power Game: How Washington Works.* New York: Random House, 1988.

Smith, John. *Description of New-England.* London, 1616. Reprint ed., New York: AMS Press, 1967.

Smith, Margaret Chase. *Declaration of Conscience.* Garden City, N.Y.: Doubleday, 1972.

————, and H. Paul Jeffers. *Gallant Women.* New York: McGraw-Hill, 1968.

Stadig, Rita B. *Our Maine Heritage.* 2 vols. Soldiers Pond, Maine: N.p., 1984.

Stanton, Elizabeth Cady, ed. *History of Women's Suffrage.* New York: Arno and the New York Times, 1969.

Stremlow, Mary V. *A History of the United States Marines, 1946–1977.* Washington D.C.: History and Museums Division, Headquarters United States Marines, 1986.

United States Capitol Historical Society. *We, the People: The Story of the United States Capitol.* Washington, D.C.: National Geographic Society, 1963.

United States Historical Society. *Washington Past and Present.* Washington D.C.: N.p., 1987.

White, William S. *Citadel: The Story of the U.S. Senate.* New York: Harper & Brothers, 1956.

Wroth, Lawrence C. *Voyages of Giovanni da Verrazano.* New Haven: Yale University Press, 1970.

Articles

"Air Marshal Vinson." *Newsweek,* 28 March 1949, 18–19.

"As Maine Goes. . . ." *Time,* 5 September 1960, 13–14.

Cook, Gay and Dale Pullen. "Margaret Chase Smith, Republican Senator from Maine." Ralph Nader Congress Project. Citizens Look at Congress. Washington, D.C.: Grossman Publishers, 1972.

Janeway, Eliot. "The Man Who Owns the Navy." *Saturday Evening Post,* 15 December 1945.

"Maggie vs. May." *Newsweek,* 8 April 1963, 23–24.

"Navy's Defenders." *U.S. News and World Report,* 26 April 1946, 67–69.

"New Air Force Test: The Senate." *Aviation Week,* 26 April 1948, 13.

"Probe's View of Arms Profits Raises Cry for Drastic Curbs." *Newsweek,* 2 February 1942, 38–39.

Rice, Berkeley. "Is the Great Lady from Maine Out of Touch?" *New York Times Magazine,* 11 June 1972, 52.

Smith, Margaret Chase. "A Remembrance of Christmas," *House Beautiful,* 13 July 1988.

Vinson, Carl. Untitled. *Congressional Digest,* April 1941, 110–13.

White, William S. "Men of More Than Distinction: Who Really Runs the Senate?" *Harper's Magazine* 214 (January 1957): 73–79.

White, William S. "Who Really Runs the Senate?" *Harper's Magazine* 213 (December 1956): 35–40.

Newspapers

Bangor Daily News, 16 June 1948.

Bangor News, 28 February 1959.

Boston Herald, 29 May 1953.

Boston Sunday Globe, 2 June 1940.

Christian Science Monitor, 3 June 1950.

Hartford Courant, 2 June 1950.

Houston Chronicle, 6 June 1950, 23 September 1993.

Lewiston Journal, 22 September 1946.

Lewiston Weekly Journal, 12 September 1934.

Maine Sunday Telegram, 4 February 1973.

Morning Sentinel, 14 December 1987.

New Hampshire Sunday News, 14 November 1954.

New York Herald Tribune, 5 February 1954.

Portland Press Herald, 6 June 1971.

Portland Sunday Telegram, 11 July 1948.

Somerset Reporter, 1898–1972.

St. Augustine Record, 3 June 1950.

Wall Street Journal, 22 December 1970.

Washington Post, 20, 29 December 1940, 7 January 1941, 2 June 1950, 6 June 1950.

Washington Star, 6 June 1950.

Waterville Sentinel, January 1990.

Video Recordings

Debate between Senator Margaret Chase Smith and Mrs. Eleanor Roosevelt. "Face the Nation." 4 November 1956. Videocassette.

King, Angus. "A Conversation in Maine with Margaret Chase Smith." WCBB. Videocassette.

Murrow, Edward R. "Senator Margaret Chase Smith and Mr. Robert Jones." "See It Now." 1954. Videocassette.

Nielson, Howard. "Senator Margaret Chase Smith." Cable News Network. 13 December 1982.

Wiggins, Patsy. *Margaret Chase Smith: A Woman of Courage.* Maine Broadcasting System, 11 December 1987. Videocassette.

INDEX

About the Author

PATRICIA WARD WALLACE is a Professor of United States History at Baylor University. *Politics of Conscience* is her seventh book. Her other works include *The Threat of Peace: James F. Byrnes and the Council of Foreign Ministers.*